Peg Woffington
and her World

Janet Dunbar

*Peg Woffington
and Her World*

HOUGHTON MIFFLIN COMPANY : BOSTON
1968

PRINTED IN GREAT BRITAIN
BY COX & WYMAN LTD, LONDON, FAKENHAM AND READING

For
C

Acknowledgments

I wish to express my thanks to the following for valued assistance in the preparation of this book:

Mr Douglas Matthews of the London Library, Miss Helen Willard of the Harvard Theatrical Collection, Mrs Jack Crawford of Yale University Library, Mr Paul Myers of the New York Public Library, Mr George Nash of the Enthoven Collection at the Victoria and Albert Museum, Mr John Collett of the Central Public Library, Newport, Mon., Miss Diana Howard of Richmond upon Thames Public Library, the Librarian of the Dublin Municipal Library, the Trustees of the National Library, Dublin, the Trustees of the British Museum.

Mr Roy Kift was very helpful with information about sources for the Paris episode.

I am greatly indebted to those who placed private papers at my disposal, and gave me access to their own collections of eighteenth-century material and to theatrical records. I wish especially to thank Lord Lansdowne for permission to use a photograph of the Pond portrait of Peg Woffington.

Contents

Contents

List of Illustrations

Preface

This is the story of one of the most beautiful and popular actresses of her day. She was not 'respectable': few eighteenth-century actresses were, though two or three clung to their well-publicized virtue and tried to use it as a bargaining counter for 'marriage and a coach' when pursued by a lord.

Peg Woffington became a legend in her lifetime, and has remained one ever since: a legendary beauty, a legendary actress, a legendary courtesan. She was the first woman whom David Garrick loved emotionally, and probably the only one. Many men desired her, and Peg took her pleasure as it came – she had a strong dash of Restoration amorality in her seductively feminine person. Yet she was no hypocrite, and cared not a fig for public opinion. Margaret Woffington, actress, took the view that if she served the public as a stage-player – and she was a superlative actress – that was as much as they had a right to expect. What she did with her private life was no concern of theirs.

Her story, set in the tempestuous world of the eighteenth-century theatre, begins in Dublin, a noted nursery of dramatic talent. It was a city second only to the capital in extravagant fashion and high living. George the Second sat on the throne of England, Ireland was a subjugated country, and the monarch's Viceroy held splendid state at Dublin Castle, attended by a court of aristocrats who might have lived on another planet for all they troubled themselves with the real Dublin of squalid poverty and a sub-human existence. The only point of contact between the two was the theatre, patronized by gentry and street-sweeper alike. In the glamour of the playhouse, lit by hundreds of candles, the aristocrat could be amused for a few hours, and the native Dubliner, outgoing and quick to respond to a charm of words, be carried for a short time into a realm of magic.

After she had established herself in Dublin, Peg Woffington decided to go to London. It was a London which springs out at you from Hogarth's canvases: teeming streets, fops and beaux, beggars and cutpurses, vice and a cynical acceptance of the way of the world. The common people squeezed the last drop of juice out of everyday life; they, as well as the Quality, crowded the theatres, and if actors failed to please them, woe betide the actors. Life in the Green-room was often as dramatic as the scenes enacted on the stage. Loves and hatreds, likes and dislikes, generosity and greed – all beat strongly in the breasts of players in a profession where intense individualism and jealousy were occupational hazards. Actresses would, quite literally, pull the dresses from their rivals' backs and the hair down from their heads if roused to fury. Peg Woffington was to witness – and take part in – scenes in London which she had not known in Dublin.

The beautiful Irish actress, young, successful, praised by the wits, pursued by men of wealth and rank, inevitably had detractors, and there were many 'private eyes' of the day to look for scandal in her private life and serve up titbits – true or exaggerated – in coffee-house and drawing-room. Her reputation as a loyal and hard-working actress, however, was sufficient to outweigh the effects of tattling tongues, and even the strait-laced Chetwood wrote nothing but good of Peg Woffington. William Rufus Chetwood, one of the most revealing theatrical chroniclers of the time, was prompter at Drury Lane for twenty years. He had strong principles:

Moral virtue, and a decent Behaviour, will gain Esteem from People of every Rank, will add Weight to the Characters they represent, and even may atone for want of Excellency . . . the Performers must be as Blameless as human nature will allow. I remember a virtuous Actress, or one reputed so, repeating two lines in *King Lear*, at her Exit in the third Act,
Arm'd in my Virgin Innocence I'll fly
My Royal Father to relieve, or die,
receive a plaudit from the Audience, more as a Reward for her reputable Character, than, perhaps, her acting claim'd; when a different Actress in the same Part, more fam'd for her Stage

Performance than the other, at the words *Virgin Innocence*, has created a Horse-laugh, and the Scene of generous Pity and Compassion at the Close, turn'd to Ridicule.

Chetwood must have had his principles trodden on every day, but during his long reign at Drury Lane, he continued to be the friend of players, frail or virtuous. In spite of his moralizing, he loved the actors, and they teased and loved him in return. He ends his book* with an Epilogue 'design'd for Mrs. Woffington in the Character of a Volunteer', prefacing it with a graceful tribute which probably gave her more pleasure than most of the flattering verses which filled the public prints during her zenith, for when old Chetwood paid a compliment, he meant it:

I shall leave this Lady to pursue in her Path of Merit where she still leads, with an Epilogue wrote purely for her Manner of Speaking; and as Prologues and Epilogues are the most difficult Tasks of both Sexes on the Stage, it is to be remark'd but few besides the Capital Performers are trusted with them, and a good Prologue and Epilogue, have often help'd a bad Play out of the Mire, or at least sent the Audience Home a little better humour'd.

* *A General History of the Stage,* Dublin, 1749.

1
Prologue

On St Stephen's Day, 1670, that lewd play *Bartholomew Fair* was presented at the playhouse in Smock Alley, a narrow, squalid lane not far from the River Liffey in the city of Dublin. During the performance, part of the theatre collapsed, killing several people and injuring a great many more, for the playhouse was crowded, lewd plays being a great attraction. It was said that the actual crashings began as a passage was being spoken on the stage 'that reflects upon a profession of holiness', and the puritan element in the city, still strong in spite of the influence of the very unpuritan King Charles the Second, seized upon the calamity as a sign, and preached many a sermon on it, both lay and clerical.

The theatre, after being patched up and used for some years, was rebuilt and reopened in 1690, under the management of a forceful actor, Joseph Ashbury. It was still called Smock Alley, though, according to a contemporary number of *The London and Dublin Magazine*:

> The proper name is Orange Street, but it took the Appellation of Smock Alley from Mother Bungy of infamous Memory, and was, in her Days, a Sink of Sin; but a Man being found murder'd in these Bottomless Pits of Wickedness, the Sheds were pulled down by the Populace, the unclean Vermin were banished, the Place purged of its Infamy, handsome Dwellings now show their Faces, in a modest Garb, and entertain modest, and reputable Inhabitants, and therefore I think ought to lose its old stained Name. But if Tyburn were removed the Spot would be called Tyburn still.

He produced what should have been considered a respectable enough repertoire, one which included *Othello, Macbeth* and *Henry VIII*; but when the crowded galleries of the Smock Alley theatre gave way in 1701 – again on St Stephen's Day, 26 December – there was another great outcry. This was a further judgement from Heaven! The play being performed at the time of the second disaster was Shadwell's *Libertine*, 'a play extremely loose, and improper for presentation'. It was asserted that the candles on the stage burnt blue, and that a stranger with a cloven hoof suddenly appeared and danced on the stage. Supernatural proof! A more mundane aggravation may have been the fact that Ashbury had been arrested and prosecuted for swearing, under an Act designed to 'prevent Prophaneness in the Theatre'.

There was opposition to the second rehabilitation of the playhouse in Smock Alley, but Joseph Ashbury held the Royal Patent, and he had no intention of giving in to a parcel of 'moralmenders'. The theatre in Dublin was considered to be quite the equal of those in London, and had the advantage of patronage in the highest quarter. Ashbury knew that actors in the English capital were glad to be offered a season in the capital of the neighbouring 'Kingdom', where the Lord Lieutenant, George the First's Viceroy, held magnificent court, and was a supporter of Smock Alley, declaring that the establishment of a theatre was 'an effective provocative of wit and grandeur'.

There had been companies of wandering players in Ireland from the sixteenth century. The first theatre in Dublin was erected in Werburgh Street in the reign of Charles the First by John Ogilby, a Scots dancing master, who became the official Master of the Revels. He went to ground during the Commonwealth, when all the theatres were closed, and reappeared at the Restoration. He had a position of great influence, for by the Royal Patent, now confirmed, he could license actors. He also licensed all plays intended for public performance, and could 'inhibit and forbid all persons whatsoever that they nor any of them presume to erect or build any theatre or stage whatsoever'. A truly formidable monopolist.

By Ashbury's time, this last prohibition was winked at; there were small, unlicensed theatres and booths where acrobats, tumblers, dancers and puppet shows drew houses at a few pence for a seat. Ashbury did not attempt to interfere with them; he detested the puritan element in the city which would have carried on the Commonwealth prohibition into an era when the music of fiddles and pipes, the glitter of tinsel, the gaiety of bright colours, were no longer sinful. Smock Alley theatre was repaired, Ashbury got a company together, plays were again produced. A clergyman, preaching before the Societies for the Reformation of Manners, denounced professors and Church members who were 'grown so loose as to frequent and plead for those nurseries and schools of wickedness, the Play houses, places the Devil claimeth as his own'; but the moral-menders, as the comedian, Hains, had drily called them, were no match for the energetic Ashbury, who continued to attract audiences to Smock Alley for upwards of thirty years, and when he died in 1720, bequeathed the management to his son-in-law, Thomas Elrington, 'a gentleman of genius and ability, well qualified for so arduous an undertaking'.

There were often English and Continental performers in Dublin, in spite of the long and tedious journey by stagecoach and packet. The sea voyage usually took four days; in foul weather

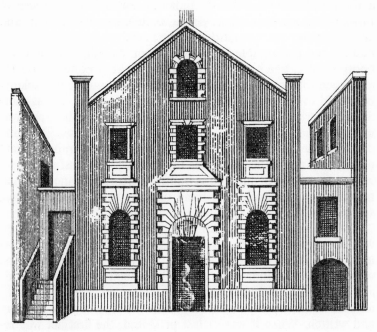

Smock Alley Theatre.

it took considerably longer. In December 1729 the *Old Dublin Intelligencer* announced: 'A few days past the celebrated Madam Violante, the most famous Rope dancer now living, arriv'd here from England after a tedious and dangerous passage of six weeks.' This was not Madame Violante's first visit to the Irish capital; she had come to Dublin some years before, bringing with her a troupe of dancers and acrobats, and herself giving a spectacular turn, walking across a tightrope with a basket containing a baby hanging from each foot. The audiences had been breathless, though Chetwood, the theatrical prompter, wrote disapprovingly that, 'Strength and Agility is a Qualification that does not render the Fair-Sex the least more amiable; the strength of the Limbs, which these sort of Undertakers expose . . . is shockingly indecent, but hers [Violante's] were masculinely indelicate.'

On this occasion Madame Violante brought with her a French dancing master, Lewis Duval, and 'Posture Master Phillips'. She was able to hire the theatre in Smock Alley for a week, presenting a mixed vaudeville performance. This was so popular that she tried to extend the hire, but was refused. Violante decided to have a theatre of her own, and confidently rented a large house in Fownes's Court, off College Green, building a covered stage and an auditorium over the garden at the back. It was ready within a month, and fashionable Dublin was soon crowding the unusual booth-theatre. She had only the vaudeville act to offer, however, and when the novelty wore off, the receipts diminished. Violante now tried to collect a company and to put on plays, but as most of the experienced actors were engaged at Smock Alley, she was unable to find others good enough to draw the town. Nothing daunted, she hit on the idea of using children and training them to act, sing and dance, and this time she was successful. She removed to a more commodious booth in George's Lane, and had no difficulty in recruiting a band of eager young people, some scarcely in their teens, and all rareing to act.

The play she chose for her 'Lilliputians', as she called them, was *The Beggar's Opera*, a witty satire which was a great success in London. It had been turned down by several London managers, who thought that audiences used to the seduction of foreign music and the novelty of those unnatural warblers, the stars of the fashionable Italian opera, would not relish the type of play Mr Gay had written. When it was at last produced, the first act was received in silence, but the audience was enthusiastic by the end of the play. John Gay had arrived. The piece was thereafter a brilliant success.

Madame Violante knew that the novelty of seeing children impersonating Gay's underworld characters would draw the crowds, and she was not mistaken. She had several clever young actors, and she was always on the lookout for fresh talent.

On her way to the booth in George's Lane, Violante had often noticed a girl of about twelve years of age who walked along regularly every evening carrying a pitcher, on her way to the river to draw water. The girl had such a charming face, and moved with such natural grace, that Violante began to look at her with a speculative eye. One day she followed the girl home, and found that she lived at the other end of George's Lane. Violante knocked at the door, and in her easy, friendly way asked if she could come in and talk with the girl and her mother.

Their name, she found, was Woffington. Mrs Woffington was a widow, and her daughter, whom the visitor admired, was named Margaret – Peg for short. There was also a younger daughter, Mary, whom they called Polly, but it was Peg Woffington in whom Madame Violante was interested.

2
Peg
❧

Peg Woffington was born in Dublin, probably in 1717 or 1718. There appears to be no baptismal record of her birth; one source gives the year as 1714, another, 1720. As she was later – like her contemporaries – reticent about her age, there is no way of fixing the actual year, but 1718 seems the most likely date, as Madame Violante judged her to be about twelve years of age when she first met Peg.

Her father was John Woffington, a journeyman bricklayer, 'a sober, industrious man married to Hannah, a thrifty, sensible woman'. They were, like most of the Irish population, Roman Catholics, though not outstandingly devout. Mrs Woffington managed very well, in a humble way, on her husband's small wage, and she was able to spare a shilling or two to have Peg taught her letters at a small dame school not far away. Being exceptionally intelligent, the child soon learnt to read, and from an early age showed signs of a bright, lively disposition. A second daughter was born when Peg was six years old, and the girl became devoted to the baby. It was a happy household. Then John Woffington died, probably of a fever. His wage stopped, and Mrs Woffington was left with two children and no money coming in.

This was a situation common to many women in her condition in life, and Hannah Woffington had to lift herself out of her grief and make shift to provide for her family. She took in washing for a time, but this was badly paid, and with the help of friends and neighbours she was able to open a huckster's shop* on Ormond Quay. Hannah was no business woman, and the shop was a

* Grocer's shop

failure after a very short time. She sank to a meagre form of subsistence, selling watercress on the street. Life was now very hard.
They left their small house and moved to George's Lane, 'a
narrow, side-walkless cul-de-sac lined on either side by low, white-
washed cabins – hardly houses'. Peg had to leave the dame school
and help her mother look after young Polly and cry their wares as
they moved slowly through the streets. Presently Peg was taking
her own tray of salad stuffs to other parts of the city, thus increasing their small earnings. Chetwood knew people who remembered her at this time, neatly shawled and barefoot in warm
weather, walking 'like a princess or a duchess', holding out
bunches of watercress and salads and Lee Lewes, a later writer,
stated:

> I have met with more than one in Dublin, who assured me
> that they remember to have seen the lovely Peggy, with a little
> dish upon her head, and without shoes to cover her delicate
> feet, crying through College Green, Dame-street, and other
> parts of that end of the town – 'All this fine young salad for a
> halfpenny – all for a halfpenny, all for a halfpenny here!'

She had a core of regular customers on College Green, where the
students from the university looked for her coming. Their teasing
brought out a facility for repartee which set them shouting with
laughter, and this delicious form of praise sharpened her wit still
more.

College Green was the centre of the aristocratic quarter of the
city. In the early part of the eighteenth century, Dublin houses
were gabled, and had high, narrow windows. The great era of
classical houses and squares was yet to come, but Trinity College,
seized by the orders of James II for a barracks at the time of the
Jacobite troubles, had been restored, and was one of the glories
of the city. Peg knew nothing about architecture, but she liked
College Green, and the students, and their boisterous friendliness
which often ended in a kiss or two. She enjoyed watching the
coaches heaving themselves over the cobbles, with liveried footmen jumping down to hand out the grand ladies attended by
gentlemen in swinging cloaks and three-cornered hats. Best of all,
she liked to return home by way of Smock Alley in the late afternoon, especially on a day when the Lord Lieutenant was attending a command performance. Then indeed there was a bustle,

chairmen carrying sedan chairs whose occupants glittered in satins and jewels, feathers adorning the powdered hair of the ladies, diamonds flashing at their ears and throats.

The Dublin slum child looked at the pageant and enjoyed it, accepting the way things were without in the least understanding their cause. The Lord Lieutenant lived in the Castle, and he was English, and there were many English ladies and gentlemen in Dublin, and they were all rich. The shopkeepers were quite rich, too, and so were the laughing students on College Green – they often paid her twice what she asked for her salads. The rest of the people she knew or saw were like herself and her mother, poorly dressed, often cold, sometimes hungry.

Peg much preferred the streets round College Green. And the houses! A servant buying her salads had once asked Peg into the kitchen and given her a mug of small beer, and the child never forgot the splendour of that place. Dark as it was, she could see enough by the light of a roaring fire: rows of pots on the wall, a vast spit, mounds of food on trays. She was given a pasty to take home, and, wonder of wonders, when they had it for their supper, found it packed full of meat. Peg and her mother enjoyed the treat, and continued in their frugal way. Life was hard, but it was uncomplicated; they seized on any piece of luck that came their way, and made the best of their lot, poor as it was. They had neighbours and acquaintances who muttered against the hated English, but Hannah Woffington did not hold with dangerous talk: it took all her time and energies to scrape a bare living for herself and her two children. She must have considered herself lucky to be living in the city, where at least there were pickings now and then, rather than in the country. Hannah had relations near Wicklow, and their conditions of existence were even worse than her own. She was too simple a woman to know the history of her unhappy country, except that all hope for those of the Faith had been crushed at the battle of the Boyne: a dreaded and execrated name to everyone she knew.

The condition of Ireland in the early 1700s stemmed from that day at the River Boyne, in July, 1690, when the Irish Catholics who had elected to support James the Second in his bid for the English throne were vanquished by the Protestant William, and so became a subject nation. Their best lands were confiscated and given to English settlers, who joined the considerable body of

English Protestants already 'planted' on estates confiscated after
earlier rebellions. Savage penal laws left the native Irish in no
doubt as to who were the rulers of their country. No Irish Roman
Catholic could buy land, or even inherit it. He could not enter
the university, or teach in a school, vote, sit in Parliament,
become a judge, serve on the Bench, or hold any office under the
Crown.

The Protestant Ascendancy were determined to keep these
abominable laws in being, though many Protestants in England
itself were appalled at such savage colonization of the sister island.
Samuel Johnson expressed himself with characteristic forceful-
ness:

> The Irish are in a most unnatural state, for we see there the
> minority prevailing over the majority. There is no instance,
> even in the Ten Persecutions, of such severity as that which the
> Protestants of Ireland here exercised against the Catholics.

The resulting standard of life for the peasants was wretched in
the extreme. As tenants of smallholdings on the estates of their
English landlords, they existed

> with the utmost Penury in the Midst of a rich Soil . . . It is
> notorious they seldom taste Bread or Meat; their Diet in
> Summer is Potatoes and Sour Milk; in Winter, when something
> is required comfortable, they are still worse, living on the same
> Root . . . Their Cloathes is so ragged, that they rather publish
> than conceal the Wretchedness it was meant to hide.

So stated *The Reformer*, and ended with the observation that
'many of our fine Gentlemen's Pageantry would be greatly tarn-
ished, were their gilt coaches to be preceded and followed by the
miserable Wretches, whose Labour supports them'.

There were rack-renting absentee owners of estates who employed bailiffs to extract rents from the smallholders, and themselves lived most of the year in England; Swift reckoned that a
third of Irish country rents were spent in England. It was these
owners of gilded coaches at whom *The Reformer* aimed its terrible
indictments. There were also 'improving landlords', who brought
new methods of agriculture from England, drained bogs, established trees, and treated their tenants with some degree of humanity; but they were outnumbered by the callous absentee

owners of the estates which had once belonged to the Irish themselves.

As time passed, and the English king's rule grew ever more despotic, many of the Anglo-Irish – the settlers themselves – became disgusted, especially when economic restrictions were put on two Irish industries which had managed to thrive – cattle-raising and the wool trade. Jonathan Swift, a Protestant, born in Dublin of English parents, who had 'a perfect hatred of tyranny and oppression', put his finger on the English attitudes to the Irish in his *Drapier Letters to the People of Ireland*, 1724, when he said that the English knew little more of Ireland than they did of Mexico,

> further than it is a country subject to the King of England, full of Boggs, inhabited by wild Irish Papists; who are kept in Awe by mercenary Troops sent from thence; And their general Opinion is, that it were better for England if this whole Island were sunk into the Sea: For, they have a tradition, that every Forty Years there must be a Rebellion in Ireland.

Politics were for grand folk: talk of rebellion among the angry-eyed workmen who lived in and around George's Lane was carefully not listened to. Hannah Woffington trudged to the outskirts of the city to buy her salad-stuffs from the market-gardens, Peg leading little Polly. Then Hannah would take the child and start on her round, while Peg went to her own beat. It was a disappointing day when either brought home unsold watercress and lettuce, a worse if the weather was so bad that the cook-maids in the big houses did not come out to do their marketing: Peg and her mother had then to go to the scullery doors of the mansions to try and dispose of their stock. They were both very weary when they reached home, often very late, and then Peg's work was not finished, for she went down to the Liffey with a pitcher, to bring water from the river.

One evening, after she had, as usual, brought back the full pitcher, Peg was sitting with her mother after Polly had been put to bed, when there was a knock at the door. It wasn't a neighbour; it was a strange lady, who asked if she might come in for a talk.

Madame Violante had no difficulty in persuading Hannah Woffington to allow Peg to join the company of Lilliputians; the half-guinea a week which she offered meant riches. Peg herself was clearly pleased with the idea. Violante studied her. The child was very pretty, with dark, glossy hair falling on her shoulders, and shining black eyes. She was tall for her twelve years, and held herself so well that already she showed promise of a good carriage – indispensable for an actress. Best of all, she was sharp and quick in understanding; the few questions Violante asked her were immediately answered. Could she read? Yes, tolerably well. Had she a good memory? Peg did not know, but she thought so. Her manner was direct and natural, her smile infrequent but charming when it flashed out.

Violante left some money for Mrs Woffington, and, well satisfied, arranged for Peg to come to her booth the following morning to join her company of juvenile players as an apprentice. As she expected, the girl was punctual, and though her clothes were shabby, she wore them with an air. It took only a few days to familiarize Peg with this new kind of life. The famous Margaret Woffington was to remark in later life that she might have been born in the booth at the end of George's Lane, so completely did she feel at home there. The other Lilliputians took little notice of her, or of one another, except on the stage in their mimic parts; already they were absorbed in themselves, pushing forward at every opportunity to attract Madame's attention. Some of them displayed temperament when Madame corrected them, thinking that they needed no more instruction. The newcomer obviously felt that she needed a great deal.

Violante found Peg Woffington an ideal apprentice. Self-confident but without the slightest traces of self-consciousness, the girl responded to training with enthusiasm. The hard-bitten, experienced Frenchwoman knew that she had found someone quite unusual, not only on account of her budding beauty, but because, from the very beginning, she gave evidence of possessing that priceless quality in a player – professionalism. Peg never complained when her mistress rehearsed for long hours, making her repeat lines again and again. She was eager to learn, anxious to be perfect, instinctively aware that perfection could only be reached by continually studying her business. Violante intended to spend as much time as she could spare on this girl, and for a cogent reason. In spite of Peg's aptitude for acting, she lacked the player's most valuable asset – a uniformly good speaking voice. Now and again there was a harsh note in her tone, probably the result of years of crying 'Salads, fresh salads!' in the streets. Violante set patiently to work to improve the girl's diction, hoping that now the need for street-selling had passed, the harshness would disappear. She often spoke in French, and was delighted when Peg, without understanding the sense of the words, repeated them with a fair approximation of the right accent. The Dublin brogue would then disappear, and with it the shrill timbre. Here, indeed, was material worth working on.

Madame also taught the girl dancing, and Peg showed a fresh versatility; she was precise to the music yet spritely and exceedingly graceful. The other members of the troupe were also talented – the Frenchwoman was shrewd in her choice of player-material – but twelve-year-old Peg Woffington was obviously going to be a special draw. She was a quick study, and Violante presently gave her the part of Polly in *The Beggar's Opera*. Betty Barnes, a strapping girl with a well-developed 'shape', played Captain Macheath – and so Peg became familiar with a girl taking a breeches part. Off the stage, Betty treated Peg with the same indifference shown by the others, but John Barrington, the boy who played Fitch, was friendly, and Peg found that he was as closely interested in the actual craft of acting as she was.

Life in the poor cabin at the other end of George's Lane was transformed. Madame Violante had increased Peg's salary to a guinea a week, and Hannah Woffington had no longer any need to range the streets in all weathers crying her watercress and salads. Besides being able to buy better food, she could afford to send little Polly to the dame school where Peg had enjoyed her own brief years of education; Peg herself insisted on this, for she had already seen how important it was to be able at least to read. At six years of age, Polly was already a biddable little girl, and Peg loved her dearly. Perhaps she, too, would grow up to please Madame Violante, and learn to be a player. Peg could think of no finer life.

The performances of *The Beggar's Opera* were a great success; Violante had prepared 'proper scenery, dresses and decorations'. Hitchcock says in his *History of the Irish Stage*.

the novelty of the sight, the uncommon abilities of the little performers, and the great merit of the piece, attracted the notice of the town to an extraordinary degree. They drew houses for a considerable length of time, and the children of Shakespeare's and Johnson's day were not more followed, or admired, than those tiny geniuses.

Apart from her lessons with Madame, every minute of which was enthralling, Peg did not find the atmosphere in the booth-theatre happy. Jealousy had already made itself felt in the youthful troupe, and Peg Woffington, with her pretty face and un-doubted promise of talent, came in for more than her share. Peg did not allow it to trouble her; what mattered was Madame Vio-lante's approbation, and with this incentive Peg was determined to do well. John Barrington, a year or so older than herself, had the same ambition. Violante noted that during the intervals in a rehearsal, Peg Woffington and young Barrington would often go over a scene in a corner while the rest of the troupe were chatt-ing and boasting and trying to catch her attention. There was not much that Violante missed.

Besides *The Beggar's Opera,* Violante put on *The Cobbler of Preston* by Christopher Bullock, based on the Introduction to *The Taming of the Shrew,* which was acted 'with great Applause', Violante herself taking the wife of Christopher Sly. Peg Woffing-ton played a country ale-wife and several minor parts, which she differentiated so skilfully that Madame congratulated her – a fact noted sourly by some of the other young actors, their mistress being sparing with her praise.

As it was necessary to vary the entertainments as much as possible in order to continue to draw good houses, Violante repeated what *The Old Dublin Intelligencer* had called 'these grotesque entertainments', in which she walked on a rope from the stage to the upper gallery, 'and also flaps down the same on her breast without being fastened thereto, and Monsieur Lalauze dances a new French dance in Wooden Shoes'. This display drew the town. Violante made enough money to put her booth-theatre 'in good order for the Reception of the Quality by wainscoting and lining it with woollen cloth'. Success of this order had its hazards for an unlicensed place of entertainment. Hitherto, the Theatre Royal could afford to ignore her, but now the manager

and actors of Smock Alley took alarm, lest they should lose
their regular audiences. They complained to the Lord Mayor
that Madame Violante had 'no Sanction or proper Authority to
exhibit such Entertainments', and the Lord Mayor, empowered
by his office to take action over illegalities, threatened to close
the booth in George's Lane.

Violante, well used to the vicissitudes of a player's life, decided
to take her troupe to London and try her fortune there, though
several of the juveniles were unable or unwilling to go. As the
booth in George's Lane would be empty, three of the company
who stayed behind, John Barrington, Luke Sparks and a girl
called Mackay, asked Violante to rent the booth to them, which
she agreed to do for three pounds a week. They intended to try
their fortune with plays themselves. Rumours of this venture soon
spread, and the young hopefuls were joined by several players,
near their own age, from the Theatre Royal in Smock Alley, who
had long been resentful of the snubbing attitudes of their seniors
at that theatre, and eagerly grasped this chance to secede from the
monopoly playhouse. 'Being all very young, they fell desperately
in Love with the Dramatic Poets,' wrote Hitchcock. They at once
began rehearsals for Farquhar's comedy *The Inconstant, or The
Way to Win Him*, in spite of having 'nothing but Rags, for their
Scenes had shewn their best Days'. Clothes were borrowed from
friends, and the brave venture began.

Peg Woffington went with Violante. It was the first time she
had been away from home, but her mother did not attempt to stop
her. Hannah Woffington willingly resigned herself to allowing her
elder daughter to order the course of their living. There was no
close emotional tie between them, but they were on affectionate
enough terms, and Hannah agreed to everything that Peg suggested. The elder daughter had always had to do the thinking and
planning for the little household: from childhood she had taken
the initiative. Perhaps she had sensed that a woman of Mrs
Woffington's simplicity could not make decisions, and that she
herself would always be responsible for her mother and sister. In
the event, she had no hesitation in agreeing to go with Violante;
it would give her a chance to act in London. It was an exciting
prospect. Her mother would not lack money, for Peg had saved
quite a substantial sum from the salary Violante had paid her, and
she left most of this at home. In August 1732 she embarked on

the packet-boat at Parkgate with her mistress and the Lilliputians, bound for the great city which was the capital of the theatre world.

Peg Woffington was now fourteen years of age, and already her early prettiness was showing promise of budding into real beauty. Her skin was fine and delicately coloured, her eyes dark and shining, her hair deep brown with auburn tints. Slender, but rounded, her figure was unusually graceful, and Violante's many lessons in posture and walking had given her a poise and confidence beyond her years. She was no longer a 'prentice-player, but a young actress who could be depended upon; Violante must have felt glad that she had spent so much time on the girl. The company was below strength, owing to the circumstance of Barrington and the others staying behind, and some of the parts in *The Beggar's Opera,* already doubled, would have to be trebled. Violante gave Peg several of the principal rôles to study, and the long journey to London was taken up with word rehearsals.

At the beginning of September 1732 several of the London newspapers carried an advertisement that 'the famous Signora Violante', who had just arrived with 'an extraordinary fine company', would be presenting, at the new theatre in the Haymarket, 'the most surprising Performance that ever was shown in the English Theatre – To which is added the Beggar's Opera after the Irish manner, which was performed 96 times in Dublin with great Applause. The part of Macheath by the celebrated Miss Woffington.' Bills were distributed.

Here, then, is the first mention of a breeches part played by Peg Woffington, the kind of part for which she was indeed to become celebrated without benefit of a puffing playbill. In that London performance she also played Mrs Peachum and Mrs Diana Trapes – which must have meant a certain amount of juggling with the scenes and lines by the enterprising Violante. Peg also took several parts in the 'surprising Performance' which preceded the play. This was a pantomime, *The Jealous Husband Outwitted,* in which Violante was Columbine, and the title part was played by a forceful, opinionated actor of about forty years of age, who thought that he was one of the best players ever seen on the stage, and did not hesitate to let everybody know it. It was evident that he had little opinion of Violante's troupe, straight from a Dublin booth-theatre.

James Quin had, in fact, begun his own career in Dublin, at

the Theatre Royal in Smock Alley – the legal, *patent* theatre. Since then he had played with *immense* success at Drury Lane and at Covent Garden. He had graced the rôles of Hotspur, Falstaff, Lear, Othello, Buckingham, *and* the Ghost in Hamlet, he would let them know. Why, after all that glory, he now condescended to act the comparatively insignificant Pantalone to a strolling trouper's Columbine he did not say. Violante herself listened to his boasting and made no remark; she was glad enough to get an experienced player in one of his 'resting' periods. The members of the troupe also listened, and were properly impressed. Peg was the only one who took scant notice of him – something which James Quin was always to remember. He did not know that Peg was applying herself to her own parts, anxious to play them so that the minutest detail came up to Madame's instructions. As always, it was the dramatic piece that mattered.

Violante remained only two weeks at the Haymarket: her venture had not turned out to be a success. The aristocrats who took boxes at the theatre were still out of Town for the summer, disporting themselves at Bath or Tunbridge Wells or some other fashionable spa. Anywhere else was considered clod-hopping country. 'Everybody' usually returned to London in September, but the weather was exceptionally warm and sunny, just like high summer, and many of them were remaining for another few weeks at the watering places, or at their country houses. This was disaster for a gamble such as Violante had embarked upon; she had relied on quick returns, and she was barely covering her outgoings. The theatre was half empty; even the cheap seats were but sparsely filled. Nobody was particularly interested in a troupe of Dublin juveniles, once the novelty had worn off. Even the critics ignored them, for there do not appear to have been any notices in contemporary newspapers or journals, and the advance advertisement was the chief publicity given to the Lilliputians.

Violante sent the company back to Dublin, but remained herself in London; when the winter season began, there would be opportunities to join some company of acrobats and dancers at one of the booths in the honeycomb of streets and alleys round Drury Lane and Covent Garden. Better still, she might be able to get together a company of her own, which Violante much preferred. It was with real regret that she parted from Peg Woffington. Peg was no acrobat; she was an actress, and already an ex-

perienced one for her age. When she came again to London it
would be with an assured reputation. As to another kind of reputation . . . Violante was realist enough to know the dangers a
young, beautiful and shapely girl would meet in the playhouse,
where every woman was fair game for the fops and bullies who
forced themselves into the Green-rooms. How much Peg knew of
life Violante could not tell, but it was unlikely that a child of the
Dublin slums, having spent years in the streets, selling salads for
pennies, could be unaware of the golden guineas which were to be
had in other directions.

Violante proffered no advice on the subject. After all, it was
some years since she had seen her Italian acrobat husband, and
there had been other men in her life. The girl must look after herself. She took affectionate leave of Peg, enjoining her to work
hard and cherish her voice. The company had been well paid in
spite of the comparative failure of the London performances and
Peg had a comfortably full purse to take back with her to Dublin.
There was enough money to keep her home going for some months
but, said Violante, she must lose no opportunity of getting into a
company of players.

Peg took her place with the other Lilliputians in the post-chaise
which was to carry them across England to the port where they
would embark on the Irish packet. A long, wearisome journey
lay before them, and already some of the juveniles had begun com-
plaining. Peg was busy with her own thoughts, sorting out possi-
bilities. There was John Barrington, who had taken on Madame's
booth. Was he still in George's Lane? She had every intention of
taking Madame's advice, for if there was one thing about which
young Peg Woffington felt certain, it was that she would spend
her life in the playhouse.

3
The Rivals

The three 'adventurous Undertakers', as Chetwood called Barrington, Sparks and Miss Mackay, had been surprisingly successful in their attempt to keep the George's Lane booth going. Chetwood says in his *General History of the Stage*:

> The Play was performed much better than was expected, and their Company soon became more numerous, being join'd by others that look'd more to Profit, than *Pleasure*; for these three Lovers of the Drama could play Heroes and Heroines without eating. Love for the Sublime was enough for them. However, other People did not relish this Camelion Diet, and hunger'd after something more substantial, therefore resolved upon Benefits, and gave the first to Miss Mackay, in order to break the Ice. *The Fop's Fortune* was the Play, and she then being a young promising Actress, several Ladies of the first Rank, espous'd her Cause and brought upwards of forty pounds to her Benefit. They might well say with the Herald in the *Rehearsal*: *They had not seen so much the Lord knows when.*

The custom of giving actors a benefit had been in being for a very long time. With salaries sometimes hardly at subsistence level – and often in arrears – a player needed to be assured of a substantial sum coming to him from time to time. On his benefit night, the other players, ordinarily paid on a nightly basis, would forgo their own share of the proceeds of the performance, and the benefit player would receive the takings, less the regular expenses of the theatre. If he was a popular actor, his aristocratic patrons would bring parties to fill the boxes, and of course the townsfolk, following the lead of the Quality, would crowd the rest of the

Peg Woffington by A. Pond.
(Reproduced by kind permission of the Earl of Lansdowne.)

Peg Woffington's First Visit to John Rich by F. Smallfield.
(Harvard Theatre Collection.)

Peg Woffington. An early
portrait by J. Lewis.
(Harvard Theatre Collection.)

house. The players seldom refused to give their services, knowing how much they depended on their colleagues when their turn came for a benefit.

Miss Mackay's forty pounds was a very large sum for a booth-theatre, and the fact that ladies of the first rank were taking an interest in her came as a second shock to the managers and actors at Smock Alley, who had thought that with the departure of Madame Violante, there was no longer any danger that audiences would fill the booth at George's Lane, and so stay away from Smock Alley. It seemed they had been mistaken; there was more potential danger from these young, enthusiastic and mettlesome players, ready to try any venture. Immediate action was necessary, and the managers of the Theatre Royal applied to the Lord Mayor, under the Licensing Law for playhouses, to have the George's Lane booth closed. The Lord Mayor ordered the youthful company to close their doors, and was with difficulty persuaded to allow them to put on a performance of *Woman's a Riddle*, which they had been rehearsing, and which they played 'to a good House'.

Peg was glad to be at home again with her mother and little sister, and Hannah Woffington was pleased and proud when she saw the purse of gold guineas this clever daughter had brought home. It was no longer necessary to sell watercress and lettuces in the street: Peg was determined that her mother should never do so again. She would be able to earn enough to keep the three of them in modest comfort.

The first shock came when she learned that John Barrington and his companions had been forced to close the George's Lane booth. The young company was disbanded, and Barrington had turned temporarily to other employment. Peg was reluctant to look for work in the shops or great houses of the city. She was intensely conscious of her talent as a player, a natural talent, trained by a mistress of the craft. There was already an improvement in her voice, for Madame Violante had taken time to give her singing lessons, which had helped to minimize the discordant

B

tone that was such a drawback. She could dance well, and Madame had insisted that she should read every book she could get
hold of, no matter what the subject was, so that she could increase
her vocabulary and learn to pronounce 'genteel Words in a genteel fashion'. Peg knew she *must* go on the stage. Yet where and
when would she get a chance to become a player in a proper
theatre?

The answer came in the form of the one person who was in an
excellent position to help her. Charles Coffey was a Dublin
schoolmaster, well known as a poet, and the author of a light
opera, *The Beggar's Wedding*, for which he wrote the music as
well as the libretto. Below normal stature, and the philosophic
owner of an ill-favoured countenance, Coffey had a kind heart
and an unforced charm which assured him of a welcome wherever
he went. He was in and out of the playhouses, knew everyone
and – more important – knew what was going on, and which way
the wind was blowing for the rumoured theatrical ventures always being talked about in the Green-rooms.

Coffey had been friendly with Violante, and had often watched
the Lilliputians act in George's Lane, going behind the scenes and
complimenting the young players. He had especially noticed
pretty, lively Peg Woffington, and when he heard that the company which Violante had taken to London had returned without
Madame, he was at once helpful when Peg Woffington came to his
lodgings and asked if he could assist her to obtain a footing in a
playhouse. Apart from the booths, there was not much choice.
A 'Music-hall' had been opened the previous year in Crow Street,
but Peg wanted to act in the playhouse. The Theatre Royal in
Smock Alley was the obvious place, especially as Thomas Elrington had raised its status.

'The stage', says Hitchcock,

> had now attained a most respectable eminence. Its professors
> were held in estimation, and their company courted. The
> manager was, most deservedly, esteemed and caressed by all
> the nobility and gentry. His grace the Duke of Dorset, then
> lord-lieutenant, was remarkably fond of the drama, and a
> princely encourager of it; he commanded plays once or twice a
> week constantly, and . . . his presence always occasioned a
> full house.

Elrington had recently died; the theatre was being managed by his brother, Francis, and two of Thomas's sons, Joseph and Ralph, were actors in the company. Coffey went to see Francis Elrington, who refused to take on a young player with such limited experience. Coffey then persuaded the manager to allow Peg to attend the theatre as an apprentice. She was not a vain, imperious miss, he said: she was a born player, trained by Violante, and wished to learn as much as she could of the business. She would keep out of the way, and be content to stand at the side and watch. Francis Elrington, like all Coffey's friends, had much respect for the little schoolmaster-poet-playwright, and he agreed to allow Peg Woffington to come to rehearsals, and to be given a seat at performances. Perhaps she could make herself useful in return, but she must not, he insisted, get in the way of the actors.

Peg was greatly delighted when Coffey told her the news. This was a chance she must not miss. It meant that she would not be earning any salary, but by careful management her store of money from the London trip could be made to last for a few weeks. Perhaps, by then, she might have the good fortune to be offered a small part. Coffey was optimistic. She would get to know the company simply by being there, day after day, and her face would become familiar to the Elringtons. There was nothing like being in the right place if an emergency arose, such as an actress feeling out of sorts – or out of humour. Charles Coffey knew the ways of players. He told Peg not to be too frugal with food, and said in his kind way that she had a friend to whom she could turn should her store of money run out before she began to earn a salary.

Smock Alley was even more exciting than George's Lane had been, or even London. In the English capital Peg had had her first experience of acting on a large stage in a full-sized theatre, but she had been so occupied with her various parts that there had been no time to stand and study others. Here, the stage of Smock Alley was not so commodious as that in the Haymarket playhouse, but everything that took place on it had a serious and business-like air. She watched experienced actors and actresses being put through their paces, repeating lines and practising movement and gesture. It was absorbingly interesting to note how the women managed their voluminous stage costumes, and, above

all, how they appeared to change their entire character according
to the parts they played.

Charles Coffey had been right in thinking that the Elringtons
would notice Peg Woffington. She came every day, and followed
everything that went on at rehearsal with close attention. Francis
Elrington could see her moving forward to listen when he was giving instruction to a player, no matter how trifling the matter.
Here indeed was a born actress. Another point in her favour was
the fact that she did not pester him to find her a part, as he had
half expected. Neither did she presume on her undoubted prettiness, which, in the manager's experience, showed unusual self-
discipline. He began to give the young Woffington lessons, when
he had time, and Peg might have achieved a small part and a
salary within a few months, had the attention of the manager and
players not been distracted by a new threat to the continued
success of Smock Alley.

The compulsory closing of the booth-theatre in George's Lane,
and the consequent dashing of the hopes of John Barrington and
his friends, had not gone unnoticed in the city; there had been an
indignant reaction from aristocracy and townspeople alike. The
Earl of Meath, who had been a patron of the young players and
admired their pluck, offered them 'an elevated tract on the western
side of the city' in his 'liberty', which was outside the jurisdiction
of the Lord Mayor. A number of liberties, or enclaves, flourished
in Dublin; the name stemmed from certain privileges and im-
munities conferred upon them. The inhabitants of the Earl of
Meath's liberty were descendants of French artisans who had
settled in Dublin after the revocation of the Edict of Nantes, and
had continued in their specialized trade of the manufacture of
silks and woollens. They married among themselves, preserving
their own characteristics, and had their own courts and customs. The Dublin authorities did not interfere with them,
and they were accepted as a separate community outside the city
proper.

A new theatre was built in Rainsford Street, in the earl's
liberty, and was opened at the end of January, 1733, when 'the Rt.
Hon. the Earl of Meath's Comedians' were advertised to begin

their season with a comedy, *Love for Love*. The new playhouse was described as being 'compleatly finished and extreamly commodious', and a promise was made that the Town would be highly diverted, 'there being an admirable Sett of Performers'. John Barrington and his young friends were among the regular performers, but Barrington was no longer in charge. The Earl of Meath's Comedians had grown into a full company, and had been put under the dual management of John Husband and Lewis Duval. Husband was an experienced actor, and in Chetwood's approving words, 'a Gentleman of exact Conduct'; Duval was the French dancer who had been brought over to Dublin by Madame Violante some years before, and had made a reputation as a dancing master. He had been employed by many of the fops and ladies of fashion to show them the art of moving gracefully, to hold a handkerchief and flirt a fan, and he had a ready-made following who would fill the boxes of the newly-built theatre. He was also a shrewd man of business, with an eye on the rest of the house.

Rainsford Street was some way from the centre of the city; it would need some inducement for the pit and galleries audience to walk such a distance, having no carriages, like the Quality, and being unlikely to hire sedan chairs. Duval let it be known that he would never raise the charge for seats at new plays – a usual practice – but would keep them 'at common Prices'. Even then, he could fill the theatre at a hundred pounds a time, a satisfactory sum. The only exception he made was for benefit nights, when the public in all parts of the house expected and were willing to pay more.

Smock Alley now had a really serious rival, and the manager and his associates lost no time in pushing ahead plans for a counter-attack. Thomas Elrington, before his death, had intended to build a bigger and better theatre than the existing Theatre Royal, which was becoming more and more dilapidated. Francis Elrington now decided to go on with the scheme. Possessing, as he did, the Royal Patent, he had no difficulty in persuading 'many of the Illustrious Nobility and Gentry of the Kingdom' to subscribe, especially as they were 'fully convinced of what great utility to a rising nation public amusements are, when properly conducted'. Two adjoining pieces of land, in the fashionable part of the city, at the corner of Aungier Street and Longford Lane, were leased, and the 'Engineer and Surveyor-General of His

Majesties Fortifications in the Kingdom of Ireland' engaged to build the new theatre.

Hoey's *Journal* declares that it was Sir Edward Pierce, the aforesaid Engineer and Surveyor-General, who laid the foundation stone; Hitchcock, who was present, states that there were no less than four stones, laid by four gentlemen, and describes the prodigious concourse of people who were assembled, and how each stone was laid with a flourish of trumpets, drums, a band of music, and the loud acclamations of the multitude. Whoever laid the stones, the workmen did well, for they had a barrel of beer given to them, 'and money enough to complete the day's drinking'.

The new theatre was built in less than a year, being opened in March 1734. Faulkner's *Dublin Journal* described it as much the finest playhouse in Europe – but then George Faulkner, a neat little barrel of a man in his tight brown suit, who went everywhere in Dublin and wrote most of his own newspaper, was intensely patriotic. His assertion was not entirely journalistic hyperbole, for Chetwood, not easy to please, says: 'The Audience Part is ornamented with rich Embellishment, that gives it a superbe Countenance', adding characteristically that this might have been achieved at less cost, and that the architect 'had more view to the Magnificent than the Theatrical', though, he allowed, it was fine enough to vie with the Haymarket playhouse in London.

The subscribers for the erection of the theatre, 'noblemen and gentlemen of the first rank and consequence', were actuated by the highest motives and started off 'without the least idea of emolument in return'. They insisted, however, on having a very active finger in the pie. They chose a committee and chairman from among themselves, and arranged to meet every Saturday 'to appoint plays, distribute the parts, and settle the great variety of business which unavoidably arises from so great an undertaking'. Francis Elrington was appalled. Choosing plays and actors by committee! The noblemen and gentlemen went further. While reappointing Elrington and two of his colleagues, Griffith and Layfield, they placed above them a Mr Swan, 'to superintend the management'. Mr Swan was affable, genteel, and possessed a good nature, but he knew nothing whatever about running a theatre, and Elrington foresaw trouble. It was a great relief when it turned out that Mr Swan, who dabbled in the art of acting in a modest way, was more than content to leave the tough, day-to-day business of the theatre to Mr Elrington, Mr Griffith and Mr Layfield, and he generally agreed to their decisions on plays and players.

The first production was Farquhar's comedy *The Recruiting Officer*, with a fine-looking actress, Mrs Bellamy, in the rôle of Silvia, who assumes a soldier's uniform. A breeches part. Peg Woffington played Rose, a country wench, but she must have envied Mrs Bellamy, for she liked the swagger and freedom of the manly young blade on the stage, and was ambitious to try such a part herself. Elrington gave her other rôles: Miss Crotchet in a satiric ballad opera, *The Rival Theatres, or a Playhouse to be Lett,* and a French peasant in a comedy. She also danced between the acts with two popular French performers, William Delemain and Henri Morceau. Delemain was of Huguenot extraction, and had been associated with the Dublin stage for twenty years; he could be depended on to draw an audience from the Earl of Meath's liberty. Morceau, a Parisian, was much sought after as a dancing master. Hard-working, excellent mimes, they earned what guineas came their way, always demanding of themselves high standards in whatever they undertook. They found Peg a light and graceful partner, quick to take instruction, and as hard-working as themselves. They were not surprised to learn that her mistress had been Madame Violante, and they talked to her in French, most of which she could understand.

Charles Coffey was a great influence on Peg Woffington at this time. An easy-going man of the theatre as playwright and librettist, he was still a schoolmaster in grain, and when he dropped in to see Peg in the Green-room at Aungier Street he often brought her books. A good command of language was essential to a rising actress, he told her: she must read and read. Peg especially liked the plays which Coffey lent her, as there were plenty of lines to be learnt. She enjoyed the facility she had discovered in herself of being able to memorize a part very quickly; she would commit long passages from play-texts to memory, and act them for Coffey afterwards, to his delight. He told her she should watch the way the actresses in the company impersonated fine ladies; better still, she must study the real Quality on every occasion, so that she could pass for one of them in earnest, when the time came for her to play these dames on the boards. Above all, she must understand 'dramatick characters' of every kind, otherwise she would never be a leading player. Charles Coffey was a very encouraging friend.

Peg continued to play small parts and dance between the acts. Then came an opportunity for which every ambitious young actress yearns. *Hamlet* was to be produced, and the player who had made Ophelia her own for many years 'became distempered, to her wild chagrin,' during the last rehearsal. There were no understudies; a player claimed certain rôles, and if he or she was stricken by illness the piece advertised for that night was changed and another from the repertory substituted. A manager avoided making last-minute changes of this kind if he could, for he had to go before the curtain in person, beg the pardon of the audience, ask their indulgence, and privately hope that they would not show too much resentment, or ask for the return of their money and angrily leave the theatre. All managers dreaded such an emergency. *Hamlet* was a popular play, and a Dublin audience would not take kindly to being done out of it.

Peg Woffington was well aware of all this, and she commanded her courage and went to Francis Elrington. Could she play Ophelia? She knew the part – indeed, she knew Gertrude, too. Elrington would probably not have been surprised to learn that she also knew Hamlet: he had long ago noted that she put the business of the playhouse before everything else. He consulted his co-managers, who at once agreed, and Peg was given the part. It was the classic situation of a relatively unknown player stepping into the breach at the last moment.

She turned out to be an adequate Ophelia: hardly more could have been expected, with only one rehearsal for moves before the performance. Charles Coffey, at the back of a box, thought she did well enough. The audience, the most critical and candid in Europe, were not in a mood to be overly critical. Here was a *young* Ophelia – and a lovely one. Hitchcock says: 'She began to unveil those beauties, and display those graces and accomplishments, which for so many years afterwards charmed mankind." Standing there with her dark brown hair falling in ringlets on her bare shoulders, eyes sparkling like jet in the light of the hundreds of candles sconced over the stage, she held the audience in thrall.

Elrington was more than pleased at the reception, and from then on Miss Margaret Woffington was in the regular acting company and had her name on the playbills – in small type, of course, for the other players felt there must be a sense of proportion in all things. Peg was Miss Lucy in Fielding's *Virgin Unmask'd*, and the maid Phillis in Steele's *Conscious Lovers*. Phillis was a delicious part. Phillis, a serving-maid, flirts with Tom, a fellow servant in a grand house. She copies the fine airs of her mistress, and Tom, when he finally wins her, chides her for her former behaviour, especially on the day when they first met, he cleaning the window sashes outside while she played with a duster inside. Seeing how hopelessly smitten he was, she was so provoking that he nearly fell off the ladder, he tells her. ' . . . You immediately grew wanton in your conquest, and put your lips close, and breathed upon the glass, and when my lips approached, a dirty cloth you rubbed against my face, and hid your beauteous form; when I again drew near, you spit, and rubbed, and smiled at my undoing.' To which Phillis replies: 'What silly thoughts you men have!' The critics especially liked Peg Woffington's Phillis, which became one of her favourite parts.

Charles Coffey persuaded the managers to put on his own comedy, *The Devil to Pay*, and coached Peg in the part of Nell, which Catherine Raftor had made her own before going off to London a few years before to seek fame and fortune. Miss Raftor, later to become famous as Kitty Clive, was a young Dublin lady of unimpeachable respectability and fiery temper, some seven or eight years older than Peg Woffington, who did not like her parts given over to anyone else. Still, she was safely in London, busy using her undoubted talent to get her a secure place on the metropolitan stage, and Coffey had no fear of fireworks from that quarter. Peg made a lively Nell, the audiences clapped enthusiastically, and George Faulkner was more than kind in his *Journal*.

Peg now suggested a character which she had long wanted to play: the name part in *The Female Officer*, a farce of no great merit but with a breeches rôle for her.

'She never displayed herself to more advantage than in characters where she assumed the other sex,' says Chetwood. 'Her figure which was a model of perfection, then free from restraints, appeared in its natural form.'

As Peg's natural form was exceedingly shapely, she was naturally not averse from displaying it, and Elrington made the most of the attraction. Miss Woffington's name now appeared in bold type on the playbills, and her salary was raised by ten

shillings. Aungier Street continued to be well filled on the nights
when Peg Woffington played, but the managers had always to look
for fresh novelties, for there were other attractions in the city.

Lewis Duval's company was, of course, the greatest threat.
They were no longer in Rainsford Street, but had actually rented
the old theatre in Smock Alley. Duval found that his audiences,
after supporting him well at first, began to fall off, and his 'neat,
compact building capable of containing a hundred pounds' was
now so thinly filled that he had to take definite action. There was
nothing for it but to eat humble pie and ask the Lord Mayor for
permission to return within that official's jurisdiction, and to
apply for a licence for the theatre in Smock Alley, empty since
Elrington's company had removed to Aungier Street. The Lord
Mayor was gracious, and Duval's company came back into the city.
The rivalry between the two theatres was now one between equals.

Smock Alley was in such a state of dilapidation that Duval
was soon on the look-out for subscribers to back a scheme for the
pulling down of the old playhouse and the erection of a new one.
No difficulty there; a playhouse was considered a good investment, and Mr Duval had been sensible and obtained the royal
licence. The money was subscribed by the nobility and gentry, the
old building was demolished, and the new one built within seven
months. The subscribers exercised a direct choice of the plays to
be presented by guaranteeing monetary support. They dined
together 'in Order to Chuse the four Plays and fix upon the Entertainments which shall be added the Nights of Performance. Ladies
may there have Votes by Proxy,' as George Faulkner noted in the
Dublin Journal.

The theatre was larger than the one in Aungier Street, but,
according to Chetwood, the stage was more cramped. Sir Jonah
Barrington, describes the playhouses in Dublin, which had not
altered from Peg Woffington's time:

> Lighted with tallow candles, stuck into tin circles hanging
> from the middle of the stage, which were every now and then
> snuffed by some performer . . . The galleries were very noisy
> and very droll. The ladies and gentlemen in the boxes always
> went dressed out nearly as for court; the strictest etiquette and
> decorum were preserved in that circle; while the pit, as being
> full of critics and wise men, was particularly respected . . . The

actresses of both tragedy and genteel comedy wore large hoops, and whenever they made a speech walked across the stage and changed sides with the performer who was to speak next, thus veering backward and forward, like a shuttlecock, during the entire performance.*

The new Smock Alley playhouse was packed for the first plays, but Duval had no outstanding actors who might compensate for the mediocre comedies which his backers had chosen, and he began to run into financial difficulties once more.

Both companies went on tour during the summer months, Elrington taking the Aungier Street company south to Carlow, Kilkenny, Cork and Limerick, while Lewis Duval travelled north to Belfast, stopping at various towns on the way. Peg Woffington went with the company, playing whatever parts were given to her. Touring in Ireland was her first experience of the summer life of the Dublin players. They had to travel as cheaply as possible, taking places in stagecoaches, or sitting on the bundles of scenery and the wardrobe baskets, piled on to carts.

There were no halls in villages; they usually had to make do with a fit-up in a barn. Hogarth has left an unforgettable record of what this must have been like in his painting, *Strolling Actresses Dressing in a Barn*. It is all there: the dimly-lit barn, flail aloft, hen and chickens at roost, bed, chamber-pot, flags, paint, drums, crowns, mitres, helmets, periwigs, feathers, baskets, hampers of clothes and stage jewellery, candles, daggers, dragons, flagons, an actress rehearsing tragedy, another with bare thighs posturing as Juno, cooking-pots and shirts hanging up, swags of artificial roses draping a column – cumulative detail that has been built up into a marvellous impression of the life of strolling players.

Most provincial towns, especially the garrison towns, had assembly rooms, and some of them also possessed theatres. There was a new playhouse in Cork, standing out in unwonted elegance above the thatched houses in the narrow, crooked, dirty streets. Kilkenny, too, had a theatre, as well as a good market hall where companies of players could set up for a night or two. This was a prosperous place; the citizens had money, and the best seats were not always taken by the grand people in the surrounding

* Sir Jonah Barrington: *Personal Sketches of His Own Times*, London 1827–32.

great houses, but were filled by linen merchants, silk weavers, tanners, tallow-chandlers and other craftsmen and tradesmen.

In the small towns, the audiences were less sophisticated, more liable to treat players with scant respect, bursting out laughing at highly dramatic moments and shouting and clapping overlong when a joke took their fancy. The repertoire was a well-tried one; not for small-town audiences the sophistication of a *Female Officer*. The drama of *Hamlet* was more to their liking, and the women in the company took care that Miss Woffington's Ophelia should not be allowed to overshadow the Queen and the ladies of the Danish Court; a few well-placed local 'friends' now and again started a laugh in the mad scene which was intended to shake Miss's nerve. It sometimes succeeded. Peg had to learn to hold her own, and it was a hard lesson. She discovered that coolness and dignity made strong armour, and she never attempted to retaliate.

The companies also entertained the ladies and gentlemen at the races of Mullingar, Carlow and Clonmell: 'Carlow was then thought of such consequence, that a great contention ensued, and after a vigorous opposition the Aungier Street company got the victory, and obtained leave to perform.' They had to take every opportunity of earning money.

Back in Dublin, the rivalry between the two companies immediately began again, but minor calamities outside their control could hit them both with equal force. In November 1737 Queen Caroline died, and the Lord Lieutenant ordered the two patent theatres to close for six weeks, as a mark of respect and mourning for George the Second's deceased consort. Coming as it did at the very beginning of the winter season, with plays already in rehearsal and stage costumes bought, this was indeed a blow. A closed theatre meant no money coming in, with consequent difficulties for the management and a company without salaries. Elrington was better than most at paying his players, but he was often in arrears if the theatre struck a bad patch and could not attract audiences. Few of the actors were ever able to save, and they suffered great hardship.

Peg, as usual, had given her mother the greater part of her earnings, and during that enforced 'rest' they did not want for necessities. Polly continued to go to a dame school, and Peg had already decided that her sister should move on to a Young Ladies' Academy when there was more money to spare. Peg was deter-

mined that Polly should have the good education which she herself lacked. Meanwhile, the breadwinner must husband what resources they had.

A piece of good fortune came her way within a few weeks of
the Theatre Royal's closing. Delemain asked her to join a company of seven mimes and dancers in Paris. His brother, Henri
Delemain, a first-class dancer who often partnered La Barbarini
at the Paris Opera House, had a theatrical booth at the Fair of
St Laurent, and William was joining him. The Fair lasted until
Lent, but Peg could return home when she wished.

Nothing venture . . ! Peg did not take long to make up her
mind. She left Dublin with William Delemain and a woman
dancer from one of the booths, reached Paris after a journey
which took nearly two weeks, and was soon at work. Little is
known about this first visit of Woffington's to the French capital.
It is probable that even her willingness and vitality were taxed by
the almost non-stop performances expected of booth-dancers.
She did not remain until Lent, but came home when Aungier
Street was ready to reopen. The Delemains must have paid her
well, for she brought good savings back to her mother.

In Dublin, the licensed theatres were in debt, not only on
account of the late compulsory closure, but because the Court
was still in mourning, and the Lord Lieutenant and the gentry
did not wish to disport themselves at the play until convention
made it seemly for them to do so. The patents of both theatres
were mortgaged to merchants and others, but the managers put
on productions nevertheless, increasing their indebtedness in the
optimistic hope that they would strike a success and so recoup
all. Elrington presented a gorgeous spectacle at Aungier Street:
'Henry the Eighth with the Coronation, at great expense, and
with much pomp and parade.' The town at once hurried to see
it – as did many of the Quality, Court mourning or no. Lewis
Duval could not vie with his competitor in stage splendour, and
'adopted the only conduct proper on such an occasion': what he
could not outdo he endeavoured to throw into ridicule. He mounted a mock coronation called *The Royal Merchant, or the Beggar's
Bush*, and burlesqued every procession and all the traditional
minutiae of a real coronation. The town now filled Smock Alley
every night. Honours were even.

At Aungier Street, Elrington and his co-managers countered

with Miss Margaret Woffington. Peg had already made it known
that she was desirous of acting Silvia in *The Recruiting Officer*,
the part she had seen Mrs Bellamy play. Mrs Bellamy had left the
company and gone to London, and no other woman in the company had taken over the rôle for herself. Peg Woffington suggested
the play to Elrington, who remembered her success in *The Female
Officer*, and thought it was an excellent idea. *The Recruiting
Officer* was quickly mounted, the bills printed, and boxes were
immediately bespoken at the box-keeper's. The charming Woffington, and a saucy play! The town was interested.

The town was also enchanted. Peg's high spirits and roguish
sense of comedy carried the house every night, and the journals
were full of praise. What a shape, what an intriguing mixture of
swaggering man and bewitching girl! Peg Woffington continued
to play Silvia in Dublin and during the summer journeys to the
towns in the south. There was now no question of her being billed
as a minor actress; she was one of the leading players from the
Theatre Royal, Aungier Street, and Mr Farquhar's *Recruiting
Officer* was allowed to be a most diverting piece. Peg claimed
Silvia as her own, though she was always ready to play small
parts, if required, in the other plays of the repertory – a willingness
unusual in one whose star was rising.

The rivalry between the two patent theatres continued, each
management doing its best to outdo the other. In June 1739
'The celebrated Mr Quin, then in the zenith of glory, accompanied
by Mr Giffard, played several nights at Smock Alley, and drew
crowded houses.' If Peg Woffington, at Aungier Street, remembered the conceited actor who had been Harlequin to Madame
Violante's Columbine during the London visit several years
before, it is doubtful whether she wished to renew the acquaintance, in spite of Mr Quin's aura of glory. Together with the
others at Aungier Street, she was alarmed at Smock Alley's
continued success, which drew away their own audiences. An
idea was growing in her mind. If she had the shape and spirit for
Silvia in a soldier's breeches, why not try something that had
never been done before by a woman – a part that was *all* man?
And the most handsome, elegant beau in the world at that?

4

Wildair

George Farquhar, an Irish actor who had been educated at Trinity College, Dublin, began writing plays at the end of the seventeenth century, after wryly accepting the fact that he would make but an indifferent actor, but might turn into a good playwright. His first play, *Love and a Bottle*, was produced in 1698; the second, *The Constant Couple*, was an immediate success when put on in 1700, mainly because of the character of Sir Harry Wildair, 'an airy gentleman, affecting humourous gaiety and freedom in his behavior', according to Farquhar's stage directions; in other words, a high-spirited rake, witty, good-natured, devil-may-care. Robert Wilks,* an actor who had begun his career in Dublin and then gone to London, made the rôle of Wildair famous; no one else dared to play it during his lifetime, and it was said that no man would venture on Wildair for at least a generation, for fear of being unfavourably compared with the incomparable Wilks.

No man – but, perhaps, a woman? Here was a breeches part indeed, one to set the imagination dancing. Peg got the play from Charles Coffey, read it, and, encouraged by him, suggested the play to Elrington and his co-managers. It was an excellent comedy she said – and she wanted to play Wildair. For once Elrington hesitated. Wildair! The rôle Wilks had made his very own. It could not possibly be played by a woman. No? challenged Peg. She reminded Elrington of *The Female Officer*, and of Silvia in an officer's regimentals. Elrington knew that women in men's garb had been popular since the days of the Restoration, and Peg Woffington had a glorious form. Why not? It would be a novelty,

* Also spelt Wilkes.

a new topic for the clubs and withdrawing-rooms – and therefore the best way of filling the Theatre Royal in Aungier Street.

Elrington put the play into rehearsal, but did not publicise this novelty to outdo all other novelties. It was only when the bills were displayed throughout the city that the news flew round: the lovely Woffington was to personate the fascinating rake made famous by Wilks. There was a rush for the box-keeper's and when the Theatre Royal in Aungier Street opened for the first performance a few nights later, a great press of carriages and sedan chairs filled the narrow streets, the chairmen cursing a passage through the milling mob. The theatre was soon packed full, aristocratic patrons in the boxes, Trinity men and well-to-do citizens in the pit, clerks, journeymen, shopkeepers and the like cramming the galleries.

From the moment of Peg's entrance, dashing and debonair, her figure set off to perfection by the close-fitting suit of satin and lace, the evening was a stunning success. Never had anyone looked so splendid on the stage. Managements could seldom afford new suits for the stage wardrobe; they were used to buying the cast-off finery of men of fashion, sold through servants of the beaux. Peg Woffington had insisted on having her suit specially made for her, and Elrington had had to give way. She had been right. The effect was wonderful, the new satin gleaming sleekly, a fall of lace from chin to waist giving her a rakish gallantry. Peg had dressed her thick, dark hair with its auburn tints into the form of a beau's wig, but had left it unpowdered.

At the end of the evening, the Green-room was packed with 'a great concourse of admirers and worshippers at the feet of the lovely Woffington'. Praise was a balm Peg had had in plenty during her theatrical life, but this was something she had not experienced before – rivers of compliments, hand on heart, as gentleman after gentleman bowed before her and took her hand to kiss. There were fine ladies, too, twinkling with diamonds, their powdered hair well curled, their hooped dresses swinging as they moved. They, too, murmured compliments, but they did not stay long, once they had stared at her beautiful face at close range. The men remained, trying to hold her attention. Hitchcock describes Peg's triumph with his usual precision:

The novelty of the attempt attracted the notice of all the dramatic connoisseurs. The house was crowded, and so infinitely did she surpass expectation, that the applause she received was beyond any at that time ever known. The former standard for acting the character was Mr Wilkes. Every one who had attempted it after him fell very far short. It was reserved for Miss Woffington to exhibit this elegant portrait of the Young Man of Fashion in a stile perhaps beyond the author's warmest ideas.

As Elrington had hoped, Miss Woffington's Wildair was the chief subject of talk in the clubs and drawing-rooms next day – with consequent full houses at Aungier Street. The town wits wrote verses in praise of her dash and charm, which the journals were only too glad to publish:

> That excellent Peg
> Who showed such a leg
> When lately she dressed in men's clothes –
> A creature uncommon
> Who's both man and woman
> And the chief of the belles and the beaux!

Scarcely a day went by without new verses of homage. Some remembered her earlier appearances with the Lilliputians:

> Peg, the darling of the town
> In Polly won each heart:
> But now she captivates again
> And all must feel the smart.
> Her charm, resistless, conquers all –
> Both sexes vanquished lie,
> And who to Polly scorned to fall
> By Wildair, ravaged, die.

It was Peg Woffington's first real success. The other women in the company might glare behind their smiles, but she could now demand to have her name on the playbills in the same size of print as the best of them. The placing and size of their names on the billing was of great importance to the players. It was the custom to print the names in order of their appearance, but the size of the type was a continual bone of contention. Chetwood, who in his time was responsible for printing many bills, writes: 'I have found it very difficult to please them, and some were so very fond of elbow room, that they would have shoved every body out but themselves.'

The managers prudently raised Miss Woffington's salary – the rival house was in financial difficulties, but Duval might be able to get backing to tempt the rising star away to Smock Alley: better be on the safe side. Peg was naturally delighted. More money meant an increased wardrobe for herself, more comforts for her mother, and the translation of her sister from the dame school to an exclusive Seminary for Young Ladies where she could live as a boarder. Polly's companions there would be the daughters of the Quality; she would be taught every refinement, she would learn to speak with elegance. Peg could *copy* the speech and behaviour of the fashionable world, but she had very different plans for Polly. At an age when she herself had been working hard in Madame Violante's booth, fighting to lift herself out of deadening poverty, Polly would be transforming herself into Miss Mary Woffington, young lady, in earnest. The Seminary for Young Ladies was another step towards an end: to make Polly accomplished, elegant, at ease in polite society. Later, she would perhaps go to a finishing establishment in France – this was where the Quality sent their daughters. Peg was strongly determined that her sister should be fitted to enter the kind of life she herself admired, the world where conversation scintillated, where manners were polished and graceful, where the men of letters, men of affairs, the writers and the wits talked of books and travel and the great world outside Dublin.

The press of admirers crowding into the Green-room after every performance of Peg's Wildair was a sign of the play's outstanding success. Peg enjoyed it all. She sparkled at the beaux's admiration and smiled at the ladies, who did not guess that she was also noting, with keen eye, their manners and modes and vapourings. Most of the men were as artificial as the women: powdered fops in brocade and satin suits, black patches on their cheeks, boldness in their calculating eyes and familiarity in their exaggerated bows and attempts to hold her hand.

One of these gentlemen was different, and Peg began to look out for him. His name was Taafe, and he was the son of an Irish peer; not a rich peer, it was true, but undoubtedly one of the Quality. He was good-looking, impetuous and insistent, and he was always there in attendance, outstaying the others and insisting on taking Peg home in a sedan chair, or his own carriage.

Peg fell in love. This was not difficult, with such a devoted follower. It was an exceedingly pleasant sensation, and Peg enjoyed it even more than she did the admiration of the fops, and the pleasant knowledge that she was a success and the managers were keeping on *The Constant Couple* as long as possible.

The success was not to last. An unexpected hammer-blow of ill fortune struck Aungier Street and the other playhouses. Hitchcock describes the tragedy – for tragedy it was – in simple words: 'The dreadful severe winter of 1739–40, for a long time put a stop to all public diversions. The poverty and distress of the lower classes of people at that time can scarcely be described.'

There had never been such a winter in living memory. The terrible weather began early in December with a violent storm of wind which not only lashed the city with unprecedented fury, but swept on inland, devastating villages and scattering carefully hoarded stores of potatoes and grain. At the end of December there came a frost which lasted five weeks, and which froze the Liffey solid. The cold was something the people had never experienced before, and they were unprepared for it. A passage had to be cut through the frozen river, so that coal boats could reach the city – the coals being sold at an exorbitant price. Snow lay several feet deep in the streets for weeks, and the life of the city slowed down to a miserable existence level.

In these conditions, it was impossible to keep open the theatres and booths of entertainment. Lewis Duval attempted to attract audiences to Smock Alley, according to the contemporary Dublin *Evening Post*, by an ingenious device: 'He has erected in the pit, which he designs to continue during the frost, a fire engine in which is kept a large fire burning the whole time of the performance, and warmed the house in such a manner as gave great satisfaction to the audience.' This device was not sufficient to fill the theatre, however, and he was obliged to close Smock Alley.

Peg Woffington, like all the other players in Dublin, was now out of work. She had, as usual, good savings, and she was not troubled by the prospect of long days at home: there were always books to read, plays to study. And there was Mr Taafe.

The closing of Aungier Street did not stop Taafe's pursuit of the lovely Miss Woffington. He now grew passionate, and implored Peg to come to him: he had a house in the country, where they would be undisturbed. He broke down her resistance, giving Peg a promise of marriage. Hannah Woffington was not one to ask questions, and Peg, as always, left her and Polly well provided for when she went away. Peg set off for the country with Taafe.

The hard weather broke in February, and life returned to the city. Taafe brought Peg back, renting a house in Dublin. They entertained his friends there, and all was laughter and raillery.

5
Love, and a Sequel

Peg Woffington was no stranger to the facts of dishonourable *amours* in the playhouse; from her early days with Madame Violante she had been aware of extra-matrimonial unions, temporary or permanent. Actresses lived with their managers: 'The resistance of ladies to a manager was modified by the danger of offending one who had the power to appoint them to parts.' During hard times, and when the theatres were closed, many of the unmarried actresses lived with protectors; it was often their only alternative to starvation. 'Marriage and a coach' might be the goal of those who had confidence enough in their charms to tease an enamoured fop into a declaration, but, more often than not, his family would extricate him before it was too late. A large enough purse of jingling golden guineas dropped into the lady's hand usually did the trick.

Women on the stage, not surprisingly, had a bad reputation, whether deserved or not. It was only after the Restoration, eighty years or so before, that they had been allowed to act at all, and they had then been recruited mainly from the women of the town. When they turned out to be first-class actresses, an indulgent eye might be turned on their private lives. Chetwood saw Ann Oldfield act with Booth early in the century, and in his *General History of the Stage* describes his sensations:

> Her excellent clear Voice of Passion, her piercing flaming Eye, with Manner and Action suiting . . . I could hardly lug him up to the Importance of Triumphing over such a finish'd piece of Perfection. Even her Amours seem'd to lose that Glare which appear round the persons of the falling fair: neither was it ever

known she troubled the Repose of any Lady's lawful Claim, and was far more constant than Millions in the Conjugal Noose.

There were notable exceptions, the most prominent being Mrs Bracegirdle: 'An ornament to the Theatre . . . Her Youth and lively Aspect threw out such a glow of Health and Chearfulness that, on the Stage, few Spectators that were not past it, could behold her without Desire.' Mrs Bracegirdle's private character was, however, blameless, and though she apparently had no objection to raising desire, she had not the smallest intention of satisfying it without a church ceremony and a gold ring. Actresses were still fair game for the fops and beaux, and it was taken for granted that they had lovers. What they hoped for was 'a noble man of large fortune and a generous disposition'.

Peg Woffington had become adept at dealing with the pressing attentions of would-be lovers. Whether she had yielded to any at this early stage of her life is a matter for conjecture; there is no real evidence, one way or the other. She was to become notorious for her *affaires*, and later pamphleteers, each more scurrilous than the last, let their fancy run free over Peg's love-life. This one begins with a description of her feminine charms in the Aungier Street days:

Her Eyes were as black as Jet, and while they beamed with ineffable Lustre, at the same time, revealed all the Sentiments of her Heart . . . her Eyebrows were full and arched, and had a peculiar Property of Inspiring Love, or striking Terror, though their artless Owner knew not their Force . . . Her cheeks were vermilioned with Nature's best Rouge, which, like the Lilies and Roses, blended in sweet Conjunction, were striving for Preference, and outvied all the laboured Works of Art. Her Nose was somewhat of the Aqueline, which gave her a look full of Majesty and Dignity. Her Lips were of the Colour of Coral, and Softness of Down; and her Mouth displayed such beauties as would thaw the very Bosom of an Anchorite, and make Monarchs themselves start from their Thrones to press so much Joy and Softness. Her teeth were white and even, her Breasts, which just then began to pout, and declared the Woman, were ravishingly delicate, and inexpressibly pleasing. Her Hair was of a bright auburn Colour, which, in artless

Ringlets flowing down the best-turned Neck in the World, enchanted the Heart before it could guard against its Force.
In short, her whole Form was beauteous to excess, and
such as could not be viewed without Emotion nor without
Desire.

The pamphleteer then goes on to 'describe' how Peg first lost
her virtue, calling up one Bob, 'a Lad of some Spirit, possessed of
true Hibernian Assurance', who lived next door and longed, not
to throw himself at the fair Peg's feet, but to 'press her to his
Breast, clasp her yielding Waist, and shew the Vastness of his
Love by the Ardor of his Kisses'. Bob was robust, masculine and
bold, his age was seventeen 'and his Desires violent'. One evening,
finding Peg alone, 'his Heart danced unusual Measures', he became furious and wild, and he 'invaded her lips and next attacked
the Breast-Work'. The rest apparently followed in logical pro-
gression, with 'the frail girl sinking into the arms of unbridled
Lust'. It is clear that the pamphleteer worked himself up as well as
his story, for he thought it prudent to end his account in Latin,
which must have been frustrating for those of his readers who had
not had a classical education.
   The next flight of fancy concerns 'a tall strapping Blade', who
swears that if Peg does not return 'Love with Love' he will hang,
drown or shoot himself. 'The tender-hearted Girl, too good a
Christian to be the Death of any one, prevented his Murder by
sinking into his Arms.' In actual life, Peg would have told the
strapping Blade to choose his weapon and cease from troubling
her. There was only one way to conquer Peg Woffington – through
her affections. Many names have been linked with hers, even in
those first Aungier Street years, but most of them rest on rumour.
Charles Coffey? There is no record of an intimate association,
only of good friendship; but the little playwright was as im-
pressionable as the next man, he saw Peg often, she was very
fond of him, and it is probable that she repaid his long years of
unfailing kindness in the one way she could.
   The idyll with Taafe did not last much longer than the great
frost. He no longer mentioned marriage. Peg knew that he would
have to bide his time before breaking the news of a misalliance
to his family, and she would have gone on, living under his
protection and looking towards a more settled future, had Taafe

not begun to absent himself for days at a time. Then she heard rumours – and Taafe did not come back to contradict them. A pamphlet printed after Peg Woffington's death gives a factual account of this affair, purporting to have the story from an authentic source; and the story has a certain amount of corroboration from other sources.*

The younger son of an impecunious Irish earl could hope for little patrimony; it was necessary for him to marry money. Taafe 'coolly contracted another engagement with a young heiress to an excellent estate', and terminated the lease of the house in which he was living with Miss Woffington. Peg's reaction was one of shock, then fury. Dressing herself as an army officer, wearing a false moustache and arranging her hair *en peruke*, she is alleged to have travelled to the village near the country seat of the prospective bride's parents. She contrived to get an invitation to the ball given in honour of the approaching wedding, and, what is more, so impressed the company by her manly bearing and refined manners, that she was able to walk a minuet with the bride-elect.

The various accounts of the episode now become melodramatic, but all agree that the 'officer' found an opportunity to inform the bride-to-be of her affianced husband's *amour* with the player, Margaret Woffington. 'He' produced letters in which the double-dealing Taafe declared his passion for the actress in most endearing terms, protesting eternal fidelity, and referring to their future state of conjugal bliss. The bride-elect was naturally indignant, and the 'officer' returned to Dublin – to learn to her satisfaction, a day or two later, that the engagement had been broken off.

The theatres began production again as soon as they could reassemble their companies. Aungier Street opened in April, with Peg Woffington playing Lappet in *The Miser*, and Silvia in *The Recruiting Officer*, always a favourite with the public. The

* There are pamphlets at the British Museum, in various libraries in the United States, and in private libraries.

managers judged it unwise to put on her Wildair again, being
superstitious about the interrupted run of a play.

Benefits for the actors were more important than ever, after
the hardships of the winter. It was not unknown for players to
court the favour of the nobility for their benefits by personal
canvassing. One announcement, printed on handbills and widely
distributed, made a direct appeal to the influential:

> At the Theatre Royal in Aungier Street on Monday next will
> be presented the celebrated Tragedy of Hamlet, for the benefit
> of Mrs Neal, who humbly hopes the gentry will be so good as
> to encourage her in it, tho' at the Disadvantage of so short a
> Warning; and in regard to her unhappy State of Health, will
> excuse her not waiting on them as usual. She will endeavour to
> play the Part of Ophelia, and hopes the artful insinuations of
> her Enemies will not prevail on the Town to her Prejudice.
> Tickets to be had at her Lodgings, the Corner of Big Butter-
> Lane, near the Church.

The playgoing public was apathetic; their very spirits seemed
still to be frozen. The gentry came, glad to resume their usual
amusements, but the pit and galleries were thinly filled.

Elrington tried *The Beggar's Opera*, with Peg as Polly Peachum;
it drew moderate houses at first, then the audiences dwindled to
a handful. Genest, the theatre historian, says that the managers
were so reduced in their finances and so exhausted in their credit,
that they were in despair. Peg Woffington grew restless and un-
certain of her future. The Aungier Street company would be
starting out on its summer circuit in June, but she was reluctant
to go with them. Her thoughts turned towards England; so many
players from Dublin had left to try their fortune in the London
theatres, finding fame there and amassing small fortunes. She
was experienced enough to try the venture; wait until they saw
her Wildair! Peg was blithely confident that if she went to see the
great John Rich at Covent Garden, he would welcome her without question.

Her heart was not broken by the Taafe affair, but she would
be glad to get away from all the associations which brought him
to mind. She shared out her store of money with her mother, and
prepared for the journey. Hannah Woffington, as usual, was
acquiescent. Whatever Peg said! Polly was settled at her genteel

school, and appeared to be very happy there. Peg could leave with an untroubled mind, and she sailed from Parkgate in the packet at the beginning of May, arriving in London a few days later. She did not travel alone. Charles Coffey had also intended a journey to London, and they departed together. Whether they went as lovers is not known; different chroniclers have different theories, but it is probable that Coffey looked after Peg and helped her to find suitable lodgings when they reached the capital. Player-folk lived in the streets round Covent Garden and Drury Lane, so as to be able to answer a summons to the theatre quickly; with a system under which a play could be substituted for another at short notice, this was important.

Peg had no large bundles of clothes, no box of stage jewels. She carried with her a velvet gown for tragedy, and her splendid satin Wildair suit. For the rest, she had a list of the rôles she had played – and her ravishing beauty. The day after her arrival, she decided to call on John Rich at his house in Bloomsbury Square, the address which Charles Coffey had given her.

6

Covent Garden

The manager whom Peg Woffington confidently set out to see soon after her arrival in London was one of the most powerful men in the world of the theatre – and one of the most heartily disliked by his own contemporaries, and the players who formed his company.

John Rich was born in 1691 or 1692, the son of an attorney, Christopher Rich, 'an old snarling lawyer, a waspish, ignorant pettifogger, who disregards the rights of all others', acording to a dramatist who may well have suffered at the lawyer's hands. Christopher Rich bought a share in the Drury Lane patent from the heirs of Sir William Davenant*, the original patentee, and he apparently spent much of his time after that gleefully using his legal knowledge to outwit his co-patentees, actors and any others who were unwise enough to question his machinations in a court of law. Rich *père* also got his hands on the King's Theatre in the Haymarket, opened in 1705, but he overreached himself in trying to run two theatres, no doubt on account of his 'disregard to the rights of all others', and lost the patents of both playhouses. A few years later he was allowed to erect a theatre in Lincoln's Inn Fields, but did not live to see its completion, and it was opened in 1714 by his son John.

John Rich was a curious, complicated character. His father had been too mean to have him educated properly: 'He could not read ten lines of Shakespeare, or, indeed, of any other author, with propriety.' It was probably secret chagrin at the deficiencies in his education which made him turn an arrogant face to the world, and he had few personal friends. He knew little about plays, and was

* See author's Note, p. 225.

bored by real drama, but he had a strain of ingenuity which led to his inventing an entirely new kind of entertainment. Christopher Rich had often brought over French and Italian troupes of dancers and acrobats, and his son had the same tastes. He had seen Continental mimes draw much applause with their Scaramouche characters, and he hit on a version of his own which became the *pantomime*. Taking a traditional nursery story, John Rich presented it in a serio-comic vein, and interlaced it with a version of the Commedia Dell' Arte figures of Harlequin, Columbine, Clown and the rest, 'with a variety of surprising adventures and tricks, which were produced by the magic wand of Harlequin, such as the sudden transformation of palaces and temples to huts and cottages, of men and women into wheelbarrows and jointstools, of trees turned to houses, colonnades to beds of tulips'. Rich understood the mechanics of stage-carpentry and effects, and he had brought out a new, successful pantomime every year since 1717. A mediocre actor in straight parts, John Rich was an excellent Harlequin, and always played this himself.

The manager's uncouth manners made him the butt of the town, as did a passion he had for cats. He was married, and had three daughters; actors said he preferred his Grimalkins, but took care he did not hear their pleasantries. It was not wise to offend John Rich. After managing the theatre in Lincoln's Inn Fields for twenty years, he leased a parcel of land from the Duke of Bedford at the north-east corner of the Piazza in Covent Garden, and built a new theatre there. Many were the veiled remarks in the public prints at this ambitious venture of the pushful Harlequin. Rich took no notice. He knew what he wanted. The scenery at the new playhouse was well painted, the decorations 'suited to the grandeur and magnificence of the building'. Covent Garden was opened in December, 1732, with Congreve's *The Way of the World*, a fair success, then continued with *The Beggar's Opera*, which ran for twenty nights – a long run. There were four Shakespearean productions: *Othello, Lear, Timon of Athens* and *The Merry Wives of Windsor*. Rich himself played Harlequin in a pantomime, and put on a posthumous play of Gay's, *Achilles*; John Gay had recently died, and Rich gave one of the performances as a benefit for Gay's sisters.

The splendid theatre in Covent Garden was a playhouse to be reckoned with. There were six Royal Command performances during that first season. George the Second had a robust sense of humour, and Rich made him laugh: 'Excellent Harlequin, Mr. Rich – excellent Harlequin!' Rich let it be known that he had grand plans for future productions. The best actors were glad to be taken into his company, and if it meant poaching now and again from Drury Lane, well, he would turn poacher. There was a sizeable strand of the rascally old Christopher in his son.

This was the manager on whom Peg Woffington called at his house in Bloomsbury Square. She had dressed carefully, and taken a sedan chair; Charles Coffey had often impressed on Peg the importance of making a good appearance. It did not occur to her that she would meet with any rebuff, and she was both surprised and indignant when the door-servant told her unceremoniously that he had no instructions to admit any stranger. Miss Margaret Woffington? The doorkeeper did not know the name. Mr Rich did not receive unexpected callers. Good day.

Peg could get no further, and was obliged to go away. She returned the following day, to be met with the same reception. The doorkeeper was well used to stage beauties, imperious or wheedling – and Peg was both on this occasion – seeking an interview with the most successful manager in London, and he was unbribable. Fitzgerald Molloy, in *The Romance of the Irish Stage*, states that Peg went to Rich's house nineteen times before the doorkeeper, impressed at last by her persistence, took her name up to his master, and she was admitted. A writer in the *Dublin Review* describes this first meeting, which Peg Woffington later retailed to friends.

The great manager, as Woffington first saw him, was lolling in ungraceful ease on a sofa, holding a play in one hand, and in the other a tea-cup, from which he sipped frequently. Around him were seven and twenty cats of all sizes, colours and kinds. Toms and Tabbies, old cats and kittens, tortoiseshells, Maltese, brindles, white, black and yellow cats of every description. Some were frisking over the floor, others asleep on the rug; one was licking the buttered toast on his breakfast plate, another was engaged in drinking the cream for his tea, two cats lay on his knee, one was asleep on his shoulder, and another sat demurely on his head. Peg Woffington was astounded at the sight. Rich, to her mind, had for years been the greatest man in the world. The menagerie of grimalkins, amid which he lay so carelessly, was so different an environment from her conception of the study of the Covent Garden theatre manager, that she was embarrassed into silence.

Rich, for his part, expecting to see a loud, assured actress full of airs and graces, was so struck by the beauty of his visitor and her calm deportment that he could only sit and stare at her.

Standing before him was a woman who was the loveliest creature he had ever seen. She was taller than the ordinary standard of height, faultless in form, dignified even to majesty, yet withal winsome and piquant. Her dark hair, unstained by powder, fell in luxuriant wealth over her neck and shoulders.

John Rich was to declare later to Sir Joshua Reynolds:

It was a fortunate thing for my wife that I was not of a susceptible temperament. Had it been otherwise, I should have found it difficult to retain my equanimity enough to arrange business negotiations with the amalgamated Calypso, Circe and Armida who dazzled my eyes. A more fascinating daughter of Eve never presented herself to a manager in search of rare commodities. She was as majestic as Juno, as lovely as Venus, and as fresh and charming as Hebe.

Miss Margaret Woffington was also as businesslike as his own treasurer at the theatre. He had not heard of her Wildair? Peg allowed herself to be faintly surprised. It had been, she admitted, a success. She had also played Silvia in *The Recruiting Officer*, and she would require a salary comparable to that paid to the leading actresses at Covent Garden. The manager demurred, as she knew he would, and she then gracefully agreed to accept a lesser figure – on condition that Mr Rich would 'pay a proper salary' if she was considered to be a success. Peg herself had no doubt that she would be: neither had John Rich. He had no intention of letting this beautiful girl offer herself elsewhere, and had been prepared to accede to her first demands if she had, as he expected, prepared to sweep out of the door. Peg, too, knew that she would have got the higher salary if she had pressed sufficiently for it, but she deemed it wiser to give in on this first occasion. Mr Rich knew little of her reputation, it seemed. Let him see her act – and listen to the audience huzza-ing. That would bring better offers from the other playhouses without her having to go seeking employment, and Mr Rich would of his own accord raise her salary. Peg Woffington had absorbed many of the lessons which Charles Coffey, that astute man of the theatre, had tried to instil into her.

The manager engaged Miss Woffington for the company at Covent Garden, and the following day she entered the Green-room there to look for acquaintances; among the many Irish players who had crossed the water to seek their fortune in England, there was always the chance of seeing a familiar face in London. Almost at once she found one player she knew, Mrs Bellamy, with whom she had acted several years ago at Aungier Street: that same player whose Silvia she had envied. Mrs Bellamy welcomed the new arrival effusively. She was now middle aged, and she liked talking. Miss Woffington was known to be good-natured, in spite of her rise in the world. Conscious of an interesting history behind her, Mrs Bellamy was always ready to impress people with the information that she had once married a lord. Well – more or less.

Mrs Bellamy had been the only child of a hop farmer in Kent, of the name of Seal, who died suddenly without leaving a will. Mrs Seal, still young and handsome, sold the farm and removed to Tunbridge Wells with her small daughter, where she invested her money in several houses, which she let to 'persons of the first distinction'. She acquired a comfortable income and was much courted by the unmarried men of the town, making a bad choice in the end, for, 'having withstood all their attacks for upwards of two years', she gave her hand to one Busby, 'a builder of some eminence'. It turned out that Busby was eminent more for the size of his debts than anything else, and the new Mrs Busby's houses and all her possessions were seized by her husband's creditors, she unaccountably having failed to make a marriage settlement. It was with thankfulness that she accepted an offer made by the Honourable Mrs Godfrey, who had sometimes rented one of her houses for the season, to take young Miss Seal and bring her up with her own daughter. Mrs Godfrey was a sister of the Duke of Marlborough, so the little girl was fortunate to be virtually adopted into such exalted society.

High society at the beginning of the eighteenth century was loose-living and licentious, a fact that Mrs Busby found it convenient to ignore. At the age of fourteen, Miss Seal, already a beauty, attracted the attention of the dissolute young Lord Tyrawley, and as she, on her part, 'found her vanity gratified by receiving the devoirs of a person of his consequence', it was not difficult for him to persuade her to elope with him. He carried her off to his apartments in Somerset House, where she assumed his name without benefit of clergy, 'and was treated with the same respect as if she had really been Lady Tyrawley'. Her lover promised to marry her, but when, some months later, he was ordered to rejoin his regiment in Ireland, there was still no wedding ring.

Lord Tyrawley was an extravagant young man and he had squandered a great deal of money. There were two ways in which a nobleman could recoup his fallen fortunes: at the gaming tables, or at the altar. Success at gambling needed time, and the daughter of Lord Mountjoy had cast amorous eyes upon him. She was wanting in femine charm, but she was endowed with a pleasant disposition – and thirty thousand pounds. Her father, however, had heard of the lady already in residence at Somerset House, and wrote her a polite letter, asking about her connexion with Lord Tyrawley and giving the reason for his inquiry.

'Lady Tyrawley' had recently given birth to a son, and the letter came as a shock. In no mood to be prudent, she forwarded to Mountjoy a bundle of affectionate letters which Tyrawley had sent her from Ireland, including the latest, which had come by the same post as the other's communication, and which she had not yet opened. She did not then know that in this letter Tyrawley informed her of his distressed financial situation, and of the sad necessity there was for his marrying a lady of fortune. He added that he would not remain longer in Ireland than the time necessary to lay hands on his wife's fortune; he would then fly on the wings of love back to Somerset House. Lord Mountjoy read the letters, and forbade the match.

Did Peg Woffington smile at Mrs Bellamy's recital? It is probable. Taafe – Tyrawley – others of whom she had heard. The

Hogarth's painting of Peg Woffington as Sir Harry Wildair in *The Constant Couple*.
(Harvard Theatre Collection.)

David Garrick by Liotard.
(Harvard Theatre Collection.)

story was already a familiar one, and Peg accepted it as she accepted everything: as part of the nature of things.

Mrs Bellamy's career had been exceptionally colourful. Lord Mountjoy's refusal to allow his daughter to marry Lord Tyrawley came too late: they married secretly. Mountjoy withheld her fortune, and Tyrawley found himself tied to a plain, dowerless woman to whom he soon took a dislike. How could he disentangle himself? He had friends at Court, and was able to secure an appointment as Minister in Lisbon, whither he went without his bride.

Miss Seal, as she was now known, was without means of subsistence, but she had friends who suggested that, with her looks, she should go on the stage. She had no particular talent, but the idea appealed to her, and leaving her baby son in the care of her mother – who had again begun to let apartments to the nobility at Tunbridge Wells – she applied to the managers of the smaller theatres in London for engagements, and managed to make a living for several years, without achieving any fame. Lord Tyrawley had not dropped out of her life; on the contrary, he often wrote to her, inviting her to come to Portugal to visit him. After several refusals, she suddenly decided to go. Tyrawley received her with the warmest demonstrations, and for a time all went well; she stayed in a merchant's house, where there was much agreeable company, and a sea captain, Captain Bellamy, fell in love with her and began to woo her with much fervour. Miss Seal enjoyed his attentions, while, at the same time, resuming the liaison with her former lover whenever opportunity offered.

Tyrawley was attentive – but he had omitted to mention that he had a Portuguese mistress. When, inevitably, the quondam Lady Tyrawley found this out, she was already pregnant again. The next time Captain Bellamy called at the merchant's house, Miss Seal smiled upon him. They were married, and left Portugal in the Captain's ship for Ireland. The marriage did not last long. A daughter was born at Fingal on St George's Day, 1731, 'some months too soon for Bellamy to claim any consanguinity with the infant'. Captain Bellamy was so angry at his wife's duplicity that he sailed away and never came back.

Tyrawley's adjutant lived near Fingal, and he sent news of the birth to Lisbon; Tyrawley wrote giving instructions for the child to be taken from its mother and put into the care of a good

c

nurse. Mrs Bellamy was quite willing to give up her daughter, for she wanted to return to the stage. Lord Tyrawley sent instructions that the child was to be called Georgiana, but the minister at the christening somehow misheard the name, and saddled the baby girl with 'George Anne'. Mrs Bellamy did not see her daughter for four years, when a nursemaid took George Anne behind the scenes at Covent Garden to make a curtsy to her mother. Mrs Bellamy's reaction was hardly maternal: 'My God! What have you brought me here? This goggle-eyed, splatter-faced*, gabbart-mouthed wretch is not my child! Take her away!'

The goggle-eyed child grew up into an attractive girl. Lord Tyrawley had her educated in a French convent, and on her return to London placed her in the care of one of his former servants. George Anne was in the equivocal position usual with the illegitimate children of the nobly born: without any real place in society. Through her father she met ladies of quality, but no secret was made of her bastardy, and she grew up with a steady eye on her own interests. She soon learned that the chief passports to the world of opulence and fashion were flattery and a reputation for wit. Tyrawley had become very fond of her, and George Anne used this partiality quite ruthlessly to get him to introduce her into the best houses. Once there, praise tripped off her tongue with charming spontaneity, and a good memory enabled her to remember other people's witticisms and give them out as her own.

Lord Tyrawley was nominated ambassador to the Court of Russia. He left George Anne in the care of a lady of quality, allowing the girl a hundred pounds a year. News travelled quickly in the enclosed world of London society; in the Green-rooms, where the fashionables met after the play to compliment the players and exchange the latest news current in their own exalted circles, a pair of sharp ears might pick up snippets of information. And Mrs Bellamy had very sharp ears.

So George Anne now had a hundred a year of her own, with Tyrawley out of the way. Interesting. Mrs Bellamy, existing on badly paid small parts at Covent Garden, decided that she longed to see her daughter again, after all these years. It was at this point in her sad saga that Mrs Bellamy resumed her acquaintance with Peg Woffington, newly arrived from Dublin, and was

* A splatter was a coal-boat in Ireland.

grateful for the friendliness of the creature who was entitled
to put on fine airs on account of her youth and beauty, but who
remembered their old acquaintance, and even sat down to listen
to her talk.

The 1740 season at Covent Garden began in September. Rich
had put down Peg's début for November, and she had several
months in which to get used to London life. Charles Coffey looked
after her, taking her about with him to the coffee houses and to
the lodgings of his various player friends; it was always useful to
know people.

Peg was accustomed to the contrasts of Dublin, to squalor
existing side by side with extravagant luxury, but it is probable
that she had never imagined such a kaleidoscope as now presented
itself in London. Charles Coffey, the arch realist, believed in his
protegée having a clear-eyed view of the city in which she had
come to live and work; only in this way would she be able to look
after herself.

It was Hogarth's world: raucous, predatory, a human jungle
where everyone was out for himself, and the devil took the hind-
most. Covent Garden and Drury Lane were surrounded by lanes
and alleyways where the very dregs of humanity existed, swarm-
ing out at night to swell the crowd watching the coaches and
chairs set down outside the theatre, or going farther west to
Leicester Fields and the Haymarket. Here was a conglomeration
of types hardly seen anywhere else in Europe. 'Bewigged dandies
with gold-headed canes and embroidered coats, bearded foreign-
ers, red-coated officers of the Foot-guards, painted whores flaunting their feathers, swaggering dandies in broad-skirted, be-ruffled
coats with hand on dress-swords.'

Sedan chairs carried ladies of quality – and ladies of no quality
at all – their chairmen pushing through the throng, while the
light-fingered gentry slunk round the unwary, ready to cut a
purse or pick a pocket. It is all there, in the masterly canvases of
this artist who was to paint Peg Woffington at the peak of her
fame, and who may well have passed her as she strolled through
the crowded streets, secure on Coffey's arm. Hogarth had a
wonderful gift for depicting the oddities he saw around him: faces

showing cruelty, snobbery, corruption. Where Rowlandson caricatured with savage satire, Hogarth set down the vices and weaknesses of mankind with a detachment that made them all the more vivid and terrible. Yet there was always compassion: 'Truth is so priceless, and so welcome in every shape, that we must be content to honour it whatever form it comes to us.' Hogarth was not afraid of life; as Johnson said of him, he had 'the attentive eyes that saw the manners in the face'.

Rehearsals for *The Recruiting Officer* began in October, and Peg now began to work in earnest. The company at Covent Garden were friendly enough; Mrs Horton and Mrs Vincent, who had been playing leading rôles, may have looked at the newcomer with some hostility, but Mrs Bellamy – in minor parts, as usual – passed the word round that Miss Woffington was good-natured and not proud, and there was a great deal of politeness in the Green-room. Among the men, there was an Irishman called Delane, who had been a student at Trinity College when Peg sold watercress in the Dublin streets, and remembered her. Theophilus Cibber, son of the actor and playwright, Colley Cibber, played Brazen; he had a reputation as a devious charac-ter, and Peg avoided him out of the theatre.

John Rich said little in advance about his lovely Irish acquisi-tion, but he was able to beg the favour of a Royal Command for Peg Woffington's first appearance, a never-failing method of filling the house. Frederick, Prince of Wales, and his Princess, graciously agreed to be present, 'as his Royal Highness is always anxious to be diverted'. It so came about that Peg's début at Covent Garden was given in the best possible circumstances.

On the evening of the 6 of November, 1740, at the hour of six o'clock, a brilliant and crowded audience had assembled in Covent Garden Theatre. In the Royal Box, under a canopy of scarlet silk most richly adorned with gold tissue and tassels of the same, sat the Prince and Princess of Wales; and in the boxes around them, the gay and witty courtiers who had turned their backs on St James's to frisk, flatter, and enjoy themselves ... In the pit, as usual, sat the students of the Inns of Court, the men about town, the young fellows from the Universities, with their periwigs, swords, ruffles, and snuff boxes; glib compliments on their lips ... and much knowledge of stage affairs in their heads, by which they would presently, over a glass of wine, try their Irish actress and pronounce judgment upon her. Presently when the fiddles had played their last long-drawn notes, and the candles had been judiciously snuffed, up went the heavy green curtain; then a silence fell upon the house, broken only by the fluttering of fans and the snapping of snuff-box lids.

Thus Fitzgerald Molloy, setting the scene for the occasion. The house was charmed by Peg's early appearance as the feminine Silvia: 'her playing indeed was nature, not art.' Then she came on in Silvia's disguise, 'in the apparel of a pretty gentleman about town with a red coat, a sword, a hat *bien troussée*, a martial twist in his cravat, a fierce knot in his periwig, a cane hanging from his button'.

The effect was marvellous. Her air was at once graceful and rakish, her delivery pert and pointed; the witchery of her glances was pronounced inimitable. There were no two opinions regarding her pronounced in the coffee-house that night, for all admitted that the satisfaction she afforded was beyond expression.

The house rose to her. Here was someone new, someone fresh, a charmer who was the very essence of gaiety. The enthusiasm was so vocal that Rich, behind the scenes, was already rearranging his programme of plays for the week.

The versifiers rushed quickly into print:

To Miss Woffington
on her playing the part of Silvia

When first in petticoats you trod the stage,
Our sex with love you fired, your own with rage:
In breeches next, so well you played the cheat –
The pretty fellow and the rake complete –
Each sex was then with different passions moved:
The men grew envious, and the women loved!

Peg was pleased with the praise, but there was little time to meet her admirers in person, except to acknowledge their homage in the Green-room after the performance before hurrying back to her lodgings. Rich was not one to keep a good player idle. *The Recruiting Officer* was repeated for three nights; then the Duke of

Cumberland and several of the princesses 'bespoke' *The Double Gallant*, with Miss Woffington, and immediately afterwards Rich gave her Audrey in *The Country Lasses,* two long parts to learn in a few days.

Her name on the playbills was now prefixed by 'Mrs', a courtesy given to all adult actresses, even when they were unmarried; the only exceptions were when a mother and daughter played together, which was not uncommon. *Mrs Margaret Woffington* had also been enlarged to a bolder size of type on the bills; more prompting from Coffey.

On 21 November Rich announced *The Constant Couple*, 'by particular desire' [his own], with Mrs Woffington in her far-famed rôle as Sir Harry Wildair. Peg's essay in the character in Dublin was not generally known, and there was speculation and incredulity at the news. Wildair was a character exactly suited to the taste of the town: Farquhar's 'airy gentleman', hiding a brave heart behind a façade of debonair rakishness. The Woffington as Wildair? It was not in nature. Peg herself, who delighted in the rôle, dressed carefully on the night, prepared to carry the doubters by storm. She succeeded. As a contemporary critic wrote:

> In the well-bred rake of quality, who lightly tripped across the stage, singing a blithe song, and followed by two footmen, there was no trace of the woman. The audience beheld only a young man of faultless figure, distinguished by an ease of manner, polish of address, and nonchalance that at once surprised and fascinated them.

Wildair as a character intrigued Peg for more than the obvious reason. True, she liked showing off her perfect form, but she also loved a play which gave her scope to make the most of her intelligence and wit. Pope's damning criticism of the dramatist: 'What pert, low dialogue has Farquhar writ!' was a typical sting from 'the little wasp in a black coat', and it did Farquhar a great deal of harm at the time with the fops and duchesses who preferred smooth, artificial language to gloss over the brutal plots of lechery and double dealing which were the staple themes of contemporary plays. Wildair may lack conventional morals, but he is not fundamentally corrupt, as are many of the characters in Wycherley, Congreve, Otway, or even Dryden. Peg Woffington caught the unquenchable high spirits of the man:

THEATRE ROYAL in *Covent-Garden*,
This present *Saturday*, being the 7th of *December* 1754

The Constant Couple;

Or, *A* Trip *to the* JUBILEE.

The Part of Sir *Harry Wildair* to be perform'd

By Mrs WOFFINGTON,

Colonel *Standard* by Mr. S P A R K S,
Vizard by Mr. R I R O U T,
Alderman *Smuggler* by Mr. A R T H U R,
Beau *Clincher* by Mr. C I B B E R,
Young *Clincher* by Mr. S H U T E R,
Dicky by Mr. C O S T O L L O.
Constable by Mr. M A R T E N, *Tom Errand* by Mr. B E N N E T,
Angelica by Mrs. D Y E R,
Lady *Darling* by Mrs. B A M B R I D G E,
Parly by Mrs. P I T T,
Lady *Lurewell* by Mrs. V I N C E N T.

To which will be added

A Comic Entertainment *of* Dancing.

TO BE PERFORM'D

By Mr. P O I T I E R, Junior:

AND

Mademoiselle C A P D E V I L L E,
Lately arrived from *P A R I S*

Likewise, A BALLAD FARCE, call'd

The CONTRIVANCES.

The Part of *Rovewell* by Mr. LOWE,
And the Part of *Arethusa* by Mrs CHAMBERS.

Boxes 5 s.   Pit 3 s.   First Gallery 2 s.   Upper Gallery 1 s.

On *Monday* next a New *Italian* BURLETTA, call'd
LA FAMIGLIA DE BERTOLDI.
And on T U E S D A Y a *TRAGEDY* (*never perform'd there*) call'd
The ROMAN MATRON.
Taken from Shakespear *and* Thompson's CORIOLANUS.

The playbill for *The Constant Couple*.

Tell me news, gentlemen! What lord has lately broke his fortune at the Groom-porter's*, or his heart at Newmarket, for the loss of a race? What wife has been lately suing in Doctors' Commons for alimony? or what daughter run away with her father's valet? What beau gave the noblest ball at Bath, or had the finest coach in the ring?

Wildair says nothing about the Battle of Landen, beyond that he was 'heartily drubbed with the butt-end of a Swiss musket', and rounds off the list of his adventures on the Continent: 'I went thence to Paris, where I had half a dozen intrigues, bought half a dozen new suits, fought a couple of duels, and here I am again in statu quo.' At this point Peg gave a swagger which brought shouts of appreciation, for it was an exact imitation of a beau's gesture.

The play was repeated for twenty nights, an unprecedented run. After every performance the Green-room was filled with the beaux, 'eager to meet the fair Peggy'. Many of them brought gifts, as was the custom of the time: fans, precious trinkets, silver boxes, lace ruffles, feathers, paste shoe-buckles. Peg 'received them with the grace of a princess', but she gave no encouragement to the crowd of idlers who so ardently wished to make her closer acquaintance. Adulation, costly presents: these were the rewards of success in the London theatre, and Peg enjoyed her triumph to the full. She kept her head at the same time, smiled radiantly at her flatterers, and when she was at last able to leave and call a chair, took with her their tributes and locked them carefully away. She had her mother and Polly to think of.

John Rich was hardly ever known to praise players – Lord knew how puffed up they might become, and they would be sure to ask for double salaries! – but he indicated to Mrs Woffington that she had done well. He could have afforded to be more generous in his appreciation: Covent Garden was crowded to the doors every night Peg appeared. In the Dublin *Evening Journal* for December 6, 1740, there appeared an item:

By a private letter from London we are inform'd, that Miss Woffington plays the Part of Sir Harry Wildair with great Applause, that the Playhouse is full every Night before five o'clock, she has played the same Part several times by his

* A gambling resort.

Majesty's and afterwards by the Prince of Wales' Command.
Mr. Cibber has promis'd to do all in his Power to Improve her,
which he thinks her very capable of.

Colley Cibber, one-time Poet Laureate and 'industrious author
of Playhouse pieces', was about seventy years of age when he
saw Peg Woffington play Silvia and Wildair. He had been a man
of the theatre most of his life, not only as playwright but as
actor and manager, and throughout his long life he engaged in
controversy – with his fellow actors, with managers and patentees, with members of his own family. An outsize character in
everything, he might be disliked by many but he could never be
ignored, and in his old age he was one of the most influential
men in the London playhouse.

Colley Cibber taught many of the actors at Covent Garden
and Drury Lane how to speak effectively on the stage, and he
now suggested to Rich that he could do a great deal for the new
Irish actress, who, though extremely beautiful, possessed a less
than perfect voice. He himself had been trained in the school of
Betterton, fifty years before; in fact, he had got his first salaried
part, after being an unpaid probationer for nine months, by
annoying Betterton, the most famous actor in his time. Cibber
relates in his *Apology for Colley Cibber* how he was assigned to
carry a message to Betterton in some play, but developed nerves
at the critical moment and threw the scene into confusion.

' Who is the young man who made the blunder?' Betterton
asked, and on being told Master Colley, said: 'Master Colley!
Then forfeit him.' The prompter replied that the young man would
be unable to pay a fine because he had no salary. 'Why then put
him down ten shillings a week and forfeit him five,' said Betterton, and so the young Colley Cibber was entered for the first
time on the treasurer's books.

Colley Cibber admired Betterton greatly, and copied the old
actor's deliberate manner of speaking lines, then considered the
height of good dramatic utterance. Every line was given equal
weight, every part interpreted with the utmost solemnity. This
intensity could be effective in some tragic rôles, but when, with
the passage of time, the style passed, Colley Cibber was too set in

his manner of speaking to change. Benjamin Victor, one of a merry party who went to see Cibber in one of his own plays in 1725, relates how they all laughed at the actor's 'quavering tragedy tones', while a spiteful journalist, Nathaniel Mist, who delighted in attacking Cibber in his *Weekly Journal*, commented in its pages on 2 January 1725: 'Mr Cibber seems to have a great aversion to the English tongue and mangles it without the least mercy. We may say of him what Sir John Falstaff did of the Welshman, "He makes fritters of English."'

Colley Cibber fumed at the impertinent upstarts who dared to criticize him in the prints, but he could afford to ignore them. He was a born actor: the stage was life to him. When he had begun his career as a stripling: 'I saw no Joy in any other Life than that of an actor . . . 'twas on the stage alone I had formed a Happiness preferable to all that Camps and Courts could offer me.' At seventy he was a grand old fop, wearing a fine wig and a velvet coat handsomely trimmed with lace: still an actor. Rouged, powdered, a patch upon his cheek, a glint in his roving eye, he followed the beau-monde to Bath and Tunbridge Wells, on to Scarborough and back to London for the theatre season. With him went his friend, Owen M'Swiney. Cibber had few close personal friends, but he had known M'Swiney for many years.

M'Swiney was an Irishman, a Wexford man originally, who had been assistant manager to Christopher Rich at Drury Lane. He formed his own company at the Haymarket in 1706, and later went into partnership with Wilks, Cibber, and Doggett; Anne Oldfield, the leading actress of the time, was to be a fourth partner, but 'Doggett, who had no objection to her merit, insisted that our affairs could never be upon a secure foundation if there was more than one sex admitted to the management of them,' as Cibber was fond of relating. M'Swiney was in many theatrical transactions during the next dozen years; some were successful, others brought him near to bankruptcy. In 1712 he was in low water through unwise speculation, and he went abroad, travelling all over the Continent and making himself at home in most of the capitals of Europe. He was away for twenty-five years in all, but his friends found him remarkably unchanged:

On the wrong side of three-score, he has yet the open spirit of a hale young Fellow of five-and-twenty . . . Time has not,

yet, been able to make a visible Change in any Part of him,
but the Colour of his Hair, from a fierce coal black, to that of
a milder milk-white.

M'Swiney and Colley Cibber took up their old friendship, and
went everywhere together. After Peg Woffington's triumphant
first night as Wildair, they were quickly round at the Green-room
to kiss her hands and express their adoration. They came again,
this time before rehearsals in the morning, and Peg was flattered
when the renowned Mr Cibber said he intended to give her
lessons. She told him she would be honoured by such attentions.
It was not easy to fix times, for Peg's days were full; there were
morning and afternoon rehearsals, fittings with the mantua-
makers and dress-makers, regular visits from the *perruquier*, and,
always, long parts to learn or polish up. Still, Mr Cibber was Mr
Cibber, and arrangements were made for him to come to the
theatre before rehearsals, or to the Green-room in the evenings
when she was not performing.

With Cibber came his friend, M'Swiney. Peg liked them both.
Colley Cibber amused her by his practised gallantries, and she
found Owen M'Swiney interesting and agreeable. His long sojourn on the Continent had given him a sophistication which
Cibber lacked, and Peg greatly enjoyed conversing with him.
They usually stayed after the lessons, and when Peg was free they
would escort her to the routs, assemblies and parties to which
she was invited; the town got used to Mrs Woffington being
escorted by these elderly beaux. Tongues began to wag. Peg
laughed when it came to her ears that the wits were alluding to
them as Susannah and the Elders.

Colley Cibber found a new lease of life in teaching this delightful Irish girl; he had taught many actresses, but Peg Woffington took her craft more seriously than most. It did not occur to
him that he was doing her an ill turn. He still kept to the sonorous, singing tone prevalent in his own apprentice days, and it was
this tone which he persuaded Peg Woffington to assume, assur-
ing her that it was the only way in which to speak the lines of
tragedy. 'Tone – more tone!' was his constant adjuration, and
Peg practised hard. She was anxious to extend her range as far
as possible, so as not to become known only as an actress of
comedy. During her Dublin days she had once taken the part of

Lothario, a tragic rôle, and it had been one of her few failures; perhaps Mr Cibber's lessons would enable her to follow the sock *and* buskin.

Meanwhile Rich put on many comedies, in which Peg excelled, and as the season progressed her reputation grew. In January 1741 Congreve's *The Old Batchelor* was performed as a benefit for Chetwood, 'late prompter at Drury Lane and now a prisoner in the King's Bench': the old man had fallen on hard times and was now being held for debt. Colley Cibber returned to the stage to act Fondlewife to Peg Woffington's Laetitia, and he played the part in good earnest, for it was soon plain that he was as infatuated with the heroine off-stage as he was on it. However, he did not deny to his friends that he was still in love with another beauty, Miss Chudleigh, who had been the toast of Tunbridge Wells during his last visit there, and who had captivated him, with the rest of the beaux; so Peg did not take his infatuation too seriously.

It was Owen M'Swiney who attracted her. M'Swiney was very companionable, he talked to her intelligently, and did not rely on extravagant compliments for her favour. Charles Coffey had returned to Dublin, and Peg missed him; M'Swiney came into her life at the right moment. He reminded her of Coffey in his lack of possessiveness, his appreciation of her as a person as well as a woman. He would come into the Green-room when she was surrounded by admirers, stand a little apart, and enjoy watching her charming the dandies. The Green-room at Covent Garden was a handsome apartment, lit by numerous lustres and well-furnished with brocaded sofas and chairs. There were animated scenes every night as the actors and actresses entertained their friends; wine was sent for, toasts were drunk, the wits made epigrams, the ladies laughed, and delightful scandals were whispered behind muffs and fans.

M'Swiney was usually in the background, waiting to take Peg to her lodgings when she grew tired, or when she rose to depart because there was a script to study for a final word run-through before next morning's rehearsal. The lessons with Colley Cibber had ceased; he was off in pursuit of another 'fair'. Owen M'Swiney remained devoted to Mrs Woffington, and was in constant attendance . . . until, one evening, it was plain that he had been forgotten.

7

The New Player

When Edward Bligh, second Earl of Darnley, came into the Green-room one night after a performance of *The Constant Couple*, Peg was soon aware of him at the back of a throng of satin coats. She had changed from her Wildair suit into a 'sacque of cherry silk', and she must have looked quite ravishing beautiful.

Presently a tall, well-made, handsome young man was bowing over her hand. He had not attempted to compete with the crowd of fops, but had waited until Peg saw him. Once he began to speak, she had no attention for anyone else that night. He was Irish – the Blighs came from County Meath – and from that moment these two recognized each other as being two of a kind. The first words he said brought a dancing retort to her lips. Witty, adventurous, challenging: Darnley had the inborn charm of the cultivated Irishman, and Peg responded to it with her own inimitable gaiety.

Darnley was twenty-five years of age to Peg's twenty-two, unmarried, very rich, an aristocrat, a member of the Prince of Wales's household. The first time he had seen Peg was at her début, when he had attended the Prince of Wales to the Command Performance; and though he had been instantly attracted to the new actress, he had not been able to join the procession to the Green-room afterwards because of the protocol of duty. Now he came alone, and that night he carried Peg to her lodgings in a sedan chair – and told her that such a jewel must have a better setting.

He came to Covent Garden every night. Then Peg left Covent

Garden, and Darnley continued his attentions at the rival house, Drury Lane. Peg had not anticipated two major changes in her life in such a short space of time, but, as usual, she accepted the inevitable without question.

She had had to be careful of money ever since her childhood, and Charles Coffey had impressed on her the absolute necessity of getting a signed agreement from managers once she was established, and of being businesslike in all matters of money. There were contradictions in her nature. Naturally prudent, she was also generous and hospitable; quite without personal vanity, she yet, at times, had inflated ideas of what she was worth to a manager. At the end of her first season at Covent Garden, she considered that her great success entitled her to a rise in salary. When she suggested this to Rich, he refused. He was, in fact, within his rights, for she was demanding a much higher amount than had been agreed on in the original terms, and he pointed this out very loudly to Mrs Woffington.

Peg was not one to listen to a bullying tone of voice, and she replied by walking out. She knew that Drury Lane would be glad to have her for the next season. So did John Rich, but he was unperturbed; the way of audiences was to demand novelty, Mrs Woffington had supplied it this season, and he would no doubt get strong enough attractions for next season to offset the loss of the Woffington.

As she had expected, Fleetwood, the manager of Drury Lane, was very pleased to engage Mrs Margaret Woffington for the following season, and once the agreement was signed, she went off with Darnley to spend part of the summer at Tunbridge Wells and Bath. Both spas were full of fashionables, and Darnley obviously enjoyed showing off his companion, who wore her fine dresses with a queenly air, and was unconcerned at the side-long glances which greeted her appearance on her escort's arm in the Assembly Rooms. Were all the genuine ladies of the Quality dancing with their own husbands under those glittering chandeliers? And were they at the Wells with their attentive partners for the sake of love alone? 'Many women besides whores found virtue a marketable commodity,' wrote a cynical contemporary observer of the social scene, and the ladies who tried to patronize the London actress on moral grounds must have been disconcerted by her cool smile and level gaze. More than one writer noted the devastating effect of Peg Woffington's 'strait look' when she took it into her head to be superior.

They returned to London when Darnley was due to resume his duties at Court. He had installed Peg in the setting he had promised her, elegant lodgings off the Strand, a short chair-ride from Drury Lane.

The company she was now to play with at Drury Lane was a strong combination of talents, and included Mrs Clive, Charles Macklin, Theophilus Cibber, Delane, and Milward. Delane, her acquaintance from childhood days, had also left Covent Garden for the rival house, and they got on well. Milward was another pleasant actor; Theophilus Cibber Peg detested. Charles Macklin was genial and polite, while Mrs Clive – was Mrs Clive. She had sensed danger from this Irish rival long before she had met Peg Woffington, and now that they were in the same company, she lost no time in showing Mrs Woffington that *she* was the most important woman player at Drury Lane and intended to remain so.

Kitty Clive was a remarkable woman – remarkable in that she was decidedly plain, and rose to the top of her profession by sheer force of personality. Born Catherine Raftor in Ireland, 'when very young she had a strong propensity to acting'. She was a great success as the blithe Nell in Charles Coffey's ballad farce, *The Devil To Pay* (in which he had also coached the young Peg Woffington), and when she came to London was soon in demand for the parts of hoyden, romp, virago, and affected fine lady. Her great ambition was to play Portia, Ophelia and Desdemona, but she could not resist introducing comic business into these straight rôles, and she was persuaded to return to parts which showed off her talent for comedy. Hot-tempered and with a formidable command of invective, Kitty Clive made enemies as well as friends. Horace Walpole might call her his 'laughter loving dame', but a pamphleteer named Hugh Kelly, who doubtless had experienced the rough edge of her tongue, set her down in bitter doggerel rhyme:

> Formed for those coarse and vulgar scenes of life
> Where low-bred rudeness always breathes in strife
> When in some blessed union we find
> The deadliest temper with the narrowest mind;

> The boldest front that never knew a fear,
> The flintiest eye that never shed a tear,
> Then not an actress certainly alive
> Can e'er dispute pre-eminence with Clive.

She married a brother of Baron Clive, but they separated soon afterwards; there is no record of the reason for such a short-lived union. 'No word of scandal ever assailed her character and she was received into the best houses.' This was a piece of information which she was fond of letting drop in the Green-room, and she took care that Mrs Woffington was about when she said it. Peg heard, but made no sign. She was not interested in being invited to the best houses; she was leading a full and interesting life of her own.

Charles Macklin, who, with Milward, played the leads, was friendly from the beginning, and on occasion he would sit by Peg in her favourite seat near the great carved chimney-piece of the Drury Lane Green-room and tell her of some of his early days.

Macklin's career was typical of many players of the time, who went through great hardships before achieving their ambition of entering the world of the playhouse. Irish by birth, he had been sent to a school in Dublin run by a bad-tempered Scotsman called Nicholson. As the boy early possessed an extraordinary talent for mimicry, he annoyed that pedant by alternately counterfeiting Nicholson's voice and that of his wife, Harriet. The boy also taught a parrot to mimic the schoolmaster, and Charles's mother was continually being asked to remove him from the school. She would come and threaten and entreat, and Charles would promise amendment – and go on as before.

It was through Nicholson, albeit indirectly, that young Macklin decided to take up the stage as a career. The schoolmaster put on a play, *The Orphan*, to show off his skill in teaching the boys elocution. Charles played a character which no one else would take on, that of the heroine, Monimia. He disliked the part but he determined to play it for all it was worth, and eclipsed everybody else. His acting astonished the audience – and himself – and the applause gave him a feeling of confidence he had never experienced before. He resolved to leave Mr Nicholson's Academy and his native country, and go to London to seek his fortune in the theatre. That was in 1708.

He had surprising luck from the beginning. A woman who had once been in his mother's service got him a bed in an attic, the other lodgers being a company of drolls and tumblers. The young Macklin's high spirits and amazing talent for mimicry soon earned him a livelihood in the same line of business. After a time his mother prevailed upon him to return home to Dublin, where she let rooms to undergraduates at Trinity College. Charles became a servant at the college, and remained there until he was twenty-one. Then his mother used some influence she had to get him into the army; her brother, a captain, promised to procure a commission for the youth. The captain and his nephew got as far as London, but when the time came for them to travel on, Charles was not to be found.

The captain would have been hard put to it to recognize his nephew in an insignificant troupe of strolling players at Hockley in the Hole, near Clerkenwell Green. Charles had discovered his old companions, and joined up with them; he wanted to be an actor, not a soldier. The captain had to go on without him.

Young Macklin felt completely at home with his companions, a happy-go-lucky, roistering crew who were serious only about their craft. Charles played Harlequin, Scaramouche, and every variety of the low life which he saw in those slums. As he was an athletic youth, he also perfected earlier skills as a pugilist and boxer. His mother, who had married again and was now Mrs O'Meally, got wind of the fact that her son was leading a wild, licentious life in London, and asked a friend to go over and persuade Charles to return once more to Ireland. The boy was fond of his mother, and he was so touched by her appeal that he agreed, and went home, though not without a great deal of regret at the loss of his free and easy existence with the players.

Mr O'Meally had an inn at Cloncurry, and Charles helped his stepfather run the place; but he found Cloncurry dull. He hankered to return to England, 'that great theatre of the world', where 'some of inferior talents, weaker bodies, and no better education than himself, were bustling and pushing their fortune in life', and where he knew 'every man got to the last farthing the value of whatever commodity he brought to market, be it what it might – merchandise, intellectual talents, or bodily labour.' The years dragged on, and then, when he was twenty-six, Charles Macklin decided to get away, this time for good. He knew there was only one thing he wanted to do in life – to act in the play-house.

He crossed to England and went first to Bristol, where he made such an impression on the manager of the theatre there with his expressive face, powers of mimicry, and 'very pertinent and ingenious remarks upon the drama in general, and actors in particular', that he quickly got an engagement, making his début as Richmond in *Richard the Third*. From that time forward he became an all-round man of the peripatetic theatre, knocking up the stage and scenes in the barns where the company had their one-night stands all through the West Country, writing Prologues, Epilogues and songs, using his fists on persons who were rude to the players, taking on every kind of part from Antony to Harlequin. He changed his name to Macklin, that being easier for the English tongue to get round than M'Laughlan, took pains to eliminate his strong brogue, and

> looked forward to future greatness . . . steeling his constitution, learning the human heart, storing up in his mind character in all its shapes, familiarising himself to the caprices of fortune, and laying up a treasure of information which he could not have acquired in any seminary in the course of an age.

Macklin often thought of London, and studied enunciation so patiently that he at last arrived at a style of speaking which was clear and strong, with little noticeable accent. At last he was ready to try his luck in the great city, and when he had finished his contract at Bristol, he took the stage-coach to London. He got an engagement at Lincoln's Inn Fields within a few days. The salary was small, less than he had been getting at Bristol, but it was a beginning. He went on to Sadler's Wells the following season, and was seldom without an engagement.

When Macklin was thirty, he fell in love with a young actress, who was very beautiful but had one fault – she was immoderately fond of drinking rum, and even carried a bottle in her pocket on the stage, so as to be able to have a tot before and after the performance. Macklin, who was acting with her, tried to cure her of the habit by hitting this pocket 'accidentally' with a cane while they were on the stage. At last he was successful: the bottle broke during one performance, and rum dripped down her gown and on to the stage, much to the mortification of the young lady. She did not, however, reform, and Macklin reluctantly but sensibly broke the connexion. He later married very happily, and acted with his wife for many years, playing the principal parts in *The Beggar's Opera* during its phenomenal run.

Macklin was in his prime when he played at Drury Lane with Peg Woffington in that 1741 season, and, unlike most of the men who attempted to get to know her, he was no philanderer. Solid, brusque on occasion, with a downright manner and few frills of speech, he had a basic honesty which showed through. He, for his part, saluted a woman of the theatre who took great pains with her business, and they were quickly friends.

Peg found Drury Lane a less pleasant theatre to work in than Covent Garden. It had a narrow stage, with stage-boxes that had canvas extensions to hold two or three further seats 'for ladies of distinction', who could hardly see what was happening on the stage but were content to be seen by the audience themselves. If the actors had to make an exit in that direction, they would bow and thrust themselves into these boxes, causing the occupants to move out of the way.

There was only one entrance to the pit and boxes on each side of the stage, and many of the beaux who crowded round these doors delighted in impeding the passage of the players. They would also bandy words with the gallery, 'who showed their resentment by dispersing golden showers of oranges and half-eaten pippins, to the infinite terror of the ladies seated in the pit, where they were so closely wedged as to preclude the possibility of securing a retreat.' Others sat on the front of the stage in rows three or four deep; a performer could hardly move or make wide gestures without risk of striking a member of the audience – who might be tipsy and aggressive.

As usual, Peg made the best of the difficult conditions, and enjoyed her parts: Nerissa to Kitty Clive's Portia, Rosalind to Clive's Celia, and Lady Brute in *The Provok'd Wife*, another of the parts with which she was to become associated. There was a novelty: '*All's Well That Ends Well*, after having lain more than a hundred years undisturbed upon the Prompter's shelf,' was revived and Peg played Helen, with Macklin as the Clown and Milward as the King. This production of Shakespeare's comedy seemed to be pursued by a malign fate. Peg had been feeling unwell for some time, but she conscientiously attended all the rehearsals, as usual. She grew worse, and on the night of the performance rose from her sick-bed and insisted on going to the theatre, in spite of the protests of her physician. Even that stubborn will was no match for what was probably some form of influenza, for after she had dressed and forced herself to go on the stage for her first entrance, she fainted away. One of the other actresses who was in the theatre had to read her part, and Peg was carried to a sedan-chair and taken home to her lodgings.

The play was billed for the following week, 'if Mrs Woffington were well enough', and though she was partially recovered, the play did not go on as Milward was ill. More misfortune followed; two of the minor actresses in the production went down with a similar distemper to Peg's. They recovered, but the unfortunate Milward developed consumption. Peg frequently went to see him, and on one occasion, when another actor asked Milward how he did, the sick man smiled and answered:

'Well, I thank you – 'twould be ungrateful to be otherwise, with such a kind nurse as Mrs. Woffington.'

Peg's friendly sympathy could not save him, however, for he died shortly afterwards, and she acted in the benefit which the management arranged for his wife and children.

On 16 May, an actor who had been playing at Goodman Fields Theatre made his début at Drury Lane at the benefit of another recently deceased player. He appeared again ten days later as Bayes in *The Rehearsal*, and for the third time as Lear to Peg Woffington's Cordelia. His name was David Garrick.

In 1729, Thomas Odell had opened a small theatre in Whitechapel, near Goodman's Fields, in spite of opposition from respectable citizens in the neighbourhood, who were afraid that their daughters and servants might be contaminated by its vicinity – a dread not without foundation, for it was soon surrounded by a 'halo of brothels'. Odell knew little about the practical side of running a theatre, and an Irish actor, Henry Giffard, who had had some experience managing companies in the provinces, took it over. Ambitious and energetic, Giffard rebuilt the place,

The PLAY BILL *that announced the first appearance of Mr. GARRICK.*

GOODMAN'S FIELDS.

October 19, 1741.

At the Theatre in Goodman's Fields, this Day will be performed,

A Concert of Vocal & Instrumental Music,

DIVIDED INTO TWO PARTS,

TICKETS AT THREE, TWO, AND ONE SHILLING.

Places for the Boxes to be taken at the Fleece Tavern, near the Theatre.

N. B. Between the Two Parts of the Concert will be presented an Historical Play, called the

LIFE AND DEATH OF

King Richard the Third.

CONTAINING THE DISTRESSES OF K. HENRY VI.

The artful acquisition of the Crown by King Richard,

The Murder of Young King Edward V, and his Brother in the Tower,

THE LANDING OF THE EARL OF RICHMOND,

And the Death of King Richard in the memorable Battle of Bosworth Field, being the last that was fought between the Houses of York and Lancaster; with many other true Historical Passages.

The Part of King Richard by A GENTLEMAN,

(Who never appeared on any Stage.)

| King Henry, by Mr. GIFFARD. | Richmond, Mr. MARSHALL. |

Prince Edward, by Miss HIPPISLEY,   Duke of York, Miss NAYLOR.
Duke of Buckingham, Mr. PATERSON,   Duke of Norfolk, Mr. BLAKES,   Lord Stanley, Mr. PAGETT,
Oxford, Mr. VAUGHAN,   Tressel, Mr. W. GIFFARD,   Catesby, Mr. MARR,   Ratcliff, Mr. CROFTS,
Blunt, Mr. NAYLOR,   Tyrrel, Mr. PUTTENHAM,   Lord Mayor, Mr. DUNSTALL,

The Queen, Mrs. STEEL,   Duchess of York, Mrs. YATES,

And the Part of Lady Anne, by Mrs. GIFFARD,

WITH

Entertainments of Dancing,

By Mons. FROMET,   Madame DUVALT,   and the Two Masters and Miss GRANIER.

To which will be added a Ballad Opera, of One Act, called

The Virgin Unmask'd.

The Part of Lucy, by Miss HIPPISLEY.

Both of which will be performed Gratis, by Persons for their Diversion.

The Concert will begin exactly at Six o'Clock.

The playbill for Garrick's first appearance.

and by 1733 he had 'an entire new, beautiful, convenient theatre, by the same architect as that of Covent Garden, where dramatic pieces were performed with the utmost elegance and propriety'. The propriety did not extend to the audiences, for the *Observator* remarked:

> The theatre would be a perfect ease to the ladies of Rag Fair, who are now forced to trudge as far as Lincoln's Inn Fields to mix themselves with quality . . . The Does in Tower Hill Park and Rosemary Lane purlieus will be foddered nearer home this winter, and the sailors will have better entertainment for their loose coin.

Giffard had got together a good company, and he prospered for several years, putting on pieces by new authors and occasional Elizabethan plays, generally of a gory and 'highly dramatick' character, showing forth 'the black passions which infect man's nature and inflame the conflict 'tween Good and Evil'. Strong stuff. Giffard might have continued on his successful course had he not, on an unlucky day, been sent the script of a new play for consideration. It was called *The Golden Rump*, and it was loaded with uninhibited abuse of King George the Second and his ministers, all very thinly disguised by mocking names and titles. It was a lively play, and the manager knew it would fill his theatre if he put it on, but he was afraid of the possible consequences should it prove offensive to those in high places.

He decided to show the script to Sir Robert Walpole, the Prime Minister, and be on the safe side. Safe! Walpole read the play and was furiously angry. He had already been ridiculed in one of Henry Fielding's comedies, and *The Golden Rump* was even more satirical. He at once brought a Bill into Parliament, confirming the existing limitation of theatres in London to the two patent houses, Covent Garden and Drury Lane, and establishing a strict censorship of plays. Every play intended for performance had first to be submitted to the Lord Chamberlain, who, if he thought fit, would issue a licence for its performance. If it had no licence, it could on no account be performed in a public theatre. The Bill was, in fact, an amended version of an Act of Queen Anne, in which players were included with persons designated as rogues and vagabonds.

There was some opposition to the Bill in Parliament. Lord Chesterfield was one of its strongest opponents, making a powerful speech against it:

My Lords, the proper business of the stage . . . is to express those vices and follies, which the law cannot get hold of, and to recommend those beauties and virtues which ministers or courtiers seldom imitate or reward, but by laying it under a licence, and under an arbitrary Court licence, too, you will . . . entirely pervert its use.

The Bill was passed – Walpole had more place-men than Chesterfield had friends – and the censorship of plays began in 1737.

Henry Giffard had cooked his own goose; his new, beautiful and convenient theatre was now an illegal one. He had been given £1000 by Walpole, probably as a kind of compensation, but this was not sufficient for the loss of his livelihood. It did not take him long to find a way of keeping Goodman's Fields theatre open and still be within the law. He got round the regulations by the simple device of putting on concerts of music 'at the late theatre', and presenting a play between the items. Admission money was charged for the music – songs, accompanied by flutes, drums, and the hautboy. The play was free. This pattern of evasion soon became common to the unauthorized theatres, and Giffard appears to have had no trouble in keeping Goodman's Fields open for the length of the usual winter seasons. In the summer he took a company of players to Bristol, Bath, York, Coventry and other provincial cities, returning to London for the winter season with new 'concerts' for his patrons.

On 9 October 1741 Giffard's gratis offering between the musical items was 'an historical play called the Life and Death of King Richard the Third', with an unknown young actor called David Garrick in the name part, the said actor being 'a young gentleman who never appeared on any stage'. This was not quite accurate, as the new actor had in fact appeared under Giffard's management at Ipswich, under the assumed name of Lyddal. At Goodman's Fields he tried his fortune under his own name. The theatre was well filled, for David Garrick had been in London some time, and had made many friends. It was well known that he had given up a secure position as partner to his brother in the

family wine trade to follow the sock and buskin, and that he had
some original ideas on the histrionic art.

Richard the Third was a testing rôle for any player, and the
audience looked forward to what had been rumoured was going
to be a fresh interpretation of Crookback. They were not disappointed: David Garrick's acting was startling in its novelty.
Where his predecessors had declaimed lines in loud, deliberate
cadences, using formal gestures hallowed by long usage, this new
actor *became* Richard: he presented in turn the hypocrisy, the
tempestuous passion, the ferocious cruelty, the death-agony of
the most subtle creature in the Shakespearian canon. At the end
of the play he was acclaimed by the shouting audience, and next
day the talk in the coffee-houses was all of this remarkable
phenomenon at Goodman's Fields.

The new actor, David Garrick, was of French Huguenot stock,
the son of an army captain with his permanent home at Lichfield.
He was born in 1716 and grew into 'a most sprightly and diverting
boy', not attracted to 'puerile diversions', or, for that matter,
to his schoolbooks. While still very young, 'he had conceived a
very early passion for theatrical representation, from which
nothing could turn him aside', and by the time he was eleven
years old, he had assembled a little company and was producing
The Recruiting Officer before an audience of relations.

After a visit to Portugal to stay with a wine-merchant uncle,
David returned to Lichfield, and at the age of eighteen became
a classics pupil, along with several other young gentlemen, of
Mr Samuel Johnson, the highly individual son of a Lichfield
book-seller who had literary ambitions. The lessons were not a
success. As Garrick's contemporary biographer, Davies, remarks: 'Dr Johnson, in his conversation, conveys admirable
lessons of instruction, and communicates knowledge with a
profusion and liberality peculiar to himself; but he cannot, perhaps, easily descend to the minutiae adapted to young and un-
formed minds.'

In any case, David was not interested in the classics; he could
think of nothing but the stage, and had already begun to write
plays. When Johnson set him some exercise, the youth brought

him several scenes of a comedy. Captain Garrick wanted a more solid occupation for his son than vagabonding in the playhouse, and sent him to London to a coach who would prepare him for entrance to Lincoln's Inn. Samuel Johnson, tired of his narrow life at Lichfield, went to London with young Garrick; he himself would try his fortune in the larger world of letters in the metropolis.

David Garrick benefited by the coach's teachings, but 'his mind was theatrically led, and nothing could divert his thoughts from the study of that to which his genius so powerfully prompted him.' The death of his father, and of his mother a year later, left him 'free from all restraint, and in a situation to indulge himself in his darling passion for acting'. He had a small income, the interest on a legacy left to him by his wine-merchant uncle, and for a time he went into partnership with his brother, Peter, who was also in the wine trade. 'Peter was calm, sedate and methodical; David was gay, volatile, impetuous, and, perhaps, not so confined to regularity as his brother would have wished.' The partnership broke up amicably, and David decided to prepare himself for a life in the theatre.

He was already an excellent mimic, and he soon made an impression on the managers to whom he was able to get introductions. He was also engaged as critic, and wrote shrewd reviews for the prints. In the summer of 1741, he had a chance of joining a company of players; they were bound for Ipswich, and Garrick made his first appearance as a professional actor in that town. From that time onwards he proceeded to learn his craft with meticulous care. 'He studied the Clown, the Fop, the Fine Gentleman, the Man of Humour, the Sot, the Valet, the Lover, the Hero, the Harlequin', as well as the chief Shakespearian rôles.

Garrick fixed on Richard the Third for his appearance at Goodman's Fields because he had an entirely new conception of how to play Crookback. James Quin, who had often played it before him, had been in the habit of 'heaving his words', his actions formal and laboured. His style had been learned in the Betterton-Colley Cibber school: the elevation of the voice with a mechanical fall of tone – loud, soft, loud. The new actor was a revelation.

'Mr Garrick', says Davies, 'shone forth like a theatrical Newton; he threw new light on elocution and action; he banished

ranting, bombast and grimace; and restored nature, ease, simplicity and genuine humour.'

David Garrick was different in every way from the generation
of actors which had gone before. His voice was natural and melodious, and his bearing was good. True, he lacked height, but this
was soon forgotten because 'he was attentive to whatever is
spoke', never dropping his theatrical character for a moment
while he was on the stage, never glancing at the audience – the
older-fashioned players' habitual sin.

Giffard was quick to exploit his new star's potentialities. He
put on a series of plays during the next weeks with parts suited to
Garrick's varied powers, and 'Goodman's Fields was full of the
splendour of St. James's and Grosvenor Square; the coaches of
the nobility filled up the space between Temple-bar to Whitechapel'. It was not surprising that the companies at Drury Lane
and Covent Garden became alarmed. James Quin, hitherto regarded as the leading tragic actor in the capital, knew he had a
serious rival. Colley Cibber was another who regarded the newcomer with hostile eyes. He was no longer acting himself, but he
was unwilling to join in the general praise after seeing Garrick
at Goodman's Fields. Garrick was well enough, he said, but not
superior to his son Theophilus. This was too much for the Green-
room, where Theophilus Cibber's character and hollow talent
were well known. The veteran Mrs Bracegirdle, on a visit to the
Green-room, turned to her old contemporary and said:

'Come, come, Cibber, tell me, if there is not something like
envy in your character of this young gentleman. The actor who
pleases everybody must be a man of spirit.'

Old Cibber was a professional at heart. He took a pinch of
snuff and presently replied:

'Why, 'faith, Bracey, I believe you are right; the young fellow
is clever.'

Giffard had been a little too cunning with his dramatic representations offered free between the musical items at Goodman's Fields; the monopolists at the patent theatres, seeing the
enormous success of the new actor, which caused 'an alarm-
ing deficiency in their own respective treasuries', exercised

their rights and had the Goodman's Fields playhouse closed down.

Fleetwood, the manager of Drury Lane, quickly got ahead of Covent Garden and engaged David Garrick at the extremely high salary of 600 guineas for the remainder of the season. John Rich, at the rival playhouse, retaliated with the singer and actress Susanna Cibber, the wife of Theophilus Cibber and a great favourite; together with James Quin, who had a considerable following. They put on *Othello*, with Quin as the Moor and Mrs Cibber as Desdemona, with 'the parts all new dressed and the theatre new decorated', but they could not compete with the attractions at Drury Lane, where David Garrick was bringing fresh life into well-known plays.

He played Plume in *The Recruiting Officer*, with Kitty Clive as Rose – but it was Peg Woffington who brought down the house in the breeches rôle as Silvia. Mrs Clive was determined to excel, and endeavoured to outplay her. Each time the piece was put on, Kitty had some fresh trick to draw the eyes away from Peg's superb first entrance in regimentals. Now, Woffington! Peg was mistress of her art, and she despised tricks; she ignored Clive.

The audience, who knew every scrap of back-stage gossip, each move made by every tragedy or comedy queen, guessed Clive's purpose and good-humouredly abetted her. Woffington and Garrick got their meed of shouts and applause at the end of the performance, but Kitty Clive had made the secondary part of Rose twice as important as the author had intended, and she did not attempt to hide her excitement and satisfaction when she got back to the Green-room. A cloud of courtiers were there when Peg Woffington entered, and pointedly moved towards Mrs Clive's chair, forming themselves into a bowing, laughing semi-circle. Peg, as usual, took no notice of deliberate discourtesy, and disdainfully moved to her favourite chair. She, too, was followed by a train of admirers – but she noted that Clive had a dozen more than herself.

In any case, there was Darnley. They had become close friends as well as occasional lovers; neither made any demands upon the other, but when Darnley was in London he often came to see Peg. He spent his time between his estates in Ireland, and his duties at the Prince of Wales's Court; and as he was wealthy and personable, he was a prize worth trying for in the marriage market. Edward Bligh, Earl of Darnley, was perfectly aware of the eyes which followed him when he appeared at routs and balls and assemblies. He was courtesy personified to the matchmaking duchesses, the essence of charm to their hopeful daughters – and completely his real, laughing self several hours later as he lay on a sofa in Peg's lodgings with his head on her lap and described his conquests of the evening. They laughed together a great deal, these two, and Peg was always delighted to see Darnley when he came to town.

M'Swiney? He, too, was as devoted as ever. He still accompanied Colley Cibber on the fashionable round, but directly he returned to London he hastened to pay his respects to his dear Peggy. He came to see her act with Garrick, and in spite of his loyalty to Colley Cibber, complimented the new player on his considerable and unusual talents. Did Peg like acting with Garrick? She was enthusiastic. It was entirely different from acting with anyone else. Mr Garrick was a little anxious about getting applause, but Peg thought he was so good, he need not be troubled on that account; he had undoubtedly a glorious future in the playhouse before him. As for his personal qualities, Peg found him very pleasant, and hoped that their acquaintance would improve still further.

Meanwhile a new admirer was making his presence felt, and Peg was in a mind to encourage him. He was a poet and a wit, and Peg Woffington always responded to a man of taste and high intelligence.

8

Hanbury Williams

To Mrs. Woffington

If when the breast is rent with pain,
It be no crime, the nymph should know it;
O Woffington, accept the strain,
Pity, though you'll not cure the poet.

Should you reject my ardent prayer,
You send not back the am'rous paper,
My pangs may help to curl your hair,
My passion fringe the glowing taper.

No more the Theatre I seek,
But when I'm promis'd there to find you,
All Horton's* merits now grow weak,
And Clive remains far, far behind you.

'Tis thus the polish'd pebble plays,
And gains awhile some vulgar praises
But soon withdraws its feeble rays
When the superior diamond blazes.

Who sees you shine in Wildair's part
But sudden feels his bosom panting?
Your very sex receive the dart,
And almost think there's nothing wanting.

S̲ir Charles Hanbury Williams sent these verses to Peg Woffington at the end of 1740, when the whole town was at her feet and
Hanbury Williams was smitten with the prevalent adoration. He

* Another popular actress.

does not appear to have attempted to make her acquaintance at the same time, and it is doubtful if Peg paid more than a smiling attention to yet another versifier's homage. Yet there was a touch of wit in the curl-paper image, and she kept the verses.

Born into a wealthy Monmouthshire family, Charles Hanbury Williams was good-looking, romantic, a man of pleasure, leading the usual rich young man's life of the period. He married Lady Frances Coningsby when he was twenty-four, went into politics, wrote verses which won some acclaim, discovered a talent for political satire, and made love to actresses.

The marriage was not happy. The couple soon found that they were totally unsuited to each other, and Hanbury Williams turned to satisfactions outside. 'Clever, witty and high-spirited, he was in close relations with a clique of young men who looked on themselves as bound by no moral law.' Several of these friends were later members of the notorious Hell Fire Club, and Hanbury Williams himself acquired a reputation for ruthlessness, especially where women were concerned.

He made Peg Woffington's acquaintance at some time in 1742, learnt about Darnley, and set himself to win her away from the Irishman. Peg responded to the age-old challenge. She was not in love with him, but she found him exceedingly attractive; he had all the qualities she most admired in a man. Hanbury Williams, for his part, found Peg Woffington very different from the kind of woman he had first imagined her to be. He had gone after a beautiful actress – and found a cultivated woman. He could talk to her, listen to her. Here was someone he could have taken into his own world, had such a thing been possible. Peg's warmth and good nature were also a revelation, something he had rarely found in an actress before. Hanbury Williams was essentially a lonely man; wedded happiness had been denied him, and though he was fond of the two daughters who had been born of the marriage, his wife took good care that he did not see them, declaring that they were so accustomed to his absence that they did not miss him. Hanbury Williams spent his time between Coldbrook, his country house in Monmouthshire, and London, where he was deep in the political arena; he was a close friend of Henry Fox, and wrote many political satires attacking the opposite party. By 1742, he and his wife had formally separated; she intended to take the children to live with her own family. He turned more and more to Peg Woffington for love and companionship, but in June of that year Peg went to Dublin with David Garrick.

The two patent theatres in Dublin had been declining for several years, and their respective managers were deeply in debt. Lewis Duval, at Smock Alley, had tried dancers, operettas, anything to draw an audience; Aungier Street replied with Shakespeare, engaging James Quin, who had a good following in the Irish capital, and 'an extraordinary actress who had been for some years rising in her profession', Mrs Cibber.

Susanna Cibber was the daughter of 'a decent upholsterer in Covent Garden' who fathered two unusual offspring: Thomas Arne, afterwards a composer and doctor of music, and Susanna Maria, who had such an excellent contralto voice that Handel altered one of the airs in *The Messiah* to bring it within her range. He had conducted the first performance of the oratorio at the new music hall in Fishamble Street the year before, and Susanna Cibber had been a great success in it.

She had an extraordinary life. Married to Theophilus Cibber, she soon found that she was tied to an unscrupulous profligate who appropriated her earnings and attacked her honour. His chief feat was to contrive a situation in which Susanna was found in equivocal circumstances with a Mr Sloper, a gentleman of wealth and position. Theophilus then took proceedings against Mr Sloper for 'criminal conversations' with his wife, and asked for five thousand pounds damages for the injury done to his married state. He got ten pounds, Susanna eloped with Mr Sloper, and continued with her career; she had been trained by old Colley Cibber as an actress, and was a draw whenever she appeared at a theatre, having 'a neat person' and pretty ways.

Mrs Cibber could sing, but she had a monotonous speaking voice. Richard Cumberland, who saw her act that season with Quin, says that her voice was

so extremely wanting on contrast, though it did not wound the ear, it wearied it. When she had once recited two or three speeches, I could anticipate the manner of every succeeding one: it was like a long old legendary ballad of innumerable stanzas, every one of which is sung to the same tune, eternally chiming in the ear without variation or relief.

Quin also had little variation of cadence; his gestures were 'a sawing kind of action which had more of the Senate than the stage in it'.

Still, Quin and Cibber were popular, and Smock Alley would have to do something spectacular to draw away the Aungier Street audiences. Lewis Duval was stimulated to make a supreme gamble. David Garrick's fame had spread to Dublin, and Peg Woffington was sure to be a great draw. Duval sent to London to invite Garrick and Woffington to Smock Alley for the summer season, 'upon very profitable conditions'. He also engaged Henry Giffard, and Mrs Furnival, good supporting players, and the best actors available for the rest of the company.

Peg was delighted to be going to Dublin, not only because it was a long time since she had seen her mother and Polly, but also because it meant taking the leading rôles with a splendid actor like David Garrick. Besides – he was more than half in love with her, that was plain. Intrigued, as always, by a man's quickening interest, Peg shamelessly encouraged him, herself untouched. Darnley? He was back in London, and they had been together: sweet Darnley. Hanbury Williams? Ah. Peg had to persuade *him* that a player must go where the theatres called. She laughed at his jealousy, telling him she was free as air: she belonged to no one.

The company began the journey in early June 1742; the Dublin *Mercury* had given them so much advance publicity that crowds waited on the quays to welcome them. Hannah Woffington was, of course, prominent in her grand black velvet cloak, visibly proud as her famous daughter stepped ashore, the admired of all beholders. Garrick was scrutinized, and his short stature quietly remarked upon. The actor knew this reaction and was not offended. Let them wait!

Smock Alley theatre was sold out: 'Boxes had been engaged by the nobility weeks previously; the doors of the theatre were besieged hours before they opened, and the scramble which eventually took place for seats was beyond anything ever witnessed.'

David Garrick as Abel Drugger in *The Alchemist*. J. Zoffany.
(Harvard Theatre Collection.)

Peg Woffington.
by H. Pickering.
(Harvard Theatre Collection.)

Sir Charles Hanbury Williams
by C. F. Zincke.
(Harvard Theatre Collection.)

The season began on a wave of popular acclaim which never diminished, and Aungier Street at once felt the draught. On 15 June 'hostilities were opened' at Smock Alley with Peg as Silvia in *The Recruiting Officer*, supported by Garrick as Plume. Three nights later Garrick appeared as Richard the Third with Peg as Lady Anne; it is recorded that for this performance there were more people struggling to get into the theatre than the number of those inside. The evening was an overwhelming triumph; the far-famed Mr Garrick and their own Woffington! All over Dublin the talk next day was of nothing else; clerks and shopkeepers were as articulate over their home-grown beauty's success as were the beaux calling at the clubs for morning chocolate and the latest gossip.

Susanna Cibber and James Quin did their best at the Aungier Street house, but they could not compete with the formidable talent at the rival playhouse, and they had to close. Smock Alley continued to draw full houses at every performance. It was hard work for the players; the weather was very warm, and they rehearsed all morning, putting on a different play nearly every night. Peg 'charmed her beholders beyond expression' with Wildair, Garrick demonstrated his versatility by playing low comedy on the same evening as he took Lear, with Peg as Cordelia; she played Lady Anne to his Richard the Third, and Ophelia to his Hamlet. There was a discordant incident at a second performance of Lear, when Lear is seen asleep in the fourth act, his head in Cordelia's lap. Peg was insulted by a 'gentlemanly ruffian' at the side of the stage, who 'thrust his hand on Mrs Woffington's bosom'. David Garrick gave the ruffian 'a look which should have resulted in annihilation'. The man was removed from the stage, but at the end of the play he and his friends rushed behind the scenes with drawn swords, searching for Garrick, who had dared look so high-and-mightily upon a gentleman. The players were safely locked in the Green-room, and the bullies departed.

A student of Trinity College, Thomas Sheridan, was in the audience that night and witnessed the scene. Long stage-struck, he had been at every performance at Smock Alley, and found a way of being presented to Mrs Woffington and Mr Garrick; the three could hardly guess that they were to be closely connected within the next few years.

D

June passed into July, and the weather grew hotter. The company at Smock Alley was tireless; Garrick was as superb in comedy as he was awe-inspiring in tragedy. 'How d'ye do?' – 'As gay as Garrick!' was the new greeting. More grimly, when an epidemic of fever broke out, and many people succumbed, the irrepressible Dubliners called the sickness 'the Garrick fever'. The audiences still crowded Smock Alley playhouse. It was an astonishing season.

There was not much time to accept all the invitations which were left at their lodgings day after day – but there was time to be together. Peg and Garrick had arrived, almost imperceptibly, at a close relationship which Peg, at least, had never experienced before. She was half-way to being in love with Garrick, emotionally as well as physically. It brought her a kind of exaltation – and rare moments of bitterness. One evening, as Garrick stood at the door leading from the stage while Peg returned to acknowledge the plaudits of the audience, he caught her hand and said: 'You are the queen of all hearts, my dear.' 'Yes,' replied Peg. 'Queen of all hearts – and legal mistress of none.'

Garrick, the least promiscuous of men, meant marriage, though he said nothing then. Peg Woffington knew what promises of marriage in a *liaison* were worth, and would have smiled at one. Sufficient to the day! She had lived for years under that banner, and now she kissed her lover and laughed. The actor was quite aware of his goddess's reputation where men were concerned, but it made no difference. This love would cry a halt to all her previous loves. He wrote a poem, addressed to Peg in her character as Silvia;

> If Truth can fix thy Wav'ring heart,
> Let Damon urge his claim;
> He feels the passion void of art,
> The pure, the constant flame.
>
> Though sighing swains their torments tell,
> Their sensual love contemn;
> They only prize the beauteous shell,
> But slight the inward gem.

Possession cures the wounded heart,
Destroys the transient fire;
But when the mind receives the dart,
Enjoyment whets desire.

The senses in your charms enjoy
A sweet but short repast,
But oh! the mind can never cloy
The soul's eternal feast!

By age your beauty shall decay,
Your mind improve with years;
As when the blossoms fade away,
The ripening fruit appears.

May heaven and Silvia grant my suit
And bless the future hour,
That Damon who can taste the fruit
May gather every flow'r.

It is probable that Peg and Garrick became lovers during the last weeks of that idyllic season. In the Green-room, the fops in their brocades and laces paid Mrs Woffington fulsomely-phrased compliments; the women of quality lionized Garrick, asked him to their soirées, and boasted to one another of his acquaintance. Away from the crowds, in the seclusion of her own lodging, Peg could send her maid away and be alone with David Garrick. They had to be prudent, for in that age of licence, Dublin audiences, both high and low, preferred their favourites to observe at least the outward forms of propriety. Garrick was by now deeply in love with Peg, but it is difficult to judge how intense was her own feeling for the actor at this stage. Her lover could not be sure if the affection she showed him was a sign of real emotion, or a facet of her gay amorousness. The young gentlemen from College Green crossed the theatre every night and joined the press in the Green-room afterwards. Peg exchanged jests with them, flirted with any who took her fancy, and thoroughly enjoyed herself. Then she went out to her chair attended by Garrick, and was amused that he was angry and jealous . . .

They were, nevertheless, very happy. Success was sweet, and they were both earning high salaries and saving money. For the future? Neither made any plans for the time ahead; it was enough that they were together, supremely content to be alone in private, each a foil for the other's popularity in public, both enormously enjoying the sensation of being the darlings of the vociferously admiring Dubliners.

The 1742 summer season ended in August with a final triumph for them as Silvia and Plume in *The Recruiting Officer*. It was time to return to London. Peg decided to remain in Dublin for a short time to settle her mother in a new house, and to make arrangements for the next step in her sister's education. The daughters of the aristocracy went on to a finishing school in Paris, and Peg was determined that Polly should go to Paris the following year, to enjoy 'all the branches of elegant learning and the accomplishments of a lady of society'. She instructed the proprietress of the seminary to include Miss Mary Woffington in the next party sent out – under strict chaperonage, of course – to the French convent where these accomplishments were properly understood.

David Garrick took the packet to England. A fellow-passenger was Susanna Cibber, who had had a disappointing season at Aungier Street because of the Woffington-Garrick furore. She and Garrick conversed perfectly amicably; stage players were practical, knowing that they might find themselves in rival theatres one week and acting together the next. In any case, Susanna was a pretty, appealing young woman, and David Garrick had the normal young man's reaction to charming good looks. Besides, Mrs Cibber had influential connexions; as well as being the sister of the up-and-coming composer, Tom Arne, her father-in-law, Colley Cibber, was still someone to be reckoned with in the world of the playhouse. Garrick thought nothing of Cibber as an actor – old ranter! – but one never knew when a word in the right ear might be useful. Susanna Cibber had a pleasant and attentive escort on the long journey by stagecoach across England.

Peg left Dublin in September, and on her arrival in London was engaged for the Drury Lane company by the manager, Fleetwood. Charles Fleetwood's reputation was a byword. Originally a man of fortune, he was a born spendthrift and gambler; he had bought part of the patent of Drury Lane in a spirit of bravado, without knowing anything whatever about managing a theatre. Fleetwood was always in financial difficulties: 'He made no scruple of obtaining money or security from everybody he could. Though conscious of his incapacity to repay any sums he borrowed he still borrowed on; his best friends were no exceptions to his arts.' He had an engaging manner 'that made his attacks irresistible', but it was a constant source of surprise to the town that he retained good players at his theatre, for he owed most of the acting fraternity long arrears of salary.

On Garrick's return to London Fleetwood had immediately opened negotiations with him to appear at Drury Lane. Garrick asked six hundred pounds for the season, which Fleetwood agreed to pay. Garrick intended to get it, too. He was aware of his drawing power, and knew that full houses were virtually certain with himself and Peg Woffington in the company, so there would be money in the treasury. Charles Macklin had also been engaged, together with Giffard and his wife, and several other excellent actors. It looked like being a very successful season.

Peg and Garrick set up house together at 6, Bow Street. Their private association was considered by the sophisticated Londoners to be a natural outcome of their stage partnership, and was accepted by everybody. Daly remarks:

> The fine thought and amiable temperament which marked their natures in addition to the pre-eminence of genius and fame that lifted them far above all their contemporaries, in the dramatic profession, were all matters which not only made their union agreeable but advised that it should be permanent.

They certainly appeared to be well suited: they obviously enjoyed each other's society, and Garrick made no secret of the fact that he was fathoms deep in love. Peg responded to his ardour, and for the first time through all her adventures she began to feel she would like to settle down with one man – and that man David Garrick. The question of 'good family' did not arise: they were both players, both set a little apart because of their profession.

Meanwhile, they were together. Charles Macklin, who had a lodging above their apartments in the Bow Street house, was then a close friend of Garrick's, and was often a guest at their table. They entertained a great deal, 'persons of the first rank . . . of the greatest character and the most eminent for learning'. Besides her great beauty, Peg Woffington had acquired an air of polite breeding and distinction which had by now become second nature. She was a constant reader of books, in French as well as in English, and her native high spirits bubbled up with unaffected gaiety. Macklin told one of his biographers, William Cooke:

> What illustrious men assembled in her rooms! What wit and repartee were exchanged round her board! Here came Samuel Foote, the most perfect of mimics, whom Garrick feared in secret, and conciliated in public; and burly-figured Samuel Johnson, now a writer for the *Gentleman's Magazine*.

Samuel Johnson was later to tell Boswell that he found Peg Woffington 'dangerously seductive', but he did not hesitate to court temptation quite often at Bow Street. Colley Cibber was another frequent guest,

> his great wig falling upon the shoulders of his velvet coat, his shrunken shanks clad in silken stockings . . . his thin, sharp features, aquiline nose, bright small eyes, together with his solemn strutting air, giving him the appearance of some grotesque bird, at once venerable and vindictive-looking.

Henry Fielding came, and other rising dramatists. Fanny Burney recorded:

> In graceful deportment and in natural magnetism and in tact she [Peg Woffington] was a hostess so attractive, that her receptions were crowded with people of distinction, and the table was never presided over so charmingly as when she was at the head of it.

The liaison was, to outside eyes, romantic and glamorous. In sober fact, once the high tides of passion began to abate fundamental differences in their respective temperaments began to show. These would not have mattered greatly had they been actually married, for then Peg would probably have made an effort to adapt herself to Garrick's ways; but in her equivocal position – one she had never minded before – disagreements and annoyances prickled out in the most unexpected ways.

A good deal of the trouble arose over money. They paid turn and turn about for the household expenses, and it was notorious that during Peg Woffington's month for paying the table was more generously laden than when Garrick settled the bills. Peg's open-handedness often infuriated Garrick, who accused her of reckless extravagance; and his extreme care over making the most of every sixpence irritated her just as much. Garrick was earning far more than Peg; he had a passion for saving. Peg, too, was able to put aside part of her earnings – she was still supporting her mother, and Polly at the convent in Paris – but she liked good living, and enjoyed entertaining lavishly. The basic incompatibility was between an instinctively generous nature like Peg Woffington's, and one that could not help counting pence.

Samuel Johnson called his friend Davy 'frugal by inclination, but liberal in principle', a tactful description laughed at by Garrick's enemies, who continually sneered at his close-fistedness. It was the usual story of the man who had had the thumbmark of genteel poverty, experienced in youth, pressed on his soul for the remainder of his life. Johnson himself well understood this, for he and poverty were familiars, and when he heard criticism of Garrick's meanness was quick to defend him, telling Boswell that the young actor had begun to feel money in his purse, 'and did not know when he would have enough of it'. But Johnson could also smile wryly at Davy, and the oft-repeated story which he told Sir Joshua Reynolds bears the stamp of credibility. According to Johnson, he was visiting Peg and Garrick one night at their lodging, and when asked to partake of some refreshment called for tea, his favourite beverage. It was Peg's month for house-keeping, and she brewed the tea – an expensive commodity in those days, kept in a locked tea-caddy in the wainscoted parlour where they sat. When Peg poured out the tea, Garrick scolded her angrily for making it so strong.

'It is no stronger than I have made it before,' said Peg. 'It is no stronger than usual.'

'No stronger than usual!' cried Garrick. 'It is, Madam, it is! All last month it would have hurt nobody's stomach. But this tea, Madam, is as red as blood!'

Inevitably they quarrelled, but a bond existed between them which had grown strong, and there were weeks when they both knew a happiness which they had not experienced before. It was at such times that they talked of marriage, though they made no definite plans. Garrick was learning part after part, and laurels came thick and fast. He played thirteen characters during his first season at Drury Lane, including a Hamlet which set the town talking because of its power.

Peg Woffington played Ophelia, as well as her other regular parts, and she was in the theatre every night that Garrick performed. His fame and extraordinary success gave her the greatest satisfaction, and she was quick and sincere in her praise when they were alone together. Garrick thought highly of her opinion, and they spent many hours discussing plays and the dramatic art.

Peg's first benefit was on St Patrick's Day, 1743. She chose *The Constant Couple*, with Garrick playing Sir Harry Wildair. Peg herself suggested his taking the part, though with his short stature he obviously was not equipped to cut the dashing figure intended by Farquhar. Garrick must have been well aware of this, for he had a superb professional sense, and rarely attempted a part of which he could not make himself master. It is possible that Peg wished to encourage him to stretch his great versatility still further, to take on an unlikely rôle and make a success of it. Perhaps she persuaded him into it against her better judgment. They were, at this time, both very much in love, and Peg, with her warm, outgoing nature, may have wanted her Davy to outshine her. In the event, it was a mistake, and Garrick's admirers decided to forget it.

Garrick could afford a failure; his reputation was in no way diminished by his inadequate Wildair. He and Peg were the darlings of the town; they were fêted wherever they appeared. It says much for both their characters that they preserved a sense of proportion amid so much flattery. One panegyrist published a pamphlet in which he begged David Garrick, Esquire, not to appear on the stage as the writer was 'so blinded by prejudice or admiration, that *he* can see no body else, *he* can hear no body else, and can bear no body else', and therefore the eminent actor should quit the stage because he eclipsed all who appeared with him on it!

9
Trio

Garrick and Peg Woffington led a strong company at Drury
Lane that season. There were sixty players, among them
Delane, Hallam, Macklin and his wife, Susanna Cibber, Kitty
Clive, Hannah Pritchard and her husband. Fleetwood had also
engaged sixteen dancers to perform in the entr'actes. At Covent
Garden, the company numbered fifty, with Quin at the head, but
John Rich had a larger number of dancers.

The actors worked hard. There were usually the main pieces,
afterpieces, dancing and musical interludes, and often other items
to round off the evening. Fleetwood had seventy different plays
in his repertory, but twenty-five of them were given for only a
single performance, having failed to promise support for more.
Shakespeare drew good houses, especially *Richard the Third* and
Hamlet, in which Garrick always made a sensation. Another of
his favourites was Buckingham's *The Rehearsal*, a satire on the
high-flown style of acting of the previous decades. He played
Bayes, the vain coxcomb, who 'thought the art of dramatic
poetry consisted of surprise and thundering versification', bringing to the part his mischievous gift of mimicry, the audience
roaring with laughter as they recognized the originals.

Quin, though a rival, was one actor he never burlesqued, in
spite of the older player's bombast and vanity; perhaps he realized that Quin's day was nearly over, and did not want to embitter
an already apprehensive man. In fact, Quin was still excellent in
parts such as Sir John Falstaff, and Garrick had the true man of
the theatre's respect for genuine talent and good work, however
old-fashioned it seemed to his own bent of mind.

In spite of the promising start to the season, and the fact that his name 'when announced in the playbills, operated like a charm, and drew multitudes to the theatre, of consequence considerably augmenting the profits of the patentee', Garrick was worried, for the actors' salaries, including his own, were continually in arrears. Fleetwood blandly ignored the bogy of mounting debts, left the management of the theatre in the hands of Pierson, his treasurer, and spent his days at White's Coffee House, gaming and drinking. Pierson had lent Fleetwood large sums of money, and he kept most of the proceeds of the performances himself, to pay off the manager's debt, treating the actors 'with insolence and contempt' when they tried to get the salaries due to them. Incensed, Garrick at last went one day to White's Coffee House to talk plainly to Fleetwood. The manager was civil and friendly, but expertly avoided the issue.

Something had to be done. Garrick, Macklin and ten other players, including Kitty Clive and the Pritchards, agreed to secede from Drury Lane, form their own company, and apply for a licence to perform plays at the theatre in Lincoln's Inn Fields, or, failing that, the theatre in the Haymarket. The first step was to get a licence. If they were not successful, they would cross to Dublin and seek work there. Macklin and Garrick drew up an agreement, which they and the other seceders signed, and Garrick went to the Lord Chamberlain, the Duke of Grafton, to present his petition.

The Duke received him with marked coldness, and asked how much he and other leading actors received as salary. When Garrick replied: 'About five hundred pounds,' the Duke cuttingly remarked that his own son earned less than half that amount in the service of his King and country; he thought it an absurdly high sum for doing nothing but acting. The petition for a licence was refused.

This was a considerable disappointment to Garrick and Macklin, but they were not in desperate straits, as they had savings behind them. The other players were appalled; except for Mrs Clive, they had never been in a position to demand high salaries and so to put money by. They wrote to Garrick, asking him to make representations to Fleetwood to take them back: at least they had at times been able to extort *some* money from Pierson, and salary arrears always stood upon the books against their names. Garrick asked Macklin to release them from the arrangement.

Macklin pointed out that they had all signed a solemn agreement to leave Drury Lane, and if they could not get permission to act in London, to go to Ireland. David Garrick said that they were afraid to go; who knew if there was enough employment in the Dublin playhouses for so many? Still Macklin refused to cancel the agreement.

In the end, Garrick went to Fleetwood, who had engaged other players to fill the gaps in his company. The manager agreed to take the seceders back – with the exception of Macklin. He had, in the past, done Macklin a great service over a serious court case which had, with his help, gone in Macklin's favour, and he now conceived a passionate dislike for the actor, accusing him of base ingratitude. Macklin remained calm. He called a meeting of Garrick and the others at his lodgings, and again demanded their loyalty to the agreement they had all signed. Garrick tried to make Macklin see reason, saying he had prevailed on John Rich to engage Mrs Macklin at Covent Garden at a salary of three pounds a week, and he, Garrick, would augment that sum from his own resources until Fleetwood relented and received Macklin back at Drury Lane. Macklin obstinately rejected the offer, and the two men parted enemies.

Macklin had been a good friend – and he was a good hater when his friendship turned to enmity. His quarrel with Garrick was kept well alive in the public prints; this was the kind of situation which amused the town. Corbyn Morris, a notorious pamphleteer and a friend of Macklin's, wrote a virulent pamphlet under Macklin's name 'showing up Mr Garrick's perfidy'. Garrick knew how important it was to obtain public goodwill as quickly as possible, and he sent a letter to *The London Daily Post and General Advertiser* which was published on 2 December 1743:

Sir, As there have been many reports to my prejudice, I desire you will publish the *true* and *only* Reason why I have not yet appear'd upon the stage this winter. Many of the Persons concerned in the late struggle with the Manager, might have been left destitute had I deserted them, therefore I thought it incumbent on me to endeavour at this reconciliation with my own, upon reasonable terms; this I have accomplish'd, and I hope I am excusable for not playing 'til it is determin'd.

Tho' I am sensible my affairs are too inconsiderable to be laid before the Publick, yet as I am their servant, and have been so much favour'd with their Indulgence, I thought it my Duty to convince 'em that it is neither Obstinacy or Exorbitancy, but a quite different motive, that detains me so long from doing my utmost to contribute to their Entertainment. I am, Sir, your Humble Servant, D. Garrick.

He also had a bill printed and distributed round the coffee-houses on the day of his first performance:

To the Public. Whereas an appeal to the town has this day been dispersed by Mr Macklin, in which are contained many false and injurious assertions, calculated merely to prejudice me this night, I humbly hope the public will suspend their judgment until, by a fair state of the case, which shall be published in a day or two, I shall endeavour to convince them of my integrity, with regard to my engagements with Mr Macklin.
5th December, 1743.   David Garrick.

Supporters of Macklin came to the theatre that night bent on mischief. They began to shout abuse the moment the curtain rose, and when Garrick appeared they yelled, 'Off! Off!' Davies relates:

The play went on in dumb show, scene by scene, from the beginning to the end; Garrick, during the whole, standing aloof at the upper end of the stage, to avoid the rotten eggs and apples, which showered down in great plenty.

Garrick was not to be intimidated. He published his explanation of the case in a pamphlet and had it distributed on 7 December, and at the same time put out playbills announcing another performance that evening of *The Rehearsal*. Mr Windham, a Norfolk landowner and a staunch friend of Garrick's, was in town, and he resolved to protect the actor from further rioting.

He [Windham] happened to be an admirer of the athletic art, which at that time was in great vogue; and, having selected thirty of the ablest in that line, he desired of Fleetwood that they might be admitted into the house, by a private way, before the doors were regularly opened. This was granted. The bruizers took possession of the middle of the pit. When the last music was playing, one of them stood up, and stopping the band said, in a loud voice, 'Gentlemen, I am told that some persons here are come with an intention not to hear the play. I came to hear it; I paid my money for it, and I desire that they who came to interrupt, may all withdraw, and not stay here to hinder my diversion.'*

This speech occasioned a general uproar, but

the bruizers knew how to deal their blows with irresistible vigour. They fell upon Macklin's party, and drove them out of the pit. The fray was soon over, and peace and good order being restored, Garrick made his appearance; and, after bowing respectfully to the audience, went through the character of Bayes without interruption.

Fleetwood himself was not averse from the same tactics. Some time later, when there were disturbances at Drury Lane, he called in the prize-fighting fraternity, and was thwarted from an unexpected quarter – by Horace Walpole. In a letter to Sir Horace Mann on 26 November 1744, Walpole describes the scene:

The town has been trying all this winter to beat Pantomimes off the stage, very boisterously; for it is the way here to make even an affair of taste and sense a matter of riot and arms. Fleetwood, the master of Drury-Lane, has omitted nothing to support them, as they supported his house. About ten days ago, he let into the pit great numbers of Bear-garden bruizers (that is the term) to knock down everybody that hissed. The pit rallied their forces, and drove them out; I was sitting very quietly in the side-boxes, contemplating all this. On a sudden the curtain flew up, and discovered the whole stage covered with blackguards, armed with bludgeons and clubs to menace the audience. This raised the greatest uproar; and among the rest, who flew into a passion, but your friend, the philosopher? In short, one of the actors, advancing to the front of the stage, to make an apology for the manager, he had scarce begun to say 'Mr Fleetwood –' when your friend, with a most audible voice and dignity of anger, called out 'He is an impudent rascal!' The whole pit huzzaed, and repeated the words. Only

* Arthur Murphy: *Life of David Garrick* 1801, p. 44.

think of my being a popular orator! But what was still better, while my shadow of a person was dilating to the consistence of a hero, one of the chief ringleaders of the riot, coming under the box where I sat, and pulling off his hat, said, 'Mr Walpole, what would you please to have us do next?' It is impossible to describe to you the confusion into which this apostrophe threw me. I sank down into the box, and have never since ventured to set my foot into the playhouse. The next night the uproar was repeated with greater violence, and nothing was heard but voices calling out, 'Where's Mr W? Where's Mr W? In short, the whole town has been entertained with my prowess, and Mr Conway has given me the name of Wat Tyler.

Peg Woffington had not joined the would-be seceders. She had told Garrick that she did not think the move a wise one, in spite of Fleetwood's irresponsibility; she may have guessed what the outcome of the secession would be, and thought it better to remain at Drury Lane. Her own salary was in arrears, but she kept on friendly terms with Fleetwood, and when the others returned to the company in December she was in a strong position where Kitty Clive was concerned, and was able to choose the parts she wanted.

Her private relations with Garrick had taken an unhappy turn. There were clashes of temperament, in spite of their mutual affection; inevitably they quarrelled, and these were not ordinary lovers' tiffs. Davy, in spite of his outward good nature, had a fine command of invective when he was angry. Peg had been schooled in a city where abuse of the most picturesque kind was the loose change of wrangling friends and enemies alike. She usually seized on Garrick's meanness when she flew into a temper. For all her fine manners, her tongue could cut a man's pride to ribbons, her splendid eyes flash contempt and ridicule. To Peg, parsimoniousness was the shabbiest of traits. David Garrick looked at money in a different way: to him, the player's traditional prodigality was multiplied ten-fold in Peg Woffington. How could he save, he demanded, when she expected him to pour money out as if it were water?

Rumour began to trickle round that Garrick was showing

marked attentions to other women; Susanna Cibber was named more than once. He had plenty of opportunities: 'With all the beautiful women in England tempting his favour, he could not confine it to one.' Peg did not create scenes; she took the view that what held good for the goose also held good for the gander. She renewed her friendship with both Darnley and Hanbury Williams, and did not mind who knew it. Charles Hanbury Williams was pleased, and soon sent her verses which she had no hesitation in showing to her friends:

'Tho' Peggy's charms have oft been sung,
The darling theme of ev'ry tongue,
New praises still remain;
Beauty like Hers may well infuse
New flights, new fancies, like a Muse,
And brighten ev'ry strain.

'Tis not her form alone I prize,
Which ev'ry fool, that has his eyes
As well as I can see;
To say she's fair is but to say
When the sun shines at noon, 'tis day,
Which none need learn of me.

But I'm in love with Peggy's mind
Where ev'ry virtue is combined
That can adorn the fair,
Excepting one you scarce can miss,
So trifling that you would not wish
That Virtue had been there.

She who professes all the rest
Make sure excel the prude whose breast
That Virtue shares alone;
To seek perfection is a jest,
They who have fewest faults the best,
And Peggy has but one.'

Edward Bligh, Earl of Darnley, was in London, and was again haunting the Green-room. Peg had always liked Darnley, and she saw no reason to frown upon him because of the other two men in her life. She cared nothing for propriety or prudence; she had never been bound by conventional moral codes, knowing that, in any case, few people followed them. Hanbury Williams sent her another set of verses:

> Once more I'll tune my vocal shell
> To hills and dales my passion tell,
> A flame which time can never quell,
> That burns for lovely Peggy.
> Ye greater bards the lyre should hit,
> For say what subject is more fit,
> Than to record the spritely wit
> And bloom of lovely Peggy.
>
> The sun first rising in the morn,
> That paints the dew-bespangled thorn,
> Does not so much the day adorn,
> As does my lovely Peggy.
> And when in Thetis lap of rest,
> He streaks with gold the ruddy west,
> He's not so beauteous as undress'd
> Appears my lovely Peggy.
>
> Were she arrayed in rustic weed,
> With her the bleating flocks I'd feed,
> And pipe upon my oaten reed
> To please my lovely Peggy.
> With her a cottage would delight,
> All's happy when she's in my sight,
> But when she's gone it's endless night,
> All's dark without my Peggy.
>
> The zephyr's air the violet blows
> Or breathes upon the damask rose,
> He does not half the sweets disclose
> That does my lovely Peggy.
> I stole a kiss the other day,
> And, trust me, nought but truth I say,
> The fragrant breath of blooming May
> Was not so sweet as Peggy.
>
> While bees from flow'r to flow'r shall rove
> And linnets warble thro' the grove,

Or stately swans the waters love
So long shall I love Peggy.
And when Death with his pointed dart
Shall strike the blow that rives my heart,
My words shall be when I depart,
'Adieu, my lovely Peggy.'

Verses – flowers – presents of jewels – Peg accepted them all, and was as airily faithless to Hanbury Williams as he and his kind were to the women they pursued. Darnley came to her lodgings when Garrick was at the theatre and she herself was not playing. This turn of events was bound to reach David Garrick's ears, and, rashly, Peg insisted that it was no affair of his. When he jealously questioned her on her reported associations with other men, she spiritedly reminded him of his reported associations with other women.

They were growing apart, and neither wished to admit it. Peg still wanted to marry Garrick; she felt that if their union were regularized things would be different. They would settle down to a new, better relationship, her capriciousness would disappear, and she would have nothing to do with any other man. The word 'insecurity' where emotional problems were concerned was not in use in an age which had not heard of psychology, but the opinions of contemporaries indicate that it was a lack of emotional security which made Peg Woffington act so wildly at this time. Macklin, in particular, to whom Peg talked very freely in later years, gives an account of the last few months of the affair which has an authentic ring. He says that when Peg now mentioned marriage, Garrick evaded the subject. He would not discuss it: he simply talked of other things, or found an excuse to go out.

The brilliant gatherings of wits and men of letters were growing fewer. Samuel Johnson rarely came these days; he saw Garrick in the Green-room at Drury Lane. There were many evenings when Peg was alone – but not for long. If she had not arranged to meet Hanbury Williams, there was always Darnley. The Irishman was by now deeply in love, and jealous of Garrick. He urged Peg to break up the ménage and come to him entirely.

Peg was restless and unhappy. Apparently Garrick made a last attempt to mend matters, and promised to marry her, actually buying a wedding-ring and trying it on her finger. The end of the relationship was not marriage, however, but a definite break. A purported eye-witness account of the last scene between them is given in 'Mackliniana' in an 1800 issue of the *European Magazine*, and is said to have been taken from a private manuscript attributed to Macklin. A similar account appears in 'Ryan's Table Talk'. As only the two characters concerned were there, it is likely the account has been dramatized; but Peg Woffington told several of her friends about the wedding-ring and Garrick's twistings and turnings on the subject of their marriage, so the rest of the story may be broadly true:

The wedding-day had been absolutely named and every preparation made by Garrick as well as by Woffington. But the numerous stories in connexion with Peg Woffington's name made Garrick restive. As the time appointed for the wedding grew near he began to grow impatient with her. His temper became ruffled over things that formerly he regarded with indifference. He specially objected to one of her most devoted worshippers, Lord Darnley, and even found fault, we are told, with her popularity on the stage and in society.

Garrick . . . grew more and more moody. He probably reasoned that he could gain little by this union. It would hurt his popularity somewhat with the feminine portion of his audience. In addition to these matters he possibly reflected that however high his *fiancée* stood in public esteem as an actress, her private character as a woman was far from being stainless . . .

On the morning of the appointed day, he tried the wedding-ring on Peg's finger. It fitted perfectly, and she gayly complimented him on his skill in selecting it. He made no answer to her pleasantries, but continued in such a morose and gloomy disposition that she rallied him on the lack of sprightly manner and flow of spirit usual in him. As her humour became more lively his increased in seriousness. Finally, giving up the attempt to coax him into a cheerfulness she bluntly asked him the cause of his depression. He declared it was the result of a bad night's sleep. The explanation was given with so much hesitation that Woffington would not accept it.

'And pray, was it this,' she asked, holding up the wedding-ring, 'which has given you so restless a night?'

'Why, to tell you the truth, my dear,' he said, 'as you love

frankness, it was, and in consequence of it I have worn the
shirt of Dejinira* for the last eight hours.'

'Then, sir,' she retorted coldly, 'get up and throw it off. I could
guess the cause of your dejection. You regret the step you are
about to take.'

He made no reply, and after a pause Woffington continued:

'Well, sir, we are not at the altar, and if you possessed ten
times the wealth, fame and ability that the world gives you
credit for, I would not, after this silent but eloquent confession,
become your wife. From this hour I separate myself from you
except in the course of professional business, or in the presence
of a third person.'

Peg kept her word. She took lodgings elsewhere, and sent back
all Garrick's gifts. He returned hers, with the exception of a pair of
diamond buckles. After a time, Peg wrote to him asking for the
buckles; he replied that he was keeping them to remind him of
their happy years together. Peg did not ask for them again, and
Garrick constantly wore the buckles in his shoes. The print-
sellers were soon on to the story, and many caricatures appeared
– with Garrick, of course, figuring as the grasping ex-lover who
could not even break off an affair of the heart in a civilized
fashion.

An entirely different version of their parting is given in the
Diary kept by Mr Windham, Garrick's friend, who said he got it
from Thomas Sheridan in 1772, when the latter was telling him
anecdotes about Peg Woffington. After remarking that Peg was a
very captivating woman, and never failed 'to get a great influence
over all men that lived with her', Windham goes on to quote
Sheridan relating

an extraordinary anecdote . . . over the ascendancy she had
over a Lord Darnley, I think an Irish peer, and of dishonourable dealing she met with from G. This Nobleman was so
passionately fond of her, that he sent one Swiney, with a proposal, that if she would give her word of honour, never to
have any more connexion with Garrick, with whom she then

* The shirt steeped in a centaur's blood which Dejinira sent to her
husband, Hercules, thinking it now had magical powers which would
keep him faithful. Instead, it caused him great agony, and, finally, his
death.

almost exclusively lived, he would settle upon her £500 a year.
He gave her a certain time to consider of his offer, declaring
that if no answer was returned by the expiration of that, His
resolution was fix't for abandoning her for ever. This proposal
was made immediately known to G., and He was asked by her,
whether He would consent to part with her, or marry her. The
last day of the time fix't for receiving her answer was arrived,
before He would give any determination. He then, according to
Sherns account, made her a promise of marriage; Swiney was
employed to get the ring and the licence; and He slept with
her that night as usual: but after some time being in bed, He
began to groan most piteously, declaring He was ruined and
undone if He married her, and, in short, signifying that He
could not bring himself to consent. In this situation they were
found by Swiney the next morning. It was then too late to
alter her determination; the answer had been given to Lord
Darnley; who either had already gone, or went soon after
abroad, and, it was supposed, died partly of grief at her loss.
This account Sherid. said He had from Swiney; and was the
story told by Mrs. Woff. Whether the representation was altogether true may be doubted.

This account, given by Sheridan almost thirty years after the
event, may contain a few grains of truth, but there are glaring
inconsistencies. Darnley did not die until 1747; after Peg left
Garrick in 1744, Darnley was still ardently pursuing her. It is
extremely unlikely that Owen M'Swiney would have consented
to be employed on such an errand.

The likelihood is that Peg, when she was friendly with Thomas
Sheridan and his wife during her second Dublin visit in 1751, told
them the bare facts of her parting with Garrick, and that Sheridan
'misremembered' the details.

'The heart must have something to occupy it,' says Augustin
Daly. 'Love or hate or avarice are ever knocking at its portal.
Failing one object we take up another to fill the craving which
comes with the first beginnings of reason.'

Peg Woffington gave her fellow-players at Drury Lane no clue to her feelings when she broke with David Garrick; but it is evident that she had grown closely attached to him during their intimate association, and even so resilient a spirit as hers must have taken some time to recover from the emotional wounds which marred their parting. But neither hate nor avarice took the place of her love for Garrick: both were alien to her temperament. She felt no hatred, either then or at any period afterwards. Her pride as well as her heart had been hurt, but she could turn to her extraordinary powers of reasonableness and commonsense – so rare in her contemporaries, and not often found in a woman of Peg Woffington's attractions. Not a word against Garrick, the private individual, was ever heard from her lips. Garrick the actor was not always immune from her criticism, when he gave less than his best, but the ex-lover now belonged to the past.

Avarice, Davy's most disagreeable trait, was completely foreign to Peg. She had always been open-handed, taking care, at the same time, to save enough money to meet those most binding of all obligations, her responsibilities to her family. John O'Keefe tells in his *Recollections* of the pleasant change that had come to the circumstances of the widow in Dublin who had once sold watercress in the streets:

> Mrs Woffington is now comfortably supported; a respectable looking old lady in a black velvet cloak with a deep silk fringe, a diamond ring on her finger, and an agate snuff-box. She has got nothing to mind but going around the Catholic churches and chatting with her neighbours about the fame and goodness of her daughter in England.

There was Polly to support at her French convent. Polly was contented enough, but she hinted in her letters that she would like to come to London. Peg began to think of bringing her sister to England, but not to live in London; she would take a country villa, not too far away, settle Polly there with suitable servants, and visit her as often as possible.

Meanwhile, Darnley and Hanbury Williams were quick to take advantage of Peg's changed circumstances. Darnley pressed her to live with him, and in the end Peg agreed; they got on very well together, and she liked making the handsome, gay young man happy. Hanbury Williams was almost beside himself with anger

when he heard that she had gone to his rival. In July, 1744, he
wrote an Ode which was savage in its fury:

> In Imitation of Ulla si Juris tibi pejerati
> Poena, Barine, nocuisset unquam
>
> Hor. Lib. 2, Od. 8

> If Heav'n upon thy perjur'd head
> Had the least mark of vengeance shed,
> For all thy hate to truth;
> Had ev'r diminish'd any grace
> Lit up one pimple in thy face,
> Or rotted but one tooth,

> I would believe its powers, but you
> More fair, as still more faithless grow,
> Charms flow from perjuries;
> The more you cheat, we trust the more,
> Each jilting tear's a fruitful show'r,
> That makes fresh beauties rise.

> By Venus, Cupid, ev'ry pow'r,
> To love propitious, you're forswore,
> Regardless of their wrath;
> By tricks, and cheats, and lies you live,
> By breach of word and honour thrive,
> Like my good Lord of Bath.

> But at each broken oath and vow,
> Indulgent Venus smiles, you know,
> Who have so often tried her;
> And Cupid can't be angry, sure,
> While thus new vot'ries you procure
> And stretch his empire wider.

> That beauteous face, those heav'nly charms,
> The cautious mother's breast alarms,
> For her young darling son;
> And each penurious father fears
> Lest their unthinking am'rous heirs
> Should gaze and be undone.

Venus, whose charms rule all above,
Is famed for fickleness in love,
And for her beauty's pow'r;
You are her copy drawn with care,
Like her, are exquisitely fair,
Like her a thorough whore.

Hanbury Williams could not, however, free himself from his
subjection to Peg Woffington's beauty. A month later he was
writing to his friend, Henry Fox, from Coldbrook, where he was
recuperating after an indisposition:

I recover strength slowly, and look pale and mighty fair. I
believe if Mrs Woffington saw me she would venture from
Darnley for half an hour's conversation. I am glad the man
has got his mare again. She is so handsome that anybody must
like her, and he is so rich that any woman must like him. I am
forced to be content with her picture* which I have hung up in
my room in the wood, which is very like her and very handsome. I sit and look at that and my paper in turns; and I believe
pleasant subjects to look at inspire very well.

Fox replied he did not know that Mrs Woffington had gone
back to Lord Darnley. 'It surprises me; for 'tis hard to think he
gives her more money, and much harder to imagine any other
reason for her leaving you. But I can't bear you should care
about it, as I see you do.'

Did Hanbury Williams care about it? He was no doubt piqued
by Peg's desertion; it is unlikely that he was heartbroken, or
even touched emotionally. In all his relations with women, his
feelings were seldom or never involved. He was to travel much
in Europe, and go to Russia on diplomatic missions; he was to
have more mistresses, and a curious friendship with the enigmatic
Empress Catherine; but there is no indication that this highly
gifted man ever knew the joy of true affection, except from a
few old friends like Henry Fox.

* By Van Loo, commissioned by Hanbury Williams the previous year.

10
Polly

Peg Woffington had saved a great deal of money, and when she heard of a 'fine handsome villa' for sale at Teddington, twenty miles from London, she drove down to the riverside village to see Teddington Place House.* It was indeed fine and handsome. The villa had been built at the beginning of the eighteenth century for Sir Charles Duncombe, Lord Mayor of London, 'the richest and most unscrupulous financier of his time', so it was not surprising that 'money was scattered broadcast on its adornment; it had ceilings painted by Verrio and carved chimney-pieces by Grinling Gibbons'. The gardens were extensive and well laid out, and the house had an air of quiet repose in spite of its luxurious fittings.

A country house meant prestige as well as a retreat from London – and it would provide the right kind of background for Polly. Peg now brought her sister back from the French convent, where 'nothing had been left undone to give her the finest education that a lady could have'. She had received more pocket money than any other pupil, her monthly allowance being 'equal to the pin-money of many a nobleman's daughter'. Polly had proved an apt and willing pupil at the convent; she well understood Peg's ambitions for her, and was more than ready to turn herself into a lady. She spoke French with the best accent, was proficient in painting, music and embroidery, read prodigiously so as to keep up to date with the literature of the day, and did not neglect 'such other matters as were deemed essential to a young person of good family and high position in respectable society'.

* The name of the villa was changed to Udney Hall in the nineteenth century. It has since been demolished.

Good family. Respectable society. There was the rub. Peg's ultimate aim was a satisfactory marriage for the cultivated and highly polished Miss Mary Woffington, to whom she had given an auspicious start in the matrimonial stakes. Polly was very pretty, with well-bred manners, always dressed in good taste, and was at ease in any society; the finishing school had prepared its young ladies for the drawing-room by specializing in 'refined and sparkling discourse'. There was no question of Polly's refinement, and she could sparkle with the best of them when it came to small talk. A desirable bride for a man of quality.

Peg Woffington, however, was a realist. Men of quality demanded more than beauty and an air of breeding when it came to matrimony. They not only entered into the state of wedlock, they formed alliances – and alliances meant Family. Polly was the daughter of an Irish bricklayer, and sister to a stage-player. That did not count as Family. Still, Peg did not give up hope. A country house was the best home for a young and accomplished girl, with a sensible housekeeper as chaperone, and servants enough at her beck and call. A great many people of quality lived in the neighbourhood, or had summer villas between Twickenham and Hampton Court. Polly, once installed, would be asked to join picnics, water-parties and other rural amusements, and at these she would meet young people of the upper classes. Having 'spared no expense to fit her sister for an elevated position in society', Peg could only watch, and wait, and hope that her ambitions for her sister would be realized.

Hannah Woffington remained in Dublin. Peg had twice brought her over to London, but Hannah found everything bewildering. Taken to Hampton Court, she thought 'the floors very neat' and the gardens pretty. She did not care for the tedious journey from Dublin, and Peg, knowing she was happiest at home, did not again attempt to persuade her to cross the Irish Sea. She gave the old lady forty pounds a year, which kept her in comfort, and Hannah was exceedingly satisfied.

Drury Lane was again in difficulties: Fleetwood owed thousands of pounds. When he could no longer push off his creditors, he decided to retire from management. He found a couple of rich bankers who were willing to buy the patent of the theatre, and they agreed to allow him six hundred a year on condition that he really did retire, and made no attempt to interfere with the running of the theatre. Fleetwood agreed. The bankers, who were not in the least interested in theatrical production but knew a good investment when they saw one, offered a high salary to Lacy, the assistant manager to Rich at Covent Garden, to manage Drury Lane for them, and sat back to wait for the profits. The players were not consulted over the transaction; it was taken for granted that they were taken over along with the patent, and the season continued.

Thomas Sheridan arrived in London from Dublin. Peg remembered him as a pleasant, stage-struck young gentleman she had met when she and Garrick had been there together, and Sheridan was gratified by her friendliness. Garrick took the principal parts in the plays. Peg played Belinda in *The Provok'd Wife,* with Garrick as Sir John Brute and Susanna Cibber as Lady Brute. Since their parting, Peg had had nothing to do with Garrick outside the theatre, but neither allowed their private affairs to interfere with their professional work, ignoring the gossip of the Green-room and the elaborately oblique questions which slipped out from the inquisitive among their social acquaintance. They acted together on the stage in complete harmony when they were cast in the same plays, and went their own ways when they left the theatre.

Kitty Clive, who had been without an engagement the previous season, returned to the Lane.

'We find Woffington,' says Daly, 'with the best grace in the world, yielding the part of Portia to Kitty, in which the latter made her reappearance.'

Peg had, in fact, no alternative; Lacy cast Kitty Clive for the part, and Peg Woffington was too sensible to attempt to argue with a manager who could cancel her agreement if she refused to accept his decisions. Samuel Foote joined the company for the season, and calmly announced that he had 'persuaded' Lacy to allow him to make a trial of Sir Harry Wildair. Everyone waited for an explosion from Peg, but it did not come. Like Lacy himself, and most of literary and theatrical London, she preferred not to declare open war on a man who was despised and disliked, 'a compound of cayenne and vitriol', whom no one trusted and everyone feared because of his complete lack of principle.

Samuel Foote was born in Cornwall in 1720. He came of good middle-class stock, went to Oxford, read for the Bar, was more interested in gaming than in the serious study of the law, and soon ran through what money he had, ending by being imprisoned in the Fleet for debt. His extravagance was probably inherited from his mother, who, it was said, was in a similar plight at the same period. She wrote to him:

'Dear Sam, I am in prison for debt; come and assist your loving mother, E. Foote.'

To which he replied:

'Dear Mother, so am I, which prevents his duty being paid to his loving mother, by her affectionate son, Samuel Foote.'

He later turned to the stage, in spite of having a harsh voice, tried tragedy as Othello and comedy as Lord Foppington – both with equal lack of success. Now he had been taken on by Lacy. Bad actor though he was, Foote's intimacy with people of importance enabled him to show off in parts that he fancied; managers were not likely to be too critical when a player could help fill the house. Thomas Davies, Garrick's biographer, finds it incredible that for three nights the boxes were crowded to see Foote 'murder the part of Ben' in *Love for Love*, 'for his acting bore no resemblance to nature and character. He had no discipline or sense of character, degenerating into buffoonery.'

It was pleasant at Teddington, with its villas and lawns sloping gently to the river, the gardens full of flowers, fields and woods shading into the distance. Peg drove down in her coach to see Polly as often as she could, staying for a week or two when she was not playing at the theatre. Darnley often went to Ireland, and then Peg gave 'well considered and carefully peopled receptions' at her lodgings, bringing Polly up for a day or two and presenting her as a young lady of quality. If the town smiled, no one actually laughed in Mistress Woffington's presence, her motives being recognized as entirely laudable. It was agreed that the girl was charming. Lee Lewes in his *Memoirs* says that Miss Mary Woffington was, in some respects, more beautiful than her famous sister; her features were more classical, and her face had 'the refinement of one that had been delicately nurtured, and her manners had acquired grace by the mastery of every accomplishment'. The town appreciated a work of art.

Peg's swan, however, had many goose's feathers. When Polly was surrounded by admirers, she was flippant rather than witty, and sometimes her liveliness got out of hand. Mrs Thrale was later to write to Fanny Burney that in her opinion the younger Miss Woffington was easily flattered and not of a thoughtful mood, and the admiration created by her loveliness and the compliments paid to her by distinguished people soon turned a head that was not too well stored with reflective qualities. Another contemporary wrote acidly that the young Miss Woffington ascribed her success in society solely to her own pleasing graces, and did not realize that she was courted mainly because of the great reputation of her sister.

There were often parties at Teddington, for Peg's own friends as well as for Polly's country neighbours, among whom by now she had made many desirable acquaintances. The Great Room at Teddington Place House was a fine setting for gatherings, and Peg was an accomplished hostess. Sheridan had taken a house at Kingston, and there entertained Trinity College men who had come to London. He invited Peg and her sister to join him and his friends, and Peg spent many pleasant evenings full of good talk, laughter, gossip and reminiscence. Even Garrick came, at times. There was no outward awkwardness between him and Peg on these occasions; they were both players, civil and courteous in the company of their own kind.

At her own house, Peg brought down her London intimates – and these often included Colonel Caesar. Peg never attempted to explain Colonel Caesar to anyone. He was a friend of long standing, one of the lovers who had not lasted long in that capacity, but who remained faithful and devoted, no matter how the wayward Peg behaved. He appears in the background right from the early London years, a shadowy rival who maddened Hanbury Williams, Darnley and Garrick in turn. Little is known about him except that he was always one of Peg's staunchest adherents. Horace Walpole described him as a colonel in the Guards and a lineal descendant of Sir Julius Caesar, who was Chancellor of the Exchequer in the reign of James the First. Polly liked him because he looked distinguished; when Sheridan and the Trinity men came to the villa and found him there, they accepted him as a gentleman and asked no questions. Peg treated him in public with her natural gaiety and open-hearted warmth.

One of the minor actresses at Drury Lane, Mrs Barrington, had attached herself to Peg, assisting her with her gowns and stage jewellery; Peg's maid was now married, and she had not yet found a new personal maid to her liking. Mrs Barrington was the wife of the John Barrington who had been one of Madame Violante's Lilliputians. A small-part player without much ambition, she had the good nature of the genuinely kind woman, and was totally without envy or jealousy. Peg Woffington had learnt to be wary of women in the world of the playhouse, but she could depend on Mrs Barrington's friendship and loyalty, and often took her to Teddington when the other was without a part. They would walk in the garden, or along the banks of the Thames, talking or not, as the mood took Peg. Mrs Barrington was not a rattle; she knew when to be quiet, and Peg found her restful and agreeable.

One sunny day at the villa, Mrs Barrington suggested an airing, and they all set out on their favourite walk by the river. There were other strollers taking advantage of the sunshine, and Peg Woffington curtsied to a number of acquaintances. Presently a party of three young ladies and two older women came by. One of the women stopped with an exclamation.

'Why, Mistress Woffington!'

It was Mrs Bellamy, rather worn and a thought shabby in her finery, but as voluble as ever. There were introductions: Mrs Jackson, the two Miss Jacksons, and Mrs Bellamy's own daughter, George Anne – a pretty girl who curtsied and eyed the famous Mrs Woffington with interest. The two parties merged, and continued their walk together. George Anne Bellamy, telling of that meeting many years later, remembered her own excitement, and her quick thought: would this encounter be advantageous to her? It is likely that Mrs Bellamy gave a sketchy explanation of how she came to be there, accompanied by George Anne, when the last time she had seen Peg she had lamented the fact that her daughter had been reft from her. Her mind also worked quickly. She, too, was pleased at this chance meeting. George Anne was exceedingly anxious to get into the theatre, and if the girl made a good impression on Peg Woffington, it might lead to something.

The elderly actress had had a run of good fortune all round in the last year. She had hung on at Covent Garden as long as possible, but small-part players without a firm 'agreement' were only paid there, as elsewhere, by the performance, and some weeks she had so few parts allotted to her that she earned hardly enough to buy food. A protector, like the others? Mrs Bellamy was no longer attractive enough; her good looks had gone. Her thoughts turned more and more to George Anne and the girl's hundred a year. Surely her own daughter would help her?

Mrs Bellamy found the very person through whom she could approach George Anne – the servant, still in the same employment, who had brought the little girl to see her years before. The actress somehow managed to spare the money for a bribe, went to see the servant, and sent a heartbroken message through the woman. She longed to have her daughter with her. She bitterly regretted her earlier conduct, she abhorred her unnatural behaviour, and now wished for nothing on earth except to clasp once more the child from whom she had parted. Would George Anne come and live with her lonely mother? This was the burden of the message the carefully coached servant took to the young lady living under the roof of the lady of quality chosen by Lord Tyrawley.

Incredibly, George Anne agreed. If she wondered whether her annual allowance had anything to do with her mother's change of heart, she suppressed the thought in the name of duty and compassion. Perhaps she was conscious of a deeply felt desire to be with her own kin, perhaps she hoped for some real affection. In the event, when she did leave the house of her fashionable guardian and returned to her mother, she knew a little happiness. Mrs Bellamy appeared genuinely to wish to make some atonement for her previous neglect by every proof of indulgent fondness. George Anne wrote later: 'This affectionate attention made me ample amends for the loss of that elegance and splendour I had just left.'

All went well so long as George Anne's money lasted. When her allowance became due at the next quarter, however, she found that it was no longer to be paid, owing to her removal from the house of her patroness. Mrs Bellamy, instead of alleviating her own difficulties, had added another encumbrance to her indigent state. Her plight would have been serious, had not help arrived from an unexpected quarter. Mrs Bellamy was intimate with the wife of a governor of the East Indies, a Mrs Jackson, who had come to England for the education of her two daughters. Mrs Jackson lived at Montpelier Row, in Twickenham, and when she heard of Mrs Bellamy's new misfortune, she generously invited her friend and George Anne to pass the summer with her at the riverside village. They were more than delighted to accept. George Anne made friends with the Jackson daughters, and it was a very pleasant arrangement for all concerned.

Sheridan and the Trinity College men were warmly welcomed at Teddington Place House, and of course young Miss Woffington came in for a great deal of admiration. They wanted to know if she intended to follow in her celebrated sister's footsteps, and go into the playhouse? Polly laughed, and said it was possible – she did not know – indeed, yes, it had come into her mind. The praise which eddied round her in the Great Room as these fine-looking blades toasted her made Polly believe it was time that she, too, was taking her place in the centre of the stage, bowing to loud applause, holding court in the Green-room.

Peg Woffington asked herself if Polly was really in earnest. She had kept the girl away as much as possible from the theatre itself; Polly had never, until now, shown any desire to be an actress. Peg wondered if this was to be an end of all her hopes. Practical as ever, she faced the fact that though Polly now had aristocratic friends, none of the men in those exalted spheres had so far offered marriage. A lovely face and shapely figure, good breeding, intelligence and charm: these were not enough. Peg Woffington had always known it, and now she must accept it, and make other plans. If Polly was of a mind to try the playhouse, then she should have her chance.

Having come to this decision, Peg proceeded to make plans.

The next time Sheridan and his friends came to Teddington, she invited them to her house for wine and mentioned her proposal to them: she wished to put on a play so that Polly's histrionic abilities could be assessed. The men were enthusiastic; they were certain that Miss Polly would turn out to be as wonderful an actress as her bewitching sister. The extravagant compliments were highly pleasing to Polly, who was of the private opinion that the gentlemen were right. Everyone put forward suggestions, and in the end they agreed that *The Distress'd Mother* would show off the young lady's person and talents to perfection.

There was a large barn in the neighbourhood, and Peg arranged for it to be fitted up as a temporary playhouse, with a stage, seats, and sconces for candles. As for casting the play, Sheridan undertook to ask several London actors if they would assist the project, together with the Trinity men. Peg remembered the proximity of Mrs Bellamy and her daughter. She herself, Mrs Bellamy and Mrs Barrington would play the minor parts. Polly, of course, would be the heroine, and Miss Bellamy the second young lady's rôle. Everything fitted in well.

Sheridan was as good as his word and got his London player friends to take part – including David Garrick. Peg would never have asked Garrick herself, but she was pleased that he should be there at Polly's first performance: he could do a lot for Polly. It did not occur to Peg that the demure little Miss Bellamy was considering that the great David Garrick could also do a great deal for *her*.

George Anne Bellamy was determined to take hold of this opportunity and use it to the full. She had no pretensions to Polly Woffington's style of classic beauty, but she was, she knew, very vivacious, and she had found by experience that people responded to liveliness. George Anne studied her part and attended every rehearsal, taking care not to outshine the lovely Polly – which would have been easy to do, for the younger Woffington turned out to be surprisingly wooden in movement and voice.

Peg noticed, with surprise and something of shock, that Polly changed completely when she began to speak the lines of her part: she became self-conscious, stilted, uneasy. Garrick could not attend many rehearsals because he had several performances in London. Peg set to work to coach Polly, hoping to work a miracle before the day of the performance. Did she remember the

Peg Woffington. As Mistress Ford in *The Merry Wives of Windsor.*
F. Haytley.
(From Augustin Daly's *Tribute*.)

George Anne Bellamy
by F. Cotes and A. Ramberg.
(Harvard Theatre Collection.)

Kitty Clive by Jos. Van Haecken.
(Harvard Theatre Collection.)

Susanna Cibber
by Thomas Hudson.
(Harvard Theatre
Collection.)

Hannah Pritchard
by F. Hayman.
(Harvard Theatre
Collection.)

Drury Lane Theatre. (*See Note, p. 233.*)
(Harvard Theatre Collection.)

Drury Lane Theatre.
(Enthoven Collection, Victoria and Albert Museum.)

far-off days when Madame Violante had taken so much trouble with her? Was it borne in upon her that Madame had had very different material to work on? Polly made little progress; she was as stiff at the last rehearsal as she had been at the first. On the night of the performance there was a change: Polly was dancing with excitement, and looking wonderfully pretty and full of spirit. Peg was greatly relieved, and thrust aside her earlier fears.

The barn was crowded with the fashionable people from the neighbourhood, as well as actors from London who had heard of the coming début of the younger Woffington. Another Peg? Was there a second being of such perfection? They were curious to see. The play started, and when Polly made her first entrance there came an encouraging hail of applause. Peg's last doubts fled, as she told herself that tonight would see her sister's triumph.

It was, however, George Anne Bellamy's triumph. She was a natural actress, and she had sensed all through the rehearsals that though Polly had a great deal of the Woffington beauty, she possessed none of her sister's gift of holding an audience. After the first few minutes, Polly's confidence dwindled away, and she spoke her lines, no more. Well drilled, she did not falter over her words, but they lacked fire.

George Anne was exultant, and played full out when it came to her turn to speak. Exerting all the force of her personality, she succeeded in taking the centre of the stage, in spite of her secondary rôle. At the end of the performance she was complimented by the great Mr Garrick himself, and by Mr Sheridan, and by personages in the audience who came into the improvised Greenroom and turned to her after a few formal civilities to Polly. Ignoring Peg Woffington's black looks, George Anne thoroughly enjoyed her success.

Mrs Bellamy and her daughter were not asked again to Teddington, and, in fact, they presently left Twickenham. Their kind patroness, Mrs Jackson, was taken ill, and as her doctors declared that the river air was too strong for her, she took a house in Henrietta Street, in Covent Garden. Mrs Bellamy wondered what she would have done without this good friend. It was clear that George Anne could expect no further allowance from Lord

E

Tyrawley, and she herself had not been offered any part at Covent Garden. Mrs Jackson allowed her to stay at Henrietta Street, but Mrs Bellamy knew that she and her daughter could not become permanent guests. John Rich, at Covent Garden, owed her a great deal of money for past performances. It was well known that his instruction to the doorkeeper at his home 'not to admit anyone under a baronet' was one of his defences against desperate players whose hunger was greater than their fear of not being engaged again the next season. Mrs Bellamy decided to go to Rich's house, nevertheless, and take George Anne with her. She had a special reason for gaining an interview with the manager of Covent Garden – with George Anne in attendance.

John Rich was not at home when Mrs Bellamy and her daughter called at Bloomsbury Square, but a judicious greasing of the doorkeeper's palm helped her at her next attempt. Rich, perhaps shamed into paying her something on account, actually became a little friendly, and introduced his daughters to George Anne. That astute young person contrived to be invited back the next day to witness some theatricals – and soon she was on terms of intimacy with the three Rich girls. They liked 'getting up' a play for their own amusement, and George Anne was prevailed upon to act with them. They chose *Othello*. George Anne was given the name part. She took a copy of the book home and was soon word perfect.

Next came rehearsals at Rich's house. George Anne gave free scope to her fancy and her voice, and while she was 'raving in all the extremity of jealous madness', Rich passed the open door of the room. 'Attracted by the powerful sweetness of the Moor's voice,' George Anne later asserted, 'which he declared to be superior to any he had ever heard,' Rich entered the room and paid George Anne many compliments on her theatrical abilities. His own daughters were playing Iago, Desdemona and Cassius, but he did not mind *them*. He had eyes and ears only for the unusual Othello, and said that if she turned her thoughts to the proper stage, he would be happy to engage her. Mr Garrick, for all his avowed admiration, had not gone so far. George Anne Bellamy returned to her mother with the jubilant news that she was now a member of the Covent Garden Company.

The only person who seemed oblivious to the fiasco of *The Distress'd Mother* was Polly herself. She believed that the polite compliments were genuine, and told her sister that she wished to continue with her 'success' – would Peg please arrange for her début in the London playhouse? She appeared to be so set on it that Peg found it hard to refuse to do something. It would be impossible to persuade any manager to engage a complete beginner, with no experience and only a pretty face to recommend her. Peg solved the matter by giving up her own benefit night, 30 March 1745, for Polly's appearance, and chose *The Beaux' Stratagem*, where Polly would have a chance to shine as Cherry. David Garrick, punctiliously professional, agreed to take Scrub, as he would have done if Mrs Woffington herself had been playing. Polly was announced on the playbills as 'Miss M. Woffington, being her first appearance on any stage'.

Peg again coached her sister every day, and hoped for the best. She herself was speaking the Epilogue. The house was quickly sold out, the boxes being taken by aristocratic admirers of Mrs Woffington, curious to see what the new Woffington was like. Polly learnt her words well and looked charming on the night. All seemed set fair for a success. It was, in fact, another failure, and a humiliating disappointment for the woman who had made the name of Woffington famous. Polly's fresh, youthful good looks were, in the event, all she had to offer. She had either not troubled to learn the lessons given by this mistress of dramatic art, or was so bemused by vanity that she thought it unnecessary to characterize her rôle: she considered it sufficient to be herself.

The large audience were tolerant, obviously making allowance for youth and inexperience, and there was scattered handclapping when Polly took her curtain, bowing with great assurance. Peg Woffington knew her play-going public, and she knew, too, that if Polly had not been her sister there would have been hisses mixed with the tepid applause. London audiences and Dublin audiences were alike in demanding talent for their money, and in showing their displeasure when they reckoned they were not getting full value for their shillings and guineas. It was clear that Polly possessed no natural abilities whatever as an actress, and Peg was forced to admit to herself that the girl had no liking for the hard work essential for a life in the theatre, either.

Peg did not waste time in reproaches, but thought much about

Polly's future. She herself had made Polly fit only for the world of polite society, and in that world the girl must stay. The search for a suitable husband must go on; there was no alternative. It was not easy. Again Peg Woffington was conscious of the unalterable fact that they had no background, no family, no suitable connexions. Money? Peg now had sufficient money, but she knew well that it would take a very substantial dowry to offset a labouring father and a mother who had been washerwoman and huckster – let alone a player-sister, however lauded. It was hardly likely that money alone would induce an offer of marriage. The only real chance would be if a suitable *parti* fell very much in love with Polly, one who would clearly understand that he would be unable to win her except through a wedding-ring.

The Old Theatre, Drury Lane

11
Uncertainties

Thomas Sheridan returned to Dublin early in 1745. Peg knew she would miss him, but she could hardly have guessed what an important part he was to play in her life. Sheridan did not himself foresee that the fortunes of this brilliant actress were to be closely bound up in his own. He went back to Ireland with some relief, for acting in London had become edged with frustration and difficulty.

David Garrick, after a quarrel with Lacy at Drury Lane over a proposed rise in salary which the manager would not give him, had gone to Rich at Covent Garden. Sheridan had taken over many of Garrick's parts at the Lane, and had been widely acclaimed. Garrick was afflicted by an unfortunate jealous streak in his character, and the result was predictable: 'A sort of competition, a rivalship, was set up between him [Sheridan] and Mr Garrick, by officious friends.' Davies, who usually knew all the current gossip from the people concerned, does not give details, but goes on: 'This occasioned a quarrel between them, which was unreconciled when Sheridan left London.'

Sheridan was returning to his native city, in fact, because he had been offered the chance in life he had long been looking for. He intended, no less, to effect the reform of the Dublin theatre. It was a task which would have daunted any ordinary experienced player, but Sheridan was no ordinary man, and the experience he had garnered so far only served to encourage his resolution.

Thomas Sheridan was the son of the Reverend Dr Sheridan, a character well known in the Irish literary world and a close friend of Swift; Thomas was Swift's godson. The boy was sent

to London to be educated at Westminster School, and returned to
Dublin to enter Trinity College. He was an excellent scholar, and
after taking his degree he could have read for a Fellowship but
'alas for learning, he had long cherished an extraordinary pre-
dilection for the stage . . . nothing could dissuade him from in-
dulging his darling passion.'

Sheridan had no obvious advantages: Davies says:

> Neither in person nor voice had nature been very kind to
> Mr Sheridan, but his judgment, his learning and close applica-
> tion to study, compensated in some degree for the want of
> external advantages . . . He had, besides, the advantage of an
> excellent character in private life.

Both his excellent character and his status as a gentleman by
birth were to be of great assistance to him in the often stormy
years which followed this good start on the boards of the Theatre
Royal in Smock Alley. 'He was twenty three years of age at the
time of his début in 1743; he seems to have been a finished actor
from the beginning,' wrote a commentator in *The Gentleman's
Magazine*, and was soon playing leading parts like Brutus, Othello, Cato and Lord Townly.

When Sheridan made his first appearance at Smock Alley,
'the town went horn-mad about him' – not because he was
another Garrick, but on account of the great care he put into his
characterizations. James Quin was in Dublin 'during the first
warm glow of Mr Sheridan's prosperity'; he had come with the
full expectation of being engaged by the Smock Alley management
without any question, but 'he was told by the proprietors that all
the acting days during the remainder of the season were engaged
to the new actor.'

In the limited world of the playhouses, news of rising stars
quickly circulated; English newspapers and journals reached
Dublin by every packet, Irish news-sheets found their way to
London. Garrick realized that here was a rising actor who could
be useful to him, one who could be relied upon to take principal
rôles yet not prove too strong a rival. He wrote to Sheridan, sug-
gesting that the Irish actor should come to London and share the
honours with him at Drury Lane the following winter.

It was, at first sight, a tempting proposal, but after thinking it
over, Sheridan replied, in April 1743, that he intended taking 'a

jaunt of pleasure' to London in May, but he did not expect to stay there, as he had been offered very advantageous terms by Smock Alley which would keep him in Dublin until the following January. In any case:

> As to your proposal of our playing together, I am afraid I have too many powerful reasons against it; a well-cut pebble may pass for a diamond till a fine brilliant is placed near it, and puts it out of countenance. Besides, we should clash so much in regard to characters, that I am afraid it is impossible we can be in the same house. Richard, Hamlet, and Lear, as they are your favourite characters, are mine also . . . I question whether the town would bear to see a worse performer in one of your characters in the same house with you, though they might endure him in another.

He then went on to suggest an alternative proposal: that he and Garrick should divide the capitals between them, Garrick coming to play in Dublin while he took Garrick's place in London. The letter concludes:

> Pray remember my best respects to Mrs Woffington . . . as soon as I have a moment to spare, I intend to do myself the honour to write to her.

Sheridan was not happy at Smock Alley. The theatre had passed into the temporary management of one Philips, 'whose reputation for honesty was not of the best,' and Philips had engaged for the summer season another of the same kidney, Theophilus Cibber. Thomas Sheridan disliked the management and 'bore no love to Cibber'. There was a continual state of resentment behind the scenes; scene shifters, carpenters and musicians were pressing for unpaid wages, the actors had been on short salaries for weeks. One evening in June, when Sheridan arrived at the theatre to prepare for his part as Cato in the play of that name, it was to learn that Philips had absconded, 'taking with him more monies than he had a right to possess', and everything was in a state of confusion.

The play had to go on, however, and Sheridan went to his dressing-room. He found that the robe he was to wear as Cato had disappeared, and he was told that Philips had taken it. This was serious; Sheridan was sensitive about his figure, which was

ungainly without suitable stage costume. He ran along to Theophilus Cibber's room, and asked what he should do in this
emergency, lacking a suitable robe. 'Play without one,' replied
Cibber. Sheridan flew into a passion, and was beginning to
expostulate, when Cibber said: 'Damn me if I care what you do –
the play shall not stand still for you.' He then went out and
ordered the prompter to draw up the curtain.

Thomas Sheridan was now in a red-hot rage, for Cibber had no
more authority than he to order anybody to do anything. He
rushed on to the stage to explain to the audience what had happened, but Cibber followed him, and with great insolence offered
to read the part of Cato. Sheridan, beside himself with anger, ran
from the stage and went home.

The next day he published a pamphlet, setting out his reasons
for disappointing the audience:

> . . . It has been said that the want of a robe is a trifling
> thing and that the audience would have been content to receive
> me in any dress; they must have but little skill in theatrical
> affairs, who think a proper habit is not necessary. This was
> more particularly my case in this character, as it is one for
> which I am naturally very unfit in my person, and in which
> nothing could have made my appearance supportable but a
> large robe to cover my defects, and give a gravity and dignity
> to my person, which I wanted, and which are so absolutely
> necessary to the character.

Theophilus Cibber replied to this with his own pamphlet,
in which he tried to present Sheridan as a conceited autocrat.
Neither the town nor the Dublin theatre world was deceived.
Cibber was held in contempt by most of his fellow-players because he was a poor actor who managed to get engagements
only because he was the son of Colley Cibber. Contemporary
writers have not a good word to say of him; typical is Hitchcock's:

> We find Mr Cibber exhibiting his beautiful person, and
> charming with his harmonious tones in tragedy. Accordingly,
> much to his own satisfaction, he played Polydore in *The
> Orphan*, Syphax in *Cato*, and Lothario in *The Fair Penitent* . . .
> perhaps the public will not readily believe that Cibber's vanity

could tempt him so far as to play Othello; such however was really the case.

The University students, as usual, took sides in the affair, and when Cibber appeared as Othello on the 21 July, the theatre was crammed with the Trinity boys and a 'party of ruffians and other desperate fellows whom Cibber had hired'. Cibber's appearance was greeted with a shower of oranges, and he beat a retreat. When he came on a second time, there was a riot:

> The pit became a battlefield, the gods looking down took part in the fight, not alone by yells of encouragement or execration, but by missiles which they rained on the combaters. Candles and lamps were smashed, clouds of dust filled the air, blood flowed freely, until at last the College Boys turned out the party of ruffians and followed their retreat with threats of throwing them into the malodorous Liffey.*

Sheridan had had enough of Smock Alley, and he went over to Aungier Street, where he was invited to act Cato in a command performance, receiving 'every tribute of applause which his late unfair treatment and masterly performance merited'. Conditions at Aungier Street were unsettled; the theatre was doing as badly as Smock Alley. Sheridan suggested to the proprietors of both theatres that they should unite their companies, under his management. This they refused to do, and Thomas Sheridan decided to go to London.

It was on this visit that he took the house at Kingston and became friendly with Peg Woffington and her circle.

The Smock Alley and Aungier Street theatres sank lower and lower, not only financially but in public esteem; it looked as if the Irish capital was going to be without its major playhouses. The proprietors of both theatres saw at last that the only hope was to do what Thomas Sheridan had suggested in the first place – to join forces and try to assemble one company under good management. Sheridan was in London. They wrote to him, asking if he would return to Dublin and take on the new venture – on his own terms.

Sheridan had always hoped to get the opportunity of managing a playhouse; he had ideas which he had been mulling over for a

* F. Fitzgerald Molloy: The Life and Adventures of Peg Woffington.

long time. He left London without regret. Back in Dublin, he lost no time in seeing the proprietors of the theatres, and laying his plans before them. They gave him a completely free hand, and he was able to set to work at once.

Hitchcock considered that Sheridan was exactly the right man for the task, for not only was he 'unremittingly persevering in accomplishing whatever he embarked in', but he always tried to convince, rather than command. Moreover, 'his understanding was clear and comprehensive, and a liberal education enabled him to behold objects in their proper light'. Sheridan was devoted to the theatre, and had long been grieved by the humiliating condition to which it had been reduced since Thomas Elrington's day, 'deserted and despised by the grave, the rational, and every lover of order and decency'. Knowing the honour accorded to the Greek and Roman drama in classical times, he was determined to raise the Irish theatre to an equal degree of respect.

He was faced with a daunting prospect. The best players had left Dublin for England, joining companies in London or the provinces. The inferior actors and actresses who took their places drew very thin audiences; besides which, both theatres were heavily mortgaged. Sheridan saw that the first thing he must do was to get the financial situation into some kind of order. The Dublin managers were notorious for the non-payment of salaries. This was the source of much slackness, for who would attend rehearsals regularly, or take pains in their profession, when they were not sure of being paid? They had miserable pittances in any case; leading actors like Elrington received only a guinea a week, and some weeks only received half of that, or less. On one occasion all the actors went to the theatre dinnerless: even the managers were without money, and their credit was exhausted. As the sparse audience arrived and paid for their seats, a messenger was sent out.

According to Genest:

> The first shilling that came into the house they dispatched for a loin of mutton, the second for bread, the third for liquor, and so on till they had satisfied the calls of nature, when they prepared for the business of the night.

Sheridan made it known that he was establishing a fund for the regular payment of players' salaries and tradesmen's bills. Years later, he was able to claim, in a pamphlet, that every Saturday saw the weekly salary of each person discharged at the treasurer's office; throughout his reign at the Theatre Royal Thomas Sheridan did not owe anyone a penny.

He next set out for London, to engage 'such a company as must from their uncommon merit ensure success'. George Anne Bellamy was one of his first recruits, from the fortunate circumstances of her mother's accidentally meeting Mr Sheridan and learning that he was getting together a company for Dublin. Mrs Bellamy was never slow off the mark.

Sheridan knew that he would have little difficulty in tempting English players to Ireland. Rebellion had broken out in Scotland; Charles Edward Stuart had roused the clansmen and was said to be marching south with an army. There was alarm, and a run on the banks. Times of uncertainty and stress always emptied the playhouses; good engagements were welcome under a reliable manager like Thomas Sheridan, and Spranger Barry and several dependable minor players were glad to be offered a season in Dublin.

Sheridan had his eye on a big prize – David Garrick. It was common knowledge that Garrick had left Covent Garden, but the actor was not in London. Sheridan found out that Garrick was in Bath, and wrote to him, inviting him to Dublin, offering to share the season's profits on an equal basis after expenses had been deducted. He said he would give Garrick every advantage and encouragement he could in reason expect, but, he added – remembering their unresolved quarrel when he had acted with him in London a few years before – 'Mr Garrick must expect nothing from his friendship, though all that the best actor has a right to command, he might be very certain would be granted.'

Garrick had been ill a few weeks earlier, and after a stay at Buxton and a visit to see his relations at Lichfield, had gone to Bath with his landowner friend, Colonel Windham. The actor was in an unsettled frame of mind. Curious items appear in unexpected places. He had apparently heard from Peg Woffington about business affairs connected with Drury Lane, for he wrote on 10 October 1745 to Somerset Draper:

At my return from Buxton . . . I found your letter, and the enclosed from Mrs Woffington, in which (I think) she gives

me very kind sensible advice from the accounts she has had
from Lacy and his followers. I have wrote her a very civil
answer, told her the whole truth, and thanked her for all
favours.

All? How much went on beneath the surface of that enigmatic
character? When Sheridan's letter arrived, he was sitting with
Colonel Windham. Garrick read the letter and passed it over to
Windham, saying:
'This is the oddest epistle I ever saw in my life.'
'It may be an odd one,' replied the colonel, perusing the letter,
'but it is surely an honest one. I should certainly depend on a man
who treated me with that openness and simplicity of heart.'
Garrick had, in fact, been considering a visit to Dublin, if it
could be arranged. The Insurrection was not yet quelled; the
Pretender had won a victory at Prestonpans, and, though no one
doubted that he would be crushed, he was still on the march.
Better consider Sheridan's offer seriously. The actor's mind was
also on other things. Later in the month he was again writing to
Draper, saying that his thoughts were bending towards Ireland
and he was planning to go there. He added:

Woffington, I am told, shows my letters about; pray have
you heard anything of that kind? What she does now, so little
affects me, that, excepting her showing my letters of nonsense
and *love* to make me ridiculous, she can do nothing to give
me a moment's uneasiness – *the scene is changed – I'm altered
quite**.

Of the many letters which must have passed between Peg
Woffington and Garrick, none appears to have survived. There is
no suggestion in the records that Peg showed Garrick's letters to
anyone; she had enemies enough who would have spread a canard
of this kind in order to belittle her. Peg had schooled herself
over long years to hide any wounded feelings she might have.
Outwardly, she was the same as she had always been, mistress of
herself, and Garrick would have found no chink in the armour of
her smiling reserve.
It is probable that in spite of what he wrote to Somerset
Draper, he was still in love with Peg Woffington.

* A phrase out of the play *The Orphan*.

Garrick replied to Sheridan's letter, agreeing to the terms of sharing profits, and departed for Ireland a few weeks later. Robert Hitchcock, in his *Historical View of the Irish Stage*, describes the curious scene which took place when he arrived there:

> On his landing at Dublin, he was met by Mr Sheridan, who offered to fulfil his promise, of sharing the profits and losses. Though nothing could be fairer than this proposal, yet Mr Garrick insisted on a stipulated sum for performing during the winter. The other objected to the demand, and persisted in his first offer, which, as he justly observed, was the most reasonable, for then Mr Garrick would receive as much money as he brought [into the playhouse], and others would not be losers. In the other case he might perhaps be the only gainer. After some little dispute, which Mr Sheridan decided, by taking out his watch, and insisting upon an answer in five minutes, Mr Garrick submitted, and the affair terminated in the most amicable manner.

12
Marriage and a Coach

It was an anxious winter at Drury Lane. The company tried their utmost to fill the theatre, but the general feeling of despondency made audiences capricious; nothing seemed to please them. There were revivals of Shakespeare: Kitty Clive, as Ariel, played that sprite as a hoyden, and was angry when the laughs came in the wrong places. Peg Woffington tried Isabella in *Measure for Measure*. Her voice was still occasionally marred by its harsh note, and she was adversely criticized. She took a breeches part in a patriotic piece, *The Humours of the Army*: even this failed to draw, though she made a handsome figure in a stirring prologue, dressed in a splendid costume with a silver helmet on her head.

Personal sadness deepened her gathering professional anxieties. News came that Charles Coffey had died. Peg was genuinely grieved; he had done so much for her when she had been on the threshold of life in the playhouse. The misshapen little man had always been proud of the way she had risen to her present heights, and though they had not often met of late years, their friendship had always been secure. It hurt her to think that little Coffey would no longer come into the Green-room on his visits to London, and embrace her, and ask how she did, himself bringing all the Dublin news and gossip. Peg had never needed to be anything else but her natural being with Charles Coffey; he was one of the few men whom she had felt she could trust completely.

The season went on, Lacy bringing out all the most popular plays. Peg played the rôles by which she was best known, but she had a good deal of spare time on her hands, and she went down to Teddington whenever possible. Polly was prettier than ever, and, as usual, good-natured. She was surprised at her lack of success on the stage, but she did not repine; she liked a social life, and as Peg gave her a good allowance she was able to entertain her young friends in style.

One day, Peg Woffington was asked if her sister would care to join a group of well-bred young ladies who were to dance for charity at Covent Garden, which John Rich had lent for the purpose. This was the kind of invitation Peg wanted for Polly, and she accepted. Covent Garden was crowded for the occasion. Polly, who could dance better than she could act, enjoyed herself immensely. She did not know that this was to be a memorable occasion for her. Dressed in a froth of tulle, with roses in her hair, she was by far the prettiest of the girls pirouetting on the vast stage, and there was at least one gentleman in the audience who fell in love with her at first sight.

He was Captain Robert Cholmondeley, the second son of Lord Cholmondeley, a connexion of Horace Walpole's. After the performance was over he hurried to the stage door, and was overjoyed to find an acquaintance who had an entrée to the Green-room and agreed to take him there. Once inside the large, ornately decorated room he was jostled in a crowd of friends, relations and admirers of the young ladies, and he would have been sadly out of it had he not had a second piece of luck: he found someone to introduce him to the one young lady who mattered.

Miss Polly Woffington smiled at him – but he got no further, for she was kept securely at the side of her celebrated sister, Mrs Margaret Woffington. The actress was gracious, and not unfriendly. When he pressed for an opportunity to see his fair charmer again, Mrs Woffington did not deny him, and invited him to call. The first call was followed by a second, then a third and fourth. Peg Woffington indicated delicately that she wished to know if his intentions were honourable. Captain Cholmondeley made it clear that they were. Within a matter of weeks he proposed marriage. Polly waited sedately for her sister's views before committing herself.

Peg weighed up the matter with great care. The gallant officer was good looking and had breeding – but no money, beyond his captain's pay. Still, Polly would be marrying into the aristocracy; she would be the Honourable Mrs Cholmondeley, with an established position in society. Peg knew her old dreams of a title and a fortune for Polly were not likely to come to anything. Better settle for the match. Captain Cholmondeley was no libertine; he appeared to be a thoroughly worthy young man. There was no need to act in a hurry. Waiting would do him no harm; if indeed he was in earnest, his ardour would remain hot.

Captain Cholmondeley asked leave to wait upon them at Teddington, and when this was tactfully evaded, wrote letters which indicated that he could not bear the suspense much longer. A firm decision had to be made. Polly was willing to have him for a husband, and enthusiastic over the prospect of a fashionable wedding, a good establishment, and the chance at last to be her own mistress. She did not question how the good establishment was to be obtained and maintained: the money would, of course, be supplied by her sister. That was taken for granted.

There was, however, a difficulty. The bridegroom's aristocratic family strongly opposed the match. They refused to come to the wedding; Lord Cholmondeley hoped until the day itself that something would happen to prevent the marriage from taking place. Lord Cholmondeley, who was 'excessively proud', was also excessively poor; he had expected his sons to marry well. The eldest, the heir, had insisted on falling in love with a dowerless girl instead of with a fortune, and here was his younger son disgracing the family by allying himself with the stage. The stage! The playhouse! It was almost beyond belief. He appealed to the Honourable Robert, cajoled, threatened exclusion from the family, but it was useless. Robert Cholmondeley was in love. He and Miss Mary Woffington were duly united one fine day in 1746. 'The wedding was attended by a tremendous company . . .' It was as well that Mrs Margaret Woffington had earned such high salaries for years, and had been prudent enough to save and make wise investments. The young couple needed a home, so Peg bought them a house in Westminster, furnished it well, and gave Polly an income which would enable them to live in modest luxury.

Lord Cholmondeley made one last effort to save his son from continuing with a misalliance. He posted up to London to find out if there were any means by which the marriage could be annulled. This involved a meeting with Mrs Margaret Woffington. Actresses, reasoned Lord Cholmondeley, were susceptible to the chink of gold, provided there was enough of it to make a satisfactory sound. And Mrs Woffington's private reputation did not lead him to expect that she would be any different from the rest. He expected to see a Lady Betty Modish, an artificial, flaunting strumpet: he found a composed, dignified woman, dressed in the height of fashion and the best of taste. She listened politely to what he had to say, and replied – with more breeding than he had shown – that her sister had been brought up as a young lady, had had the best education, was highly accomplished, and would in no wise 'bring down' the position of Captain Cholmondeley, as his lordship feared. She also added, still with politeness, that whereas before she had one beggar to support, now she had two. Lord Cholmondeley was surprised, nonplussed, and finally charmed. There was no more talk of the possible annulment of the marriage.

In the event, Polly turned into a fine lady without any effort, and was soon holding her own with the society women who invited her to their houses out of curiosity, and continued to invite her for her own sake. The Cholmondeley relations remained aloof, and had their own opinions as to the probable reasons Lord Cholmondeley had been 'got round' by Peg Woffington. Robert Cholmondeley's uncle, Horace Walpole, wrote to his friend, Horace Mann: 'I have been unfortunate in my own family. My nephew has married a player's sister' – ignoring the fact that his own mother had been a wealthy timber-dealer's daughter.

Captain Cholmondeley now wished to leave the army, and he resigned his commission and took Holy Orders. He was not particularly religious, but a younger son had to have a profession, as he could expect no great patrimony when his father died and his elder brother, Viscount Malpas, succeeded to the estates. Like many incumbents of the day, the Reverend Robert Cholmondeley paid a curate to do most of the parish work, and spent as much time as he could with his attractive wife. Polly did not allow this devotion to inconvenience her; she had already decided that she was going to do exactly as she liked, go where she wished, accept what invitations she chose, without the need to consult the Honourable Robert.

He was not a person of outstanding personality. In later years, when Fanny Burney found him attending his wife on some social occasion, she thought him grim in person and glum in manners, though, she observed, 'he appears to have humour in himself, and to enjoy it much in others.' Robert Cholmondeley had need of a sense of humour, right from the beginning of his marriage, for his wife showed no respect for him, either in private or in front of other people, and she did not disguise the fact that she found him excessively dull. Polly herself was the reverse of dull; she had opinions on every subject, and was fond of expressing them with a pretty air of authority. She was a skilled and practised flatterer, with a quick reaction to people's foibles, and she knew how to use her beauty and liveliness to charm women as well as men. Polly was ambitious to have her own *salon*; now that she had achieved through her marriage a secure position in society, she was determined to consolidate it by making as many influential friends as possible.

Garrick had reason to be glad of his decision to go to Dublin. Sheridan soon showed the public that the theatre was going to be worth patronizing that season. He and Garrick played Richard the Third and Hamlet alternately, and each agreed to be Iago to the other's Othello in turn, with George Anne Bellamy as Desdemona. Garrick also played Bayes in *The Rehearsal*, Lothario in *The Fair Penitent*, Macbeth, the Bastard in *King John*, and Sharp in his own farce of *The Lying Valet* for his benefit night. Thomas Sheridan was no niggard.

Everyone was talking of the revitalized playhouse. In the preceding winter, the Theatre Royal had been nearly empty; now it was always full. 'The nobleman and man of fashion, the sons of science, the grave citizen, and the modest fair, long banished from the theatre, now with pleasure enjoyed once more their favourite national amusement.' The Earl of Chesterfield had succeeded the Duke of Dorset as Lord Lieutenant of Ireland, and as he was just as partial to the playhouse as his predecessor had been, he frequently commanded performances during that season – a sure guarantee of a full attendance of the fashionable world.

The Lord Lieutenant had exceedingly extravagant tastes; he

was to leave behind him memories of 'costly splendour that equalled, if not eclipsed, the glory of St James's'. He added a new ballroom to the Castle, in which he gave splendid entertainments. Benjamin Victor, who, with Sheridan, had been bidden to one of these, describes the supper-room adjoining the ballroom as being,

> most elegantly disposed and ornamented with transparent paintings, through which was cast a shade-like moonlight; flutes and other soft instruments playing all the while, but, like candles, unseen. At each end . . . were placed fountains of lavender water that diffused a most grateful odour through this fairy scene.

Chesterfield was witty, enigmatic, equivocal; a subtle, complex man. He sat in his box and applauded Garrick the actor, but he had taken a dislike to Garrick the man. Davies states:

> Though he [Chesterfield] was very gracious to Mr Sheridan, and admitted his visits to the Castle, he took not the least notice of Mr Garrick; nay, when they both waited on him with candles on the night of Garrick's benefit, he spoke very kindly to Mr Sheridan, but did not even return the salute of the other.

Garrick was not unduly offended. He was making a considerable sum from his share of the profits, and the house was bespoken for many nights to come: a lordly frown or two did not trouble him.

Spranger Barry, who had already acted at Smock Alley, was almost as popular as Garrick. Six feet tall, he was 'elegantly shaped, and his natural bearing was full of grace and dignity. His features were regular, his eyes bright and blue, his hair pale gold, whilst the extraordinary mobility of his face gave expression to every sentence he spoke.' Barry's chief charm was his melodious voice, which a contemporary said could wheedle a bird off the bush; he is often referred to as 'silver-tongued Barry'. He was an excellent actor: 'Men held their breath at the outpourings of his fury, and women were melted by the tenderness of his love.'

George Anne Bellamy was the young lead in the company, and the rest were 'useful and capable players': Elrington, Vanderbank, Morris, and Mrs Furnival, who had always wanted to step up from the useful class into the leading rôles but had not been able to achieve this ambition. She disliked George Anne, who had established herself as a favourite, and had also managed to get herself into the most exclusive social circles. George Anne had an aunt in Dublin, Mrs O'Hara, sister to Lord Tyrawley. Mrs O'Hara was not sure of the propriety of owning to an illegitimate niece, and an actress to boot; but George Anne's manners were flawless and her fragile, youthful charm betokened an innocence and gentility hard to resist. Mrs O'Hara received her, and as she was an invalid, asked the Honourable Mrs Butler to be kind to her niece. Mrs Butler was a lady of the first rank and importance, and George Anne soon found that she had a powerful patroness, at whose house she met the first figures in the land.

The chief players relied a great deal on patronage, especially that of the leading Ladies of Quality, for whom it was modish to attend a favourite's benefit and bring all her friends. Benjamin Victor, in his *History of the Theatres of London*, tells of one dame, an admirer of Spranger Barry, who even tried to dragoon her tradesmen into helping to fill the house for his benefit performance:

> The great Lady of the Night, goes early into the Box-Room, to receive her Company. This Lady has sent out Pit and Gallery Tickets to all her *Trades-People*, with *Threatenings* of the Loss of her Custom if they did not dispose of them: And the Concern she was under, when the Time was approaching of the drawing up of the Curtain, at the Sight of a thin Pit and Galleries, introduced the following Entertainment. The Lady was ready to faint, and after Smelling-Bottles were applied, she cryed out *She was ruined and undone! She would never be able to look dear Mr. B— in the Face any more, after such a shocking Disappointment*! At many of these repeated Lamentations, the box-keeper advanced, and said, *I beg your Ladyship will not be so disheartened; indeed your Ladyship's Galleries too, will certainly mend, before the Play begins*. At which the Lady cry'd, *Out you nasty, flattering Fellow! I tell you I'm undone! Ruin'd and undone! that's all! But I'll be reveng'd; I am resolved I'll pay off – no – I'll turn off, all my saucy Tradesmen Tomorrow Morning*.

George Anne had no fear of thin houses; her patroness Mrs Butler could be relied upon to fill the boxes with her friends, and

her own ingratiating ways had brought her a following among the
students who crowded into the pit. The confident young actress
had enemies, however.

She fell foul of Mrs Furnival, 'who owed me a grudge, on
account of my eclipsing her, as the more favourable reception I
met with from the public gave her room to conclude that I did.'
Sheridan had revived the tragedy of *All for Love, or the World
Well Lost*, with himself and Spranger Barry in the characters of
Ventidius and Anthony, and George Anne Bellamy as Cleopatra.
As usual, the heroine's costume had been purchased from a lady's
cast-off wardrobe, the lady in this instance being the Princess of
Wales, who had worn it only once, on a state occasion. Sheridan
had been able to procure it during the last visit to London, out-
bidding the wardrobe-masters of the London theatres.

Managers often bought clothes from royalty. Costumes were
extremely important, hence the many squabbles and quarrels over
them among the players. Audiences demanded handsome apparel
on the stage, and the critics were sure to be fierce over costumes
which did not please them, often to the detriment of their critical
faculties when judging a play of the actual performance of the
actors. There were established conventions about the kind of
clothes worn by stock characters. Queens and empresses were
confined to black velvet, except on special occasions, when they
added an embroidered petticoat; the younger actresses usually
appeared in the little-worn satin gowns of fashionable ladies, for
whose maids had sold them to the managers at low cost.

Sheridan had allotted George Anne the ex-royal gown, a gorgeous affair made of silver tissue. It was a little roomy for its
new wearer, and the stage mantua-maker and George Anne's
maid, Nancy O'Bryen, spent several hours altering the waist and
making other adjustments so that it would fit George Anne's trim
figure. There was a further enhancement of the already splendid
costume. Mrs Butler wished there to be no doubt that her young
protegée should outshine – quite literally – all others on the stage,
and she offered to lend George Anne some of her own diamonds
to sew on the corsage of the gown. Mrs Butler actually went
further, and borrowed diamonds from several of her friends for
the same purpose.

George Anne was delighted, accepted the loan, and thanked
her benefactress profusely. The mantua-maker made the

alterations and sewed on the diamonds; Nancy spread the glittering gown carefully over a chair in Miss Bellamy's dressing-room and they both went out, carelessly omitting to close the door.

Mrs Furnival, who was taking the rôle of the Roman matron, Octavia, in the play, happened to pass by on the way to her own dressing-room. Through the open doorway she caught sight of the splendid gown, the front shining with diamonds. In a matter of moments she had nipped in, taken it, and borne it along to her own dressing-room. There she tried it on, found it too tight, and set to work to let out the waist to fit herself. It did not occur to her that there was any incongruity in enrobing a Roman matron in the habiliments of the Egyptian Queen. All Mrs Furnival wanted was to outwit George Anne Bellamy, and to appear marvellously attired on the stage herself.

The maid returned to George Anne's dressing-room, and was horrified to find the costume gone. She 'ran about the theatre like a mad thing', looking for it. Mrs Furnival had been observed with the load of magnificence on her arm, and a whisper told Nancy where she must go. Bursting into Mrs Furnival's dressing-room, she saw that lady holding up the gown with an appearance of great satisfaction, and saw, too, that the waist had been undone, and the mantua-maker's and her own careful work gone for nothing, George Anne later described what happened:

> My damsel's veins, unfortunately for Mrs Furnival, were rich with the blood of the O'Bryens. And though she had not been blessed with such an education as such a name was entitled to, she inherited at least the *spirit* of the Kings of Ulster. She at first demanded the dress with tolerable civility, but meeting with a peremptory refusal, the blood of her great forefathers boiled within her veins, and without more ado, she fell tooth and nail upon poor Mrs Furnival. So violent was the assault, that had not assistance arrived in time to rescue her from the fangs of the enraged Hibernian nymph, my theatrical rival would probably have never had an opportunity of appearing once in her life adorned with real jewels.

The rescue operation by Mrs Furnival's friends left her in triumphant possession of the gown, which she proceeded to put on, the Hibernian nymph being thrown out of the room. Nancy returned to her mistress, sobbing, but George Anne was amused rather than angry at the affair, knowing how absurd a figure the Roman matron would look in that paraphernalia. There were, however, the diamonds – real diamonds. George Anne sent a civil request to the purloiner to ask for the return of the borrowed jewels, for which she was responsible. Mrs Furnival sent an equally civil reply, to the effect that the jewels would be returned after the play.

George Anne composedly chose a dress of white satin from her wardrobe, put it on without any ornament, and awaited events. They were not long in coming. Reports of the richness and elegance of her royal costume had been well circulated in advance of the performance, mainly by Mrs Bellamy, and there was a gasp when she made her entrance, attired in a plain white satin gown. There was a greater sensation when Mrs Furnival entered later, resplendent and sparkling. Mrs Butler, sitting with a party of friends in a stage box, was outraged.

'Good heavens, the woman has got my diamonds!' she cried in a loud voice, which penetrated to the farthest corners of the theatre. The gentlemen in the pit concluded that Mrs Butler, who was a well-known and respected figure in Dublin society, had been robbed of the diamonds by the actress, and there was uproar. The act went on, but at the end there was a shout of: 'No more Furnival! No more Furnival!' At this, 'the actress promptly called hysterical fits to her aid' and the performance was held up while another actress from the company, who happened to be in the audience, hurried backstage, dressed in the proper Roman matron's robe, and finished the performance. Mrs Furnival had by then 'very prudently left the theatre'.

The silver tissue gown was returned to George Anne, the diamonds counted and returned to Mrs Butler. It was considered by all who heard the story – which meant all theatrical and society Dublin – that George Anne Bellamy had come out very well in that affair.

Garrick returned to London in May, 1746, parting from Sheridan with the greatest cordiality. Sheridan closed the theatre a fortnight early, having the satisfaction of knowing that not only had the season been exceedingly lucrative, but he had achieved his primary object of lifting the Dublin stage to a high degree of repute in the minds of the citizens. There was one evil, however, which he had been powerless to reform: the admission of gentlemen behind the scenes at rehearsal and at the performances. Every idler who wore a laced coat, says Hitchcock tartly, thought it entitled him to this privilege.

It was the custom of the fops, and the students of Trinity who were not otherwise occupied, to crowd on to the stage at morning rehearsal,

> and many times have the poor distressed actors been seen rehearsing within a circle of forty or fifty of these gentlemen whose time ought to have been better employed. At night they used to take a pride in standing on the stage in sight of the audience, indulging themselves in very improper liberties, and often disturbing the performance with their irregularities.

Much was written in the newspapers and journals about this reprehensible practice, but it had been too long established for remedy. Benjamin Victor thought that 'it was highly necessary the legislature should take the theatre under their protection, and secure it from the insolence of wanton and dissolute men,' since every remonstrance to the offenders was treated with laughter and contempt. Then chance brought about what private appeals had never been able to accomplish.

> At the representation of the comedy of Vanburgh's *Aesop*, on January 19, 1747, a young gentleman of the name of Kelly went to the pit much intoxicated with liquor, an indecency at that time too frequent there, when climbing over the spikes which divided the stage from the auditorium he got upon the stage, and very soon made his way to the green-room where several of the female performers were assembled. Unawed by the decorum which constantly reigned there, he addressed Mrs Dyer, an actress of excellent character, in such gross and indecent terms, as obliged all the women quickly to retire and take refuge in their dressing-room. Thither he pursued them, and on being refused permission made such a noise as disturbed the business of the stage then going forward. Miss Bellamy ... being then wanted to go on, was afraid to venture out, till Mr

Sheridan, dressed for his character as Aesop, had the offender taken away and conducted back to the pit.

Enraged at this disappointment, the intrepid hero took a basket of oranges which stood near him, and the next time the manager came on the stage, amused himself by throwing oranges at him. Mr Sheridan, justly provoked at the indignity offered him instantly addressed the audience for protection, who immediately interfered, and with some difficulty silenced Mr Kelly, but not before he had loudly and repeatedly called Mr Sheridan scoundrel and rascal. Who with the most becoming spirit and propriety answered 'I am as good a gentleman as you are'.

As soon as the play was over, Mr Kelly, not content with the mischief he had occasioned, forced his way in at the stage door and up to Mr Sheridan's dressing-room, and there repeated the names he had so liberally bestowed on him from the pit.

This naturally provoked Mr Sheridan to strike him several times,

> which the doughty hero took with the utmost patience, and retired to a club of his companions, to whom he related his sad disaster, who, incensed that a scoundrel player should presume to strike a gentleman, united in denouncing vengeance against the offending manager, and all who should take his part.

The manager was now to experience the full spite of so-called gentlemen who considered players to be no better than servants. A few nights later Sheridan, who was taking a leading rôle in *The Fair Penitent*, was prevailed upon by his friends not to go to the theatre. He sent one of the company on to the stage to apologize for his non-appearance, and to give them his reasons. Kelly was in the pit, with about fifty of his friends; they drew their swords and climbed on to the stage, ran to the Green-room, and on to the dressing-rooms, slashing out in all directions as they went. The presses of stage clothes were broken open and the contents cut to pieces. The bravos then left the theatre and made for Sheridan's house in Dorset Street, 'but finding he had provided for their reception, thought it proper to retire'.

Next day, of course, the fracas was talked of throughout the town, and feelings ran high. On the following Saturday, an unsigned letter appeared in *Faulkner's Journal* – actually written, unknown to Sheridan, by Benjamin Victor. In it, he gave a 'portrait of this actor', establishing that he was a gentleman, son of the late Rev. Dr Sheridan, a scholar of Trinity College and a class-fellow of most of the nobility and gentry of that time. The letter went on to state that though Mr Sheridan might, in the opinion of some, appear to have *degraded* himself by becoming an actor, his moral character had remained unsullied. Having begun with this solid groundwork, Victor proceeded to build up a case for Sheridan:

> As the manager of the theatre, his ambition has been to cultivate good manners and decency, and his labours and good example have hitherto been attended with good success. The actors live in unusual harmony and have pursued their business with the utmost regularity; they are rewarded with their salaries . . . and the town (it is usually confessed) has been better entertained this winter than ever was known by so thin a company of tolerable actors. To what can this be owing, but to the good conduct and ability of the manager?

Victor set forth the circumstances of Sheridan's being insulted by Kelly. He reminded them that in London a riot was committed at the theatre in Lincoln's Inn Fields by 'a set of profligate young men of quality', and that the legislature, by the King's direction, 'entered so warmly into the affair, that the rioters thought proper to make the suffering manager ample satisfaction'.

The letter aroused a certain amount of support for Sheridan, but Kelly's friends answered it with a spate of pamphlets blackguarding the manager, and actors in general; within a month 'there were enough pamphlets published, for both sides, to have filled a large octavo volume'. Not only the players, but the entire city, seemed involved, and there were incessant public arguments on the subject of 'the honour of an actor, a defence of decency, and the decorum of the stage'.

Sheridan realized that he could not keep the theatre closed, as the actors depended on it for their bare living. He reopened a month later with *Richard the Third*. When the bills came out, there were loud threats that Sheridan would not be allowed to perform until he had made a proper submission – though Kelly and his friends were vague as to what form this humiliation should take. Sheridan had, besides his own friends and followers, some unexpected supporters:

> Several citizens advanced in years, who were seldom seen at a theatre, were so sensible of the advantages and importance of a well-regulated stage, that they declared to Mr Sheridan that they would now, more than ever, appear there, and doubted not being able to protect the manager, and the actors in general, in the discharge of their duty.

On the night of the performance, the house filled early. Kelly and his friends had assembled in the boxes: there were groups of young men from Trinity College in the pit. The play opened quietly, but when Sheridan, as Richard, appeared near the end of the first act, voices from the boxes burst out with: 'A submission – a submission – off! off! off!' There was an immediate response from the pit: 'No submission! No submission! Go on with the play!' A burly figure rose in the pit, one Lucas, who forcibly voiced his opinion of those who brought their private quarrels into the theatre. Every sober person in the house, he said, had come to receive the entertainment promised in the bills, and had paid good money for that purpose. The actors were under the protection of the audience during that entertainment. Every insult or interruption offered to them in the discharge of their duty was offered, in effect, to the audience. He moved that those who were for preserving the decency and freedom of the stage should hold up their hands. The result was so overwhelmingly in Sheridan's favour that the would-be rioters left the theatre, and Sheridan was able to continue the performance in peace.

This was by no means the end of the affair. Sheridan put on *The Fair Penitent* for the annual benefit of the hospital for incurables. The governors of the hospital assured him that no one would oppose the performance of a play for charity, and undertook to defend him if there was any trouble. The house was crowded; about a hundred ladies were in the expensive seats, and more would have been accommodated had not thirty or so gentlemen taken possession of the middle benches near the orchestra. Sheridan was playing Horatio, and at his entrance the thirty gentlemen, all armed, rose up and ordered him off, joined by several groups in the galleries. In order to avoid a riot, Sheridan immediately withdrew, but the hospital governors challenged the trouble-makers, and there were high words. One of the governors was a scholar of Trinity, at whom one of the 'gentlemen' threw an apple, calling him a scoundrel at the same time. 'Justly incensed at this affront, away flew the scholar like feathered Mercury to the college, and returned . . . with as many youths armed for the combat.'

The rioters had prudently withdrawn, but they had made themselves conspicuous, and the following day a number of them were recognized and seized by the Trinity men. The ringleader was made to kneel down in one of the college courts on his bare knees, and make submission; the others were compelled to apologize formally to Trinity College for the insult to one of its sons.

Sheridan had won a moral victory, but he suffered loss, nevertheless. Fearing further troubles, the lords justices ordered the Master of the Revels to close the theatre. Then Kelly was apprehended, and indicted for assaulting Sheridan. Thomas Sheridan was also indicted for assaulting and beating Kelly. Dublin hung eagerly on the result of these proceedings. Kelly was a gentleman of leisure: Sheridan was a player. Nobody believed that a jury would find a gentleman guilty! The case drew as crowded a house to the court-room as it would have done to a theatre.

There was a full Bench, and the Lord Chief Justice was present. Kelly's counsel, 'eminent though not very mannerly', got up and said he had often seen a gentleman soldier and a gentleman tailor, but he had never seen a gentleman player. Sheridan bowed and said: 'Sir, I hope you see one now.' It was clear from the evidence that Sheridan had had good cause, in the first place, to lay hands on Kelly, who had forced himself into the dressing-room and had abused and threatened him. Kelly's counter-charge fell to the ground. He was fined five hundred pounds and sentenced to three months' imprisonment, the Lord Chief Justice observing that anyone else who forced himself behind the scenes of a theatre, if apprehended and brought before the court, should feel the utmost severity of the law.

Kelly had been confident that his friends would subscribe to pay his fine, but he was quickly deserted. After serving a week of his sentence, he sent to Sheridan, begging the manager to use his influence to have the fine remitted and the rest of the sentence annulled. Sheridan, the most quixotic and generous of men, was able to accomplish this, himself standing surety for the young man's future good behaviour. So ended the episode which finally put a stop to the nuisance of the fops demanding access to the stage, for until that verdict was given in a court of law, 'every person who was master of a sword, was sure to draw it on the stage door-keeper if he denied him entrance'.

13

Green-room Scuffle

In London, the theatres were still in the doldrums. The Rebellion was over. The Battle of Culloden had stamped the Pretender's hopes into the ground, and everyday life was getting back to normal; but the general business of the country had been disrupted by the insurrection. More banks had failed, among them the one which had backed Lacy at Drury Lane. The manager faced bankruptcy, but his company stood by him. Led by Peg Woffington, they offered to take their salaries as and when the money came in, and were prepared to wait for better times.

David Garrick had gone to Rich at Covent Garden on his return from Ireland. Lacy was anxious to attract Garrick to Drury Lane, but he could not offer a better salary than the actor was getting at Covent Garden. Then he had an idea. He had long known that Garrick was very ambitious to have some control in theatre management, and he offered the actor a partnership in Drury Lane. Garrick was to pay £8,000, in return for which he was to get a half-interest in the theatre, with an appropriate share in the profits, a stated sum every time he gave a performance, and another sum for any plays he might write for the theatre. Garrick seized on the proposal, and replied that he would come over to Drury Lane after his contract ended with the current theatrical year at Covent Garden.

Peg took the news calmly. The barbed shafts of Kitty Clive – 'The return of Mr Garrick, Mrs Woffington – is it not fortunate?' – evoked a slight smile and no more. There was a valuable addition to the company when Lacy engaged Spranger Barry to come over from Dublin. 'Silver-tongued Barry' was an immediate success, and Drury Lane began to fill. The Prince of Wales came to see him act Lord Townley, and sent him a message next day offering the services of his own dancing-master for three months, saying that in his opinion, Mr Spranger 'wanted only the addition of a little manner, to make him the first Lord Townley in the world.' There does not appear to be any record of Spranger Barry's accepting the offer, but one may be sure it was talked about – especially at Covent Garden. David Garrick had a formidable rival, that was clear. Spranger Barry was making the most of his opportunities at Drury Lane before Garrick came over to the Lane as a partner in the management.

Garrick was content to bide his time. He intended to finish his season at Covent Garden in a burst of glory, and his farewell nights there were brilliant, drawing fashionable London to crowd the boxes. He acted with James Quin and Susanna Cibber in *The Fair Penitent, Henry the Fourth,* and *Lear,* and the town echoed with fresh praise of his magnificent performances, all tension, fire and passion.

He went over to Drury Lane in the autumn of 1747, taking with him Mrs Cibber and Mrs Pritchard, a stately actress who had disliked Peg Woffington from the day she had appeared in the London playhouse. The dislike had grown into jealous hatred. Pritchard was about ten years older than Peg, and in her early days had appeared at Bartholomew Fair, the annual Cloth Fair in the city where theatrical booths were the principal attractions. She was noted for her interpretation of scolds and viragos; in serious parts she lacked delicacy and was apt to 'blubber her sorrows'. When she played the name part in Samuel Johnson's play, *Irene,* its author, sure that she had not read the play through, declared: 'She no more thought of the play out of which her part was taken than a shoemaker thinks of the skin out of which the piece of leather of which he is making a pair of shoes is cut.'

The company at Drury Lane could now show a dazzling display of talent. Besides Peg Woffington, Kitty Clive, Cibber and Pritchard, Macklin and his wife were back, at good salaries:

Garrick, like a true politician, neither loved nor hated in the way of business; if the parties were useful to him, that was sufficient: it was his duty to form as strong a company as he could. Mr and Mrs Macklin could do so many things, and so well, he thought his *corps* could not be complete without them.

Spranger Barry's contract at the Lane had not yet expired; David Garrick with his new power as part-manager, would have liked to get rid of the Irish actor, but was forced to keep him until the end of the season. Barry was certainly a powerful rival, and the regular audiences, amused, soon took sides; each actor had his violently partisan followers. Garrick, as part of the theatre Establishment, was at an advantage, but Spranger Barry kept his head and his spirits high, and acted with all the intensity at his command. The rivalry became so acute that the news-sheets, with great gusto, printed items which might credit or discredit one or the other. On balance, Garrick was given rougher treatment than Barry, because 'he descended to curry favour with writers of his time: to meet, to solicit, to entertain and to flatter them to a degree'. The author of this comment added that these methods of trying to gain support were not necessary to 'one who really could, as Garrick might, have afforded to stand independently and proudly upon his own merits'.

Rich, at Covent Garden, had in his company Ryan and Giffard, two good actors, and Theophilus Cibber and Foote, neither a great catch. Foote, as incorrigible as ever, had invented a new kind of entertainment. A pamphleteer of the time wrote: 'There is a common saying that all Acts of Parliament have a Hole to creep out of', and Samuel Foote was an adept at finding legal holes. A new morning entertainment was advertised, 'Mr Foote's Tea, or the Diversions of a Morning', an astute device for getting round the patent laws. Foote invited his friends to come and drink tea at the Little Theatre in the Haymarket every morning, 'at playhouse prices'. While the tea was preparing, he advanced before the curtain, and told the audience that he was training some young actors for the stage, and would proceed to put them through their paces in the play they were rehearsing.

The manœuvre was highly relished by the town. Samuel Foote kept within the letter of the law; no money was taken at the door, all tickets being bought in advance from Waller, the bookseller, or George's Coffee House at Temple Bar. Foote, who knew the snags, announced that 'Any Gentleman, or Lady, with or without

George Anne Bellamy in *The Elopement*.
(Harvard Theatre Collection.)

The interior of Drury Lane Theatre.

Covent Garden Theatre. (*See Note, p. 233.*)
(Harvard Theatre Collection.)

Tickets, will be admitted', so that, if challenged, he could claim that gain was not his sole object.

James Quin, who had retired to Bath to take the waters, now thought it was time he returned to the limelight, and sent a letter to Rich:

'Dear Sir, I am at Bath. Yours, James Quin.' The reply came quickly: 'Dear Sir, Stay there and be damned. Yours, John Rich.'

Drury Lane was undoubtedly in the lead for the favour of the town, and Garrick prepared a programme of well-tried and popular plays. Lacy looked after the details of management, leaving the choice of casting to his partner. Garrick did not find this to be without difficulties. Mrs Pritchard had heard rumours that Susanna Cibber was to be given *her* rôles, and made forcible complaint; Garrick had to use a great deal of tact in mollifying her, without indicating that her increasing bulk made her unsuitable for the young parts she used to play. She was a good character actress, and had a large following, so he did not wish to antagonize her.

Then Susanna Cibber's archness had to be parried. Mrs Cibber often used her appealing manner to filch parts from other actresses. Clive was playing Ophelia, but Susanna had played it in Dublin, and mentioned the fact to the managers. She also hoped to take some of the rôles which Peg Woffington had made her own in the past. Now that Woffington was no longer Garrick's mistress, Susanna reckoned that there would be many changes in the leading parts.

Kitty Clive did not attempt to ingratiate herself with Garrick; she plagued him with her temperamental tantrums, and never cared what she said. Once, when he entered the Green-room magnificently arrayed in a glittering, silver-spangled costume, looking so splendid that he drew murmurs of admiration from the people there, Clive called out: 'Oh, my God! Room! Room! Make room for the Royal lamplighter!' Garrick was so disconcerted that he trembled for the rest of the evening – the first night of a new part in a new play. Yet, astonishingly enough, there was genuine friendship and mutual esteem underlying their relationship in the playhouse. It is probable that he laughed as loudly as others at stories about the actress – so long as he was not at the receiving

F

For the BENEFIT

Of Mrs. WOFFINGTON.

AT THE

THEATRE ROYAL in *Covent-Garden*,

On THURSDAY next, being the 24th of *March*,
Will be prefented a TRAGEDY, call'd

The FAIR PENITENT.

Lothario by Mrs. WOFFINGTON,
Being the Firſt Time of Her Appearing in that Character,

Horatio by Mr. BARRY,

Sciolto by Mr. SPARKS,

Altamont by Mr. DYER,

Roſſano by Mr. ANDERSON,   *Meſſenger* by Mr. HOLTOM,

Lavinia by Mrs. ELMY,

Lucilla by Miſs CONDILL,

Califta by Mrs. GREGORY.

With *SINGING*

By Mrs. CHAMBERS,

And *DANCING*

By Mr. POITIER, Mad. CAPDEVILLE, *&c.*

To which will be added a *Comedy* of *Two Acts*, call'd

The FRENCHIFIED LADY

Never in *PARIS.*

Being the Laſt Time of performing IT.

The *Lady* by Mrs. WOFFINGTON.

Boxes 5*s*.   Pit 3 *s*.   Firſt Gallery 2 *s*.   Upper Gallery 1*s*.

☞ TICKETS *to be had, and* PLACES *for the* BOXES *taken, of* Mr. CRUDGE,
at the Stage Door of the Theatre.

Playbill of the Benefit for Mrs. Woffington.

end of her tongue. One oft-told tale was of Kitty, addicted to gaming, playing at quadrille with a dowager who had been winning throughout the game. The dowager, an imperious dame with white hair and eyebrows, triumphantly slapped down two black aces and demanded payment for the new win. 'Two black aces!' cried the enraged Kitty. 'Here, take the money, though I wish I could give you two black eyes instead, you old white cat!'

It was Kitty Clive whom Peg Woffington most disliked meeting in the Green-room. Peg had known jealousy in the playhouse from her earliest years, but she had never come across such naked loathing as that shown to her by Kitty Clive. It was so violent that Peg soon found herself returning it, with interest.

'No two women in high life ever hated each other more unreservedly than these great dames of the theatre,' says Davies:

> But though the passions of each were as lofty as those of a Duchess, yet they wanted the courtly art of concealing them, and this occasioned now and then a very grotesque scene in the Green-room. Woffington was well-bred, seemingly very calm, and at all times mistress of herself. Clive was arrogant, high-tempered and impetuous. What came uppermost in the mind she spoke without reserve. Woffington blunted the sharp speeches of Clive by her apparently civil, but ever-keen and sarcastic replies. Thus she often threw Kitty off-guard by an arch severity which the other could not easily parry.

Kitty Clive possessed 'a volume of language and a command of vituperation . . . that was not hindered by delicacy nor confined by wit'. On one occasion, Peg came excitedly into the Green-room after a loudly applauded performance as Sir Harry Wildair, and said: 'By God, half the audience thinks me to be a man.' 'By God, madam,' returned Kitty Clive, 'the other half knows you to be a woman!' Their quarrels were not confined to exchanges of strong language. There was an explosion that season, during the production of *Henry the Fourth*, with Spranger Barry as Hotspur and Peg Woffington as Lady Percy. It was a small part, but Peg thought it worth doing, because of her conviction that small parts needed as skilful acting as leading parts.

The applause naturally went to Hotspur, and Kitty Clive, who was not in the play, made it her business to go into the Green-room and commiserate with Mrs Woffington on the slenderness of her part and the consequent lack of opportunity to show off to the audience. Peg ignored the taunt; she was very tired that evening, and not in the mood to bring out her natural weapon of sarcastic wit. Kitty Clive interpreted this silence as vexation at not getting her usual lion's share of applause, and immediately followed up her advantage. What a pity the famous Mistress Woffington was being relegated to minor rôles!

Peg made a sharp retort: contemporary reports do not say in particular what she called Kitty Clive, but it must have been something very unpleasant. Clive flew into a high passion, and abuse poured from her lips. Peg Woffington, unusually for her, retorted in kind: she had had about enough of Mistress Kitty Clive. The Green-room quickly filled with the nightly habitués, and anyone else who could push themselves in; all were ready to take sides, all eager to pile fuel on a quarrel that had actually broken into flame. Woffington and Clive at each other's throats in good earnest! How amusing! Nobody would want for a subject of conversation in the drawing-rooms and coffee-houses for weeks after this!

The two women grew more savage in their language. The discipline of the stage did not extend to the Green-room; both women were Irish, and the primitive urges of that hot-blooded race were never far beneath the surface. Clive's bitter jealousy, Woffington's long repressed resentments, flared up as they shouted at each other. Then Kitty Clive shot out her fist and struck. Peg's reaction was swift: she replied with a smack on Clive's cheek that could be heard throughout the large room.

According to an eyewitness of the scene:

> While the two great actresses were entertaining each other in one part of the Green-room, the admirer of Lady Percy, M'Swiney . . . and Raftor, the brother of Kitty Clive, were more seriously employed. M'Swiney struck the younger man with his cane, whereupon Raftor calmly laid hold of the old man's jaw.
>
> 'Let go my jaw, you villain!' and 'Throw down your cane, sir!' were repeatedly echoed by the combatants.

At the other end of the room, the two actresses were fighting like spitting cats. The excited onlookers joined in, the followers of Kitty Clive assaulting Peg Woffington's partisans. In a short time there was a pitched battle raging in the Green-room; the uproar could be heard on the stage. The play had ended and the audience were leaving the theatre, but several people stopped as the distant sounds of shouting grew louder. Were they missing an after-piece that was not on the play-bills?

Several of the actors, still on the stage, ran to the Green-room, took in the situation, and tried to separate the combatants – no easy matter in the struggling mass of scarlet faces, open mouths and bulging eyes, the chaos of torn satins, broken feathers, splayed-out wigs and broken canes. The two women were ultimately separated by Spranger Barry, who rushed in and pulled them apart, panting and still calling each other names. The dishevelled company also drew away, straightening disarrayed clothes, trying to regain their wigs and a little dignity, adjusting torn neckcloths and shredded lace. No great mischief had been done, beyond a few cuts here and there and a broken head or two. Neither lady had won the day, but there was a general feeling of satisfaction that honour had been upheld – though nobody knew whose honour.

It was, in fact, an extremely disagreeable episode, and Peg Woffington openly regretted, on more than one occasion, that she had allowed 'that she-devil, Clive' to cause her to lose her temper. The public sheets were quick to seize on the incident, and exaggerated caricatures of the scene in the Green-room sold well in the print-shops. Samuel Foote lost no time in making capital out of his fellow-players' fall from ladylike grace. He wrote and produced a piece for the stage which he called 'The Green-Room Scuffle', a highly dramatic scena showing how rival queens of the stage comported themselves when they left the boards after a performance in which they had played high-born dames with manners to match. Foote was out to make quick money, and this was an opportunity too good to miss.

Peg Woffington disliked quarrelling, and she was angry and ashamed at the recollection of such an outrageous scene. She was deeply unhappy at this time, and it was an effort to keep up the appearance of calm composure which was the strongest armour she could wear.

She had not seen Lord Darnley for some time; she missed his companionship, but no deeper feelings had ever been touched. Charles Hanbury Williams had passed out of her life – as so many women had passed out of his. Peg had no heart for new adventures.

With Garrick now permanently at Drury Lane as part-manager, it was inevitable that they should constantly meet; they acted together, and on the surface they were cool and courteous. There were times, however, when emotion broke through Garrick's calm manner. It became evident that he was still strongly attracted to Peg, and he tried on several occasions to win her over to a resumption of their former intimacy. Peg would have none of him as a lover. The past was finished with: she was not going to open that wound again. Besides, she had heard that Garrick was attracted to an Austrian dancer, Violette, who had come to London under the patronage of my Lady Burlington; an exceedingly respectable young lady of good family. It was also said that Mr Garrick's intentions were honourable, and he was seeking to become friendly with Lord and Lady Burlington, who were guarding their pretty young protégée like dragons. Peg made it clear to Garrick that she had no intention of going back to their earlier relationship, and succeeded in arousing something she had not had to face before – his personal enmity.

Garrick was angered and humiliated by her attitude. His revenge was unexpectedly petty. In the days of their happiness, he had celebrated her beauty and their mutual love in verses which he had been proud to publish. Now he wrote another set of verses, the terrible 'Epistle to Mrs Woffington', in which he savagely told the tale of her lovers:

Silvia, to you I dedicate my lays
No flattering bard, or love-sick youth;
Regardless of your censure or your praise,
I come to expose the naked Truth.

To you, and to your heart my muse appeals,
And if not tainted to the core,
Freely confess the action she reveals,
Which all your various arts explore.

And now my muse in greatest order move,
In just succession facts impart;
Pursue the rovings of a woman's love,
And sing the progress of her heart.

From *forty-two* I take my present date,
When Darnley's gold seemed void of charms,
And driven by whims, inconstancy or fate,
You flew from him to Garrick's arms.

No mercenary views possessed your mind,
'Tis love!' cried out the public voice;
To Silvia's virtue we have all been blind:
By fate a mistress, not by choice.

But soon these paeans cease – 'twas worse and worse,
(For fame will err and make mistakes)
She revels with the man she ought to curse,
And riots with her quondam rakes.

I know your sophistry, I know your art,
Which all your dupes and fools control;
Yourself you give without your heart –
All may share THAT, but not your soul.

But now her thirst for gold must be allay'd,
The want of show her pride alarms:
It must, it shall be gratified, she said,
Then plunged in hateful W-ll-ms' arms.

O peer!* (whose acts shall down time's torrent roll)
If thus you doat, thus love the dame,
In nuptial bonds unite her to your soul,
And thus at once complete your fame.

Your spring is past but not your summer gone,
O reap before the sun descends!
When autumn's fall or winter's blasts come on,
Farewell to lovers, flatterers and friends.

* Darnley

But now, advice apart, the theme pursue.
Follow the damsel in her wild career!
Say what gallants, what keepers are in view –
Behold the Colonel* in the rear!

Some say you're proud, coquettish, cruel, vain,
Unjust! She never wounds but cures;
So pitiful to every lying swain –
Flatter or pay, the nymph is yours!

This outburst was bad enough, but, far worse, Garrick now
began lessening Peg's status as an actress. New plays were produced without her being offered a rôle; old plays were revived,
and Peg's well-known parts given to other actresses – one of the
worst slights which a manager could inflict on one who had for
years been a principal player.

Peg accepted lesser parts with as much dignity as she could
achieve, but the outlook was bleak. She could face the sneers and
triumphant smiles of Kitty Clive, Susanna Cibber and Hannah
Pritchard: she could not face the prospect of her career on the
stage dwindling until in the end she would be reduced to walking-
on parts.

Her old manager, Rich, was aware of the state of affairs, and
made her a good offer to come over to Covent Garden for the
following season. In April 1748 she told Garrick that she intended
to leave his company. Daly declares that she severed her connexion with Drury Lane very abruptly, going in 'a fit of frenzy'. This
is very unlikely. Where her work was concerned, Peg Woffington
usually acted in a completely professional and reasonable way. It
is probable that the atmosphere at Drury Lane was now so re-
pugnant to her that she would have been glad to get away from
it in any case, but the deciding reason for her leaving was almost
certainly her conviction that she had no more future there. She
would accept Rich's offer of Covent Garden, or perhaps go to
Dublin, where she knew she would always find a welcome. First,
however, she would have a holiday.

* Colonel Caesar

14

Paris

Peg Woffington had long wanted to visit Paris, so that she could see the classical plays produced there. Above all, she was anxious to study the methods of the great Marie Dumesnil, who was reputed to be the finest tragic actress in Europe. Peg was aware of her own weakness in heroic parts; the lessons she had received from Colley Cibber during her early days in London had set her on the wrong tack. Garrick had often tried to persuade her to throw aside Cibber's old-fashioned ideas about tragedy, but she had told him it was useless to cast away a style without having something better to put in its place. Peg knew now that she could profit by watching Dumesnil's methods. She had not lost her knowledge of the French tongue, which she had learnt from Madame Violante in her youth, and she had always read many books in that language. After some hesitation she wrote to Dumesnil, and received such a cordial reply from the tragedienne that she decided to spend the summer in Paris.

Owen M'Swiney, after his wide travels on the Continent, knew many people in the French capital. Peg consulted him, and he at once offered to accompany her. Here was a chance to spend several weeks with the bewitching Woffington! Peg was nothing loth, and they set out for Paris in May 1748. They found lodgings in one of the fashionable quarters, and after Peg had installed herself, visited the dressmakers and ordered several gowns, she and M'Swiney presented themselves at the Green-room of the theatre where Mme Dumesnil was appearing in a summer season.

Marie Dumesnil was one of the two leading dramatic actresses in France: the other was Hyppolyte Clairon. Dumesnil at that time was in her thirties, and an exponent of the new natural school of acting. Clairon, ten years younger, had been trained in the declamatory style, and she was violently opposed to any kind of change. There was the fiercest rivalry between the two players, each setting out her own ideas, and attacking those of the other, in articles and books.

The French tragic drama was in a state of development from one style to another. Molière, in the previous century, had imposed a strict discipline on his troupe of players; he did not want his carefully written plays to be travestied by egotistical actors with a talent for improvisation. This discipline led to declamation and a rhetorical style. There were reactions and counter-reactions; after Molière, came actors who insisted that, 'The sacred fire of the great passions are the same in all and each individual of the human species, and can be lit only by the hands of nature.'

This was rather raw stuff for the early eighteenth-century French stage; a counter-reaction set in, with a return to formality and declamation, and 'the sacred fires of the great passions' were soon damped down to candle power. The audience must not be made to feel uncomfortable! By the 1740s, with *Le Drame*, the mode of acting had again swung round to the 'natural'. Costume was no longer a parade of finery, 'but in conformity both with the suggested time of the play, and the rôles played by the characters'. Players did not stand on the stage declaiming to the audience; they moved about as they would have done in their own rooms at home. They used gestures, instead of relying on facial expression to convey meanings; spoke to each other, instead of taking up a commanding position and addressing the audience directly. The old style was to insert gobbets of plot into a soliloquy, making nonsense of the presence of other players on the stage, who presumably had to be kept in ignorance of the plot otherwise there would have been no play.

Marie Dumesnil took instinctively to the 'new' method of acting. She was a player of great sensibility, 'electric, passionate and demonic', and she declared that no deep study of a work was necessary if nature had endowed a player with the inflammable soul of a tragic actor or actress. She believed firmly that 'love, jealousy, vengeance, ambition, maternal and filial love are the same the world over . . . to enter into these great feelings, to experience them straightaway and at will, to forget oneself in the

flash of an eye and replace oneself by the character one is playing
is exclusively a gift of nature beyond all the works of art.'

Clairon believed the opposite. Her work was the result of
long training; each word, each intonation, every movement on
the stage, had to be exactly calculated beforehand. Aspiring actors
she said, should be schooled in this method, preferably in provincial companies. And be taught to act automatically, and learn
bad habits which would last them all their lives and be uncorrect-
able! So countered Dumesnil in the paper war waged by these
two queens of the Parisian theatre. Clairon insisted that it was
only by long training and what her rival called 'tricks' that an
actress could make the public admit that she professed the most
difficult of all arts. Dumesnil immediately slapped her down:

> More difficult, then, than that of Homer, Virgil, Corneille,
> Molière, Racine, Voltaire; the greatest painters, the greatest
> sculptors, both classical and modern, etc. etc.? Whence it
> follows that Mlle Hyppolyte, believing she has implicitly
> proved in her Mémoires that the 'palme' of her art belongs to
> her, and this art being the first of all other, that the famous
> Clairon holds the first position among the most famous men
> and women who have ever existed; she is the first woman of the
> universe.*

Clairon, in her *Mémoires*,† had unwisely come down from the
high plane of dramatic art to spiteful personalities: 'No child
reproved by custom and law makes me blush for its existence.' In
other words, she had never given birth to a bastard. Dumesnil's
comment was a devastating

> There she is, boasting, either of having betrayed the vow of
> nature [practised contraception?] or having been sterile . . . I
> cannot remember ever having read that a woman has claimed
> to be worthy of praise because she had no children, after having
> worked her best for the propagation of the human species.
> Mlle Hyppolyte is certainly the first person who has got the
> idea into her head that she will be glorified for her sterility.

Dumesnil then dismissed the *Mémoires* of 'this august concu-
bine' in language that must have put Clairon into a passion which

* Translated from *Les Grands Comédiens* by Van Tieghem, 1960.

† *Mémoires de Mlle Clairon, Actrice du Théâtre Français*, Ponthion,
1798.

owed nothing to dramatic training, ending with the observation that, 'Mlle Clairon was born before her time. Her birth was the first fight she had with nature, and her first breath was a violation of its laws.'

It might have comforted Clairon, if she read the English prints, that not everyone agreed with Dumesnil, and that she, Clairon, was praised at least for being free from 'the disagreeable hiccough so epidemical in France'.

The human situation, then, in the French theatre was not very different from that in the English playhouse: a compound of jealousies, clashing personalities, cliques, feuds, and the inevitable move away from old ideas. Peg Woffington must have felt at home. There were, however, no personal animosities to harry her, and 'Dumesnil imparted to her all that she herself possessed of the dignified passion of the French drama'. The Parisian actress had heard much of the celebrated Mrs Woffington, and she felt flattered that such an experienced and notable player should wish to sit at her feet and learn. For all Dumesnil's avowed contempt for schools of acting, there were certain basic principles of the art which could be explained to an intelligent auditor, and Mrs Woffington was certainly that. She begged Peg to come to the theatre as often as she wished, and received her in the magnificent players' room of the theatre, where Peg met the rest of the company.

It was a wonderful experience for Peg Woffington to learn something more of her craft. Dumesnil recognized that Colley Cibber had taught Peg to recite tragedy 'so pompously, that nature and passion were not seldom sacrificed to a false glare of eloquence'. His insistence on *tone*, which meant sonorous sound without true feeling, went right against Dumesnil's instinct. She insisted that a player must look inside himself for the true manifestations of tragic drama. 'You must *be*!' was the Frenchwoman's constant exhortation. This was not an easy injunction to follow; Peg had got the habit of conventionalized movements in tragedy, together with a deliberate rhythm of speech which sometimes betrayed the harsh note in her voice which she had never been able to eradicate. Marie Dumesnil took the most elaborate pains with her guest, giving examples of how a more natural tone could be made sufficiently flexible to avoid the danger. She showed Peg that emotion, if imagined strongly enough, could bring the right depths of tone without resort to tricks and artificialities.

Peg Woffington at the age of thirty was as receptive and devoted a pupil of Dumesnil as she had been of that other Frenchwoman, Violante, at the age of twelve. A great liking developed between the two accomplished women during those summer weeks. Dumesnil invited the English actress and her *cher ami*, Monsieur M'Swiney, to her home, where the élite of Paris assembled at her soirées: poets, dramatists, Ministers of State, men of affairs and their wives or mistresses. Dumesnil knew everyone worth knowing. Peg met Voltaire, and talked to him in faultless French, much to his surprise and delight. They discussed the theatre – what else? – and Peg, basking in the great little man's admiration, was at her most scintillating, excelling herself in wit and sparkling comment.

Owen M'Swiney did not obtrude, or attempt in any way to interrupt his beautiful Peggy's triumphant progress. Sophisticated, fine looking, with his 'milk white hair' and dandified grooming, he was a perfect escort. They were, in fact, perfect companions. They walked in the Gardens, hired a coach to drive them out to Louis the Fourteenth's magnificent palace at Versailles, visited new-made friends in the city and were visited by them, at their lodgings, in turn. There were balls, and concerts of music, and fairs – Peg had not forgotten her first visit to Paris, long ago, to dance at a fair with Delemain and his brother. The sun shone, Peg's new gowns turned out to be masterpieces, M'Swiney was ever at hand to carry out her slightest wish, and there was always the theatre.

There were also other attractions. For instance, Signor Domenico Angelo Malevolti Tremamondo's fencing exhibitions. The Italian fencer, who went by the name of Signor Angelo, was a native of Leghorn, living in Paris; he was well-educated, and a noted horseman, swordsman and fencer. He had 'a singularly graceful person, and this rare gift was not bestowed in vain; he cultivated with assiduity every external accomplishment, and became proverbially one of the most elegant men of the age.' His son, Henry Angelo, writing of his father some years later, may have been filially biased, but by all accounts the noted swordsman and fencer did indeed cut a fine figure.

Signor Angelo was persuaded by his patron, the Duc de Nivernois, to enter a public fencing match at a well known *hôtel* in Paris. Henry Angelo describes the scene:

> No sooner was his name announced, than a celebrated English beauty, Mrs Margaret Woffington, the renowned actress, then on a visit to this gay city, who having met my father at a party, became suddenly captivated by his person and superior address, and following him thither, in presence of a crowd of spectators, she stepped forward and presented him with a small bouquet of roses. The company, as well as ladies and gentlemen of rank, surprised at this, were no less struck by the gallant manner with which he received the gift. He placed it on his left breast, and addressing the other knights of the sword, exclaimed 'This will I protect against all opposers.'
>
> The match commenced, and he fenced with several of the first masters, not one of whom could disturb a single leaf of the bouquet.

The incident is mentioned, with embroideries and variations, in several accounts of Peg's sojourn in Paris that summer. One source states that Signor Angelo left Paris with Peg, but from his son's account,* this is highly unlikely. Signor Angelo wanted to come to England, and it is probable that Peg and M'Swiney encouraged him in this desire, saying that they would help him to establish himself.

Peg returned from Paris happier than she had been for many months. The kindness and assistance which she had received from Madame Dumesnil had proved to be a restorative of the most exhilarating kind, and she was conscious of new powers. The strident note which had always plagued her voice was still there; she had not been able to eliminate it, in spite of continual effort and daily vocal exercise. Dumesnil had taught her how to minimize its effect, however, and Peg now felt confident of being able to master tragic rôles.

* Henry Angelo, *Reminiscences of H.A., with memoirs of his late father and friends.* 2 vols. London 1828–30.

Rich, her former manager, knowing that Peg was free, offered her a tempting salary to join the company at Covent Garden. Peg was glad to be away from Drury Lane, from Kitty Clive, Mrs Pritchard and Susanna Cibber – a triumvirate of enemies who had invariably banded together to humiliate her when opportunity offered, no matter what the state of war was among themselves. She accepted Rich's offer.

At Covent Garden, Peg soon found herself in an equally hostile atmosphere. John Rich had been going through a lean period, owing mainly to the 'company of all the best talents' at Drury Lane, which had drawn the crowds. It was the familiar story. The theatre with the best players got the audiences. Now that he had secured the talented Mrs Woffington, Rich proceeded to build up, for the 1748–9 season, a company which he hoped would rival that at Drury Lane. He engaged the pert, lively George Anne Bellamy and several dependable character actresses; and, for the men, James Quin and Delane; Quin was again in favour, and soon established himself in his former position as head of the company.

Peg played a number of parts in which she had always been popular: Silvia in *The Recruiting Officer*, Mrs Ford in *The Merry Wives of Windsor*, Jane Shore, Rosalind, Portia in *Julius Caesar*, the Lady in *Comus*, Lady Betty Modish, and several new parts. She was as good as ever – but something had happened to the audience. It was with dismay that Peg realized that the applause was sporadic instead of sustained. There was a chilling coolness in the theatre, instead of the warmth and enthusiasm to which she had always been accustomed.

This was a shock. It was even more of a surprise when she listened to the clapping and loud shouts of approval which rewarded George Anne Bellamy's efforts. George Anne did not possess half Peg Woffington's talent, but these audiences showed unmistakably that they had decided on a new favourite this season. It was a bitter fact to have to accept, but Peg was not in the habit of deceiving herself. The Bellamy was twenty: she was thirty. And Peg was aware that stories had been whispered about that she had left Drury Lane earlier in the year without any real reason beyond pique and temper. She had never troubled to justify herself, or attempted to deny rumours; long experience had taught her the uselessness of trying to refute every slander put about in the treacherous world of the theatre. Now, faced with this unexpected indifference, she knew that she would have to charm her public afresh, and it would be no easy matter to regain their former allegiance.

The outlook was unpromising. Little Bellamy was doing her best to dazzle the audience, and she was succeeding. George Anne was gleefully aware of Peg Woffington's predicament, and set out to exploit the situation with all her skill. She lost few opportunities of spitting venom at Peg Woffington in her memoirs:

> Mrs Woffington, highly offended at her quondam admirer, Mr Garrick, chusing rather to appear with Mrs Pritchard than with her, had engaged herself with Mr Rich . . . Theatrical revolutions are as frequent, and owe their rise to the same principles, as those in the political world. Pique, resentment, ambition or interest, which ever motive happens to preponderate, brings them about. And the arrangement lasts in both as long as convenience suits.

She also relates, with relish, her recollection of an evening when Sir George Metham visited her in the Green-room 'and showed transports of delight at my presence'.

> The tender respect he showed me seemed to hurt her [Woffington's] pride . . . the attention of a person whose dress, deportment and appearance proclaimed him a man of fashion seemed to excite the jealousy of Mrs Woffington, who expected to have the tribute from every one paid to her.

Bellamy disliked Peg Woffington more than ever after an incident which caused her great chagrin. It was at the end of a benefit for James Quin, when Peg had taken the part of Cleopatra and George Anne the junior lead. The Duchess of Queensberry, who had constituted herself patron of Miss Bellamy, came to the performance, and expressed a desire to visit the Greenroom, which she had been informed was superior to a drawingroom for the wit and politeness to be met there. George Anne had found out that the unpredictable Kitty, Duchess of Queensberry, could be formidable if all did not go as she expected or desired, and hoped that, for once, the Green-room would live up to Her Grace's idealized picture. After her last exit in the fourth act, George Anne threw on a cloak and joined the Duchess in her box.

They instantly attracted the attention of the whole house. Quin was delighted, for the Duchess of Queensberry was looked up to as one of the leaders of society, and to be thus visibly shown as the gracious patroness of his young protegée helped his own prestige, and diminished that of his rivals.

George Anne was excited by the Duchess's smiling condescension, and at the end of the act she led the way, in the best of spirits, to the Green-room. There was a good deal of noise coming from the other side of the door, and George Anne paused, a little apprehensive, before entering. It was usual for persons of rank to come in after the play, but sometimes friends of the players would meet there, too, and gamble at 'Woman or Head', spinning coins against the chimney-piece: thousands of guineas were lost or won in an evening. George Anne very much hoped that the gaming would have ceased, and that none but the Quality remained in the room. She opened the door.

The first thing that struck her view was Peg Woffington, still attired as the Egyptian queen, sitting at a long table with a pot of porter held high in her hand, crying out:

'Confusion to all order! Let Liberty thrive!'

That firm, slightly discordant voice was louder than usual, for a motley crowd, most of them holding their drinks at arm's length, were calling out their own toasts in high voices. The din was indescribable, and George Anne saw with renewed horror that the table was covered with an assortment of very plebeian mutton pies.

The Duchess of Queensberry had entered the room in the greatest good humour and high dignity, as befitted her station. She stood for a few moments in a state of amazement, gazing at the scene. At length, recovering herself, she exclaimed: 'Is hell let loose?' turned about and hurried out to her sedan chair.

The 1749–50 season at Covent Garden opened without George Anne Bellamy in the company; she had been 'abducted' by an admirer in the interval of a performance, and had not returned.

Peg played Lady Macbeth to James Quin's Macbeth, and the title rôle in *Lady Jane Grey*. These were dramatic parts, and she had the satisfaction of knowing that the hard study she had put in with Madame Dumesnil was showing results: she had more control over her lower register. *Lady Jane Grey*, which she acted for seven successive nights, added greatly to her reputation as heroic actress. A command performance was given before Frederick, Prince of Wales, and the Royal Family at Leicester House, and the critics were so full of praise that Mrs Margaret Woffington again became the talk of the town, and knew once more the heady sensation of popularity and success.

George Anne Bellamy, tired of the 'abduction' story, resolved her complicated love affairs for the time being and returned to Covent Garden in January 1750 to play Belvidera in *Venice Preserv'd*. She immediately resumed her sly, pin-pricking tactics. Peg was in good heart after her recent successes, and treated the younger rival with icy courtesy. The next months brought more formidable hostility. Rich decided to strengthen his company by engaging Susanna Cibber, Peg's old antagonist. He also took on Macklin, who had been to Dublin for a season and was again in London. Spranger Barry, discontented at having to share leading parts with Garrick at Drury Lane, went over to the Garden.

The manager congratulated himself on such an assemblage of famous, talented players – and closed his eyes to the fact that such a team would be difficult to lead, let alone control. Outwardly, the company maintained an appearance of harmony, but there were strains and stresses behind which soon made cracks in the façade. Mrs Cibber did not have the feline suavity of Bellamy, nor were there any fish-wife scenes such as had often provided the town with gossip when Kitty Clive had been unable to hide her hatred of the lovely Woffington. Susanna Cibber's method of showing her intense dislike of Peg was indirect and deadly effective. She would pay ironic compliments at rehearsals, or just before a performance:

"'Tis a pity you do not appear tonight in your usual excellent form. I trust you are well, Mrs Woffington?'

In the Green-room, whisperings and laughter would be heard between Mrs Cibber and her friends; cold laughter, ostentatiously repressed if Mrs Woffington rose from her favourite chair by the chimney-piece and rustled out.

There was continual bad feeling among the men, too. James Quin was jealous of Spranger Barry, who now had a firmly established reputation and was ambitious to rise as high as he could in the theatre. He, in turn, disliked the way the older actor calmly assumed control over everything to do with the management; Quin was constantly asserting his authority and long association with Covent Garden. He treated Spranger Barry as a newcomer, a novice, an upstart, and though Barry had too much self-control to quarrel openly with Quin, he could not always hide his resentment at the other's rudeness to him.

John Rich, the manager, far from pouring oil on troubled waters, exacerbated the ill-feeling which plagued the company. Never a tactful or conciliatory individual, Rich had turned sour of late years, mainly because of a new marriage which brought him real unhappiness. He had chosen, as his third wife, Priscilla Stevens, an actress in his company who had earlier been an attendant at Brett's Coffee House in Drury Lane. She had lived with him for some time under the cloak of being his housekeeper, but had, in the end, insisted on a wedding ring.

On their marriage, she became 'a serious character after having been a very contrary one'. This seriousness took the form of conversion to Methodism, an unfortunate circumstance for John Rich, for Priscilla now declared herself to have an abhorrence of everything theatrical. Rich was, at that time, putting on Handel's opera *Alceste*, written on a libretto by Smollett, and it is said that she asked the composer to set to music the three hymns: 'Sinners, obey the Gospel Word', 'O Love Divine', and 'Rejoice the Lord is King'. Mrs Rich was interfering as well as newly-religious; Smollett disliked her, and described her in his novel *Roderick Random* in uncomplimentary terms; she was the original of the woman whose husband 'laboured under the tyranny of a wife and the terror of hell fire at the same time', while she also 'set about censuring anyone who she considered had departed from the paths of respectability'.

Rich now spent more time than ever in the theatre, and his sardonic presence brought an atmosphere of unease to rehearsals. Having earlier made his name in pantomime, he was conditioned to think that pantomime was the most desirable form of entertainment; he had taken up dramatic production only because it made more money than pantomime. He had never had any great

regard for serious players, apart from their financial value, and
now he did not trouble overmuch to hide his contempt for them;
his idea of real talent was a trouper who could turn a somersault
and wield a string of sausages in a harlequinade. High-tempered
players who strutted and fretted on the stage irritated him – but
he continued, as always, to engage them, well aware of their
powers to pack a theatre and fill his pockets. Meanwhile, he
watched the feuds in the company with sarcastic amusement. He
openly compared Mrs Woffington with Sarah Malcolm, and
Mrs Cibber with Katherine Hayes – two women who had recently
been hanged for a joint murder. Neither Peg nor Susanna Cibber
were pleased by the comparisons, and Peg told him sharply to
keep his tongue in civil order. Rich laughed afresh. Players!
Faugh!

David Garrick, at Drury Lane, was well aware of the disharm-
ony at the Garden. He decided to do some poaching. First he
lured George Anne Bellamy over to his company with the offer of
a much higher salary than she was getting from Rich, and he tried
to get Quin at the same time. The old actor was tempted, but did
not yield. He enjoyed being a power at Covent Garden, where Rich
often left the choice of plays entirely to him, and he knew that he
would have very little influence at Drury Lane with a dominating
personality like David Garrick in command. Quin decided to stay
where he was – but before giving the rival manager a reply, he
went to Rich, told him of Garrick's approach, and asked for a
salary of a thousand pounds a year. This was an enormous sum,
more than any player had ever received before, and Rich was in a
quandary. Should he give in to such an extortionate demand?
The alternative would be the loss of Quin to Drury Lane. Rich
thought it better to retain his man, and paid the enhanced
salary.

The rivalry between the two theatres was the chief subject of
conversation in London society during that season. Both managements had put on *Romeo and Juliet*, with Spranger Barry and
Susanna Cibber at Covent Garden, and Garrick and George Anne
Bellamy at Drury Lane. London was 'divided into two vast
partisan armies'. Garrick then struck at Rich in a very vulnerable
place: he produced a pantomime at Drury Lane which he called
Queen Mab, with an agile young actor, Henry Woodward, as
Harlequin.

Rich was aghast. He was so accustomed to being the King of Pantomime, the motley Harlequin, it seemed incredible that anyone should attempt to oust him from a part which he had always considered to be entirely and uniquely his own. Garrick! John Rich was really angry now, a detail which did not trouble David Garrick. Young Woodward had a gift for comedy, his Harlequin was talked of after the first night, and he drew the town. Henceforth pantomime should have a place in the repertoire. At Covent Garden, Rich decided, in disgust, to take pantomime out of *his* repertoire that year.

The print-shops, as usual, were quick off the mark. A caricature soon appeared, entitled *The Steelyards*, in which a huge pair of scales was depicted, with Peg Woffington, James Quin, Spranger Barry and Susanna Cibber grouped in one pan, and Woodward and *Queen Mab* triumphantly weighing down the combined talent on the other side. Rich's temper was not improved by this pleasantry.

He had further troubles during the season. *King John* had been substituted for the usual pantomime, with Susanna Cibber playing Constance. One afternoon, Mrs Cibber was taken ill, and sent word that she would be unable to play that night. Rich's first reaction was one of extreme annoyance; he did not know if this was a real or pretended illness. Susanna Cibber made the most of a delicate physique; it was not uncommon for her to be indisposed, especially if she did not like a part, or had been upset in any way. Was she indeed unable to appear? Rich sent a henchman to try to find out, and had to accept that Mrs Cibber was genuinely ill on this occasion.

He was in a dilemma. It was too late to substitute another play; he must find another actress, one who knew the part. This, inevitably, would be Mrs Margaret Woffington, who had played Constance at some time in her career, and had a phenomenal memory; he knew that she would spend the few hours before curtain-rise going over the lines. Rich took a chair to Peg's lodgings and asked her to play the part that evening. Peg hesitated. She had not been asked to play any leading rôle lately, and, in the event, she had never cared for the part of Constance; but Rich did not have to plead with her for long. There was no other experienced actress in the company who could step into Constance at short notice, and Peg Woffington was not one to let either her

manager or the audience down. She went at once to the theatre
with her maid, who began to alter Mrs Cibber's stage costume to
fit her mistress.

Peg settled down to the script. When the curtain went up that
evening, she stood on the stage, dressed as Constance. Quietly,
with a dignity which was as high bred as that of any woman of
quality, she explained that Mrs Cibber was indisposed, and asked
the indulgence of the audience for her own appearance as a
substitute. Tate Wilkinson was in the theatre, and he described
the scene which followed:

> The spectators, instead of meeting her address with approba-
> tion, seemed to be entirely lost in surprise. This unexpected
> reception so embarrassed Woffington that she was preparing
> to retire, when Ryan, one of the actors, who thought that they
> only wanted a hint to rouse them from their insensibility,
> asked them bluntly if they would give Mrs Woffington leave to
> act Lady Constance. The audience, as if at once wakened from a
> fit of lethargy, by repeated plaudits strove to make amends for
> their inattention to the most beautiful woman that ever adorned
> a theatre.

Early in 1751, there was much dissension in the company, and
'illness' became endemic, especially among the women. Lee
Lewes wrote:

> In the course of my theatrical career, I have known several
> principal actresses, who have been suddenly seized with a
> variety of fevers; particularly one, which our fraternity knows
> by the name of the box-book fever. Sometimes, when the
> boxes were not well taken, and there is likely to be a thin
> house, the hero or heroine will have a violent cold, hoarse-
> ness, etc.

Mrs Cibber had attacks of a stomach complaint and made the
most of it. Mrs Barry had, or pretended to have, frequent sore
throats. When these actresses could not or would not play, the
productions in which Peg had leading rôles were substituted;
Rich knew he could rely on Mrs Woffington in these emergencies,

and did not hesitate to call upon her on every occasion when he was in difficulties over an actress who sent word that she was indisposed, and could not possibly, as God was her witness, appear that night. Minor actresses who were paid on a nightly basis instead of on a weekly 'agreement' enjoyed remarkably good health, and were seldom absent.

Peg's willingness to assist the manager at these awkward times did not call forth his gratitude in the one way that mattered to her professionally: by the size of her name printed on the playbills. She had for years been accustomed to having her name set in large type at the top of the bill, which was the accustomed position for leading players. At Covent Garden this season, her name had been set at the foot of the playbill, along with the supporting players. This had been Susanna Cibber's doing. Backed by Quin, Mrs Cibber had gone to the manager and insisted that her name and James Quin's, and no other, should appear at the head of the playbills. Susanna Cibber was triumphantly aware that Rich looked on her as a valuable property, and his handling of this situation of the size of the name on the billing – a very important one to actors – would indicate his assessment of Mrs Woffington's drawing powers. James Quin had urged Susanna to stand firm on the matter and not to give way 'one particle'. When they all appeared in a play together, Mrs Woffington's name must be 'in small'.

John Rich stood in awe of Quin, and had no wish to offend the popular Mrs Cibber. He gave instructions that Mrs Woffington's name should appear in small print, at the bottom of the bill. Peg Woffington was incensed. She had obliged Rich again and again by taking parts at short notice, sometimes putting off social engagements to do so, and even denying herself a few days at her villa on one occasion. And the manager continued to treat her in this contemptuous manner! Angrily she told him that if he printed her name among the small part players once more, she would refuse his next plea to substitute for another actress. Nor would she take her usual leading rôle in a play that was hastily put on because of the alleged illness of the principal actress in the play announced for performance.

Two or three weeks later, Susanna Cibber was indisposed, this time genuinely so, on the day she was to play the name part in *Jane Shore*. Peg Woffington had played the rôle and knew it, but

Rich did not ask her to substitute for Mrs Cibber. Instead, without consulting Peg, he gave orders for *The Constant Couple* to be put on that evening, and quickly had bills printed with Mrs Woffington's name down as Sir Harry Wildair. Peg knew nothing about it until she saw the theatre runners posting up the bills on walls and taking them into the coffee-houses. When a messenger arrived at her lodgings, as he had so often done, with the news that she would be playing Wildair, Peg was ready for him.

'Pray take Mrs Woffington's best compliments to Mr Rich,' she said. 'Mrs Woffington sends regrets, and is not able to play tonight because she is indisposed.'

Rich was astonished and alarmed, until he remembered Peg Woffington's threat. He ordered his chair and was carried post haste to her lodgings. Peg received him equably, and without any attempt to feign illness; she was, in fact, in the bloom of perfect health. Indeed, she was 'indisposed', she calmly informed him. She would not be able to play Wildair that evening. John Rich could hardly believe his own ears. Woffington actually intended to carry out her threat. He argued with her, but he could not move her from her resolution. She was 'indisposed'. She could not play. John Rich had always disliked 'dramatick actresses', but now he hated Mrs Woffington – actually hated her. He left her lodgings in a black fury, and took his chair back to the theatre, cursing heartily. There was just time to give orders for *The Miser* to be presented that evening; it had a cast of lesser players, but it was better than having to empty the house and pay back the admission money because there was no play at all.

The audience that night were angry at being fobbed off with an indifferent piece and secondary actors. They had come to see *The Constant Couple*, Farquhar's amusing comedy which had been advertised all over the town, with the attractive Woffington as Wildair. Why had the play been changed again? Rich sent the prompter before the curtain to apologize and crave their pardon and their patience, but he was greeted with cries and catcalls. When he tried to tell them that sickness had – ahem – unfortunately robbed them of – ahem – of their favourites – ahem – alas, distemper struck suddenly – ahem, the catcalls increased. The regular theatregoers felt that their favourites, the leading players, were growing too independent altogether, and that Mr

Rich was being very badly treated. After the performance a number of men-about-town, who spent most of their evenings at the theatres, met together at a coffee-house and resolved that next time a billed player failed to appear, he or she should be made to feel the town's disapproval.

Peg Woffington knew nothing of this. Neither was she aware that word had been passed round that Mrs Woffington had failed to keep pact with the public through whimsy and temper. A few judicious guineas distributed among certain hacks in Grub Street, and a paragraph appeared in one journal, a hint or two in another, while 'Honest Critic' let loose a few darts in a third: all to the effect that a certain celebrated Queen of the Stage was taking a larger size in Muslin Caps, and should consider her duties to the faithful admirers who had exalted her – and who could throw her down again. If Peg Woffington saw the malicious lines, she made no sign; attacks in the public prints were part of London life, and were forgotten as soon as a new victim to abuse was found.

Having made her protest to Rich in the one way he could understand, Peg put the affair behind her and went on to study her next part, Lady Jane Grey. She had no premonition of the ordeal that awaited her on her first appearance in the play. The bucks who had been indignant over the withdrawal of *The Constant Couple* were in the pit. As Peg stood on the stage, ready to begin her lines, these men shouted 'Off! Off!' The hateful, familiar sound which every player dreaded. The rest of the audience, with the exception of the ladies and gentlemen in the boxes, took up the cry, and Peg was brought to a standstill.

Tate Wilkinson was at the side of the stage that evening, and he later wrote a vivid account of the scene:

> Whoever . . . saw her that night will own that they never beheld any figure half so beautiful since. Her anger gave a glow to her complexion and added lustre to her charming eye. The audience treated her very rudely, bade her ask pardon, and threw orange peels on the stage. She behaved with great resolution, and treated their rudeness with glorious contempt. She left the stage, was called for, and with infinite persuasion was prevailed on to return. However, she did so, walked forward to the footlights, and told them she was ready and willing to

perform the character if they chose to permit her – that the decision was theirs – on or off, just as they pleased – a matter of indifference to her. The ayes had it, and all went smoothly afterwards, though she always persisted in believing that the clique against her was originally formed by Rich's family and particular friends, some of whom she did not scruple to name, though, I believe, she always acquitted Rich himself of any knowledge of it.

Peg Woffington had won that round, but, as at Drury Lane the previous year, she was aware of mounting hostility against her. She knew well that her own quick tongue made her enemies, when she was incautious enough to allow her temper to break through. It was getting more difficult to keep an outwardly cool demeanour; she was weary of the constant jealousies which bedevilled her life in the London theatre, and not only that of women. James Quin, who had always sneered at her popularity, had more than once pushed her aside on the stage during an ovation, when he considered it should have been reserved for him alone. Peg had never shown Quin the uncritical flattery which he demanded from everyone; she could not resist pricking his colossal vanity with the lance of her Irish wit on every occasion that offered – and there were many.

James Quin's dislike of Margaret Woffington was kept nicely simmering by his protégée, George Anne Bellamy. Little Bellamy, an adept at dealing with egotistical actors who might be useful to her, had been friendly with Quin for a long time, and she often dined with him. One of their common interests – possibly their chief one – was their detestation of the spirited, lovely Woffington, and it is probable they hatched little plans to humiliate her when it was safe to do so. Continual pin-pricks eventually had an effect, for Peg, though able to hold her own in any Green-room, had sensitive areas behind her cool manner. She decided to get away from their stupid hostility, and go to Dublin. It was some time since she had seen her mother, and it would be pleasant to return once more to the boards of the Dublin theatres; the audiences there were vociferous and demanding, as they were in London, but laughter was never far away. They were her own people.

When she told Rich that she was leaving Covent Garden at the end of her agreement and going to Dublin, the manager immediately offered to re-engage her for the following season. Mrs Woffington still had a big following in London, and John Rich never allowed his personal likes or dislikes to interfere with his business instincts. Peg, however, had had enough of Rich, and Covent Garden, and London. The one being she was really sorry to leave was Polly, but in any case, she did not see much of her nowadays, and when she went to Polly's town house, to say goodbye, it was to find a rout in progress.

The Honourable Mrs Cholmondeley was now the mistress of a *salon:* Polly's instinct to cultivate the friendship of influential women had produced results. It was the heyday of the Bluestocking, and young Mrs Cholmondeley aspired to be one of them. Thanks to the good education her sister had given her, and to her own quick brain, she could hold her own in any drawingroom.

The Cholmondeley family and their aristocratic relations had softened. When Horace Walpole, hearing such rapturous descriptions of Robert's wife, at last consented to meet her, he was soon captivated by her beauty and deferential manner towards him. He had her presented at the English Court. He took her with him on a visit to Paris, where she made her curtsy to the Dauphin and Madame du Barry, as well as to members of the oldest French families. There is no record that anyone knew this elegant young lady with the air of refined hauteur was the daughter of an Irish labourer. Neither did anyone mention Mrs Margaret Woffington, the renowned actress. If people did not know she was the sister of a player, Mrs Cholmondeley was certainly not going to tell them. Mr Horace Walpole, brother of the Earl of Orford, introduced her to everyone as 'my niece'.

It is probable that when Peg Woffington was announced on that day she came to take leave of her sister, Polly showed a dutiful regret at Peg's departure. Polly had left her guests and received the visitor in her private parlour, and it is also probable that after she had accompanied her sister to the front door and seen her off in a sedan chair, she returned with relief to entertaining her guests. It was an increasing embarrassment, in the world of the Quality in which she now moved, to be connected with a stage-player, however eminent. The Honourable Mrs Cholmondeley had convinced herself, quite genuinely, that she had no connexion with any world save the one which she now adorned, a world of wealth, taste, fashion – and family.

15

Return to Dublin

Peg Woffington had not arranged an 'agreement' in Dublin, but Colley Cibber had told her that he would write to Thomas Sheridan at Smock Alley Theatre; the playhouse in Aungier Street had become dilapidated, and Smock Alley was now the only theatre of consequence in the city.

The actress did not travel alone. Signor Angelo wished to see Dublin. He had had a profitable two years in London, where Peg and M'Swiney had helped him to establish himself as a *maître des armes*. He had taught fencing to the young princes, sons of the Princess Dowager of Wales, and to many of the nobility. Now he wished to make a further reputation in the Irish capital, where, he was told, affairs of honour were the order of the day among the high-bred Anglo-Irish gentry. Besides, the lovely Woffington should have an escort on the tedious journey. Peg was not discouraging. Angelo was handsome and gallant: they understood each other.

They arrived in Dublin several days later, and once the news of Peg's arrival became known, there was no doubt of her reception. The beaux welcomed her with verses in the newspapers, and George Faulkner wrote a graceful column of eulogistic welcome. Peg stayed with her mother, now established in a good small house, close by the Catholic church where she regularly worshipped. Hannah Woffington was more devout than ever, and spent most of her time 'visiting the poor, tapping her agate snuff box, and feasting her soul with good works'. Peg had never been devout, and did not pretend to any religious convictions. Still the least hypocritical of women, she believed in freedom of conscience to worship as one wished – or not to worship at all.

Dutifully pleased to see her mother, she quickly tired of her company: there was little common ground between these two. Hannah must have felt that she was entertaining a bird of paradise. She was, as ever, exceedingly proud of her daughter, but she also stood a little in awe of her, and probably felt relief when Peg decided to take a house in the centre of the city. The old, high, narrow, timbered houses were disappearing, and fine brick houses with pillared doorways and ornamental fanlights over the doors were taking their place. 'Stately and magnificent mansions, faced with sparkling granite native to the Wicklow Hills, and adorned by the genius of foreign artists' now made Dublin one of the handsomest cities in Europe, and there were daily accounts in the journals of the balls, the quadrille parties, the banquets with 'flutes and soft instruments playing', at which the Quality whiled away their time.

Signor Angelo found lodgings near by, and Peg showed him the city. She waited for two or three weeks before calling on Thomas Sheridan. He received her civilly, but he was reserved, knowing why she had come. Yes, he admitted, he had received a letter from Colley Cibber. He did not tell her that Cibber had sent an enthusiastic report of Mrs Woffington's triumphs in the London playhouse, and urged Sheridan to engage her. Sheridan was not sure that it would be wise to do so; he already had a reigning star, Mrs Bland*, and it would be extremely awkward to have a celebrated player new come from London in the same company. Besides, Mrs Woffington was very expensive. Tentatively he asked Peg what salary she was asking. Four hundred pounds a year, replied Peg Woffington. Sheridan had expected a high figure, but he was astonished at the amount she named, and showed it. Peg remained cool. She would not lower her price: she was well aware of her value as an actress, and knew that it was a bad sign to come down, once a salary figure had been named.

Four hundred pounds? Sheridan was incredulous. Four hundred pounds. And two benefits. The manager said he would think it over, and would wait upon her soon. Peg took a chair back to her lodgings, not doubting that Mr Sheridan would agree to her terms. Thomas Sheridan hesitated for an entire day. Colley

* The mother of the actress who achieved fame, and a royal lover, as Dora Jordan.

mistress to K. Wm IV

Cibber praised her, true – but everyone knew that the old pea-cock was smitten with Peg's charms, and was bound to be entirely in her favour. Sheridan had not seen her act for several years: had she deteriorated, become 'set', as so many actresses did at her age? It would be taking a chance to engage her . . .

In the end, he reluctantly decided that it might be a risk worth taking. Those verses and flattering paragraphs in the journals – they indicated a permanent popularity, not affected by her absence in London. The Woffington's old admirers in Dublin were probably elated that one of their own players had had London at her feet, and they would be sure to come and see her. Yes, it might be worth it. As for Mrs Bland – Sheridan hoped that it would be possible for two 'dramatick queens' to share the honours.

He waited on Peg, as he had promised, and agreed to her terms, the highest he had ever paid. The season had not officially begun, but he put *The Provok'd Wife* into rehearsal. At the first performance, watching Peg Woffington walk on to the stage in her costume, her slender figure superbly outlined in a brocade gown, her dark eyes snapping with mischief, the audience rising to her wit and charm, it was immediately evident to Sheridan that he had made a good bargain. Mrs Woffington's magic still held them.

The Lord Lieutenant, once again His Grace of Dorset, had commanded a performance at the Theatre Royal in Smock Alley, and the 1751 season could now be said to have begun. 'A vast number of persons of distinction flocked from England in the wake of the viceroy, and most of the Irish county families settled in the capital for the winter,' says Fizgerald Molloy, in his *Romance of the Irish Stage*.

Mrs Woffington from the Theatre Royal in Covent Garden was the great attraction at the command performance, and she was to be supported by Thomas Sheridan, Theophilus Cibber, West Digges, and the best of the minor players in a performance of the comedy, *The Provok'd Husband*. To oblige the Duchess, the play did not begin until half-past seven, an hour later than usual, but the usual audience got there well in time, for the Lord Lieutenant went to the theatre, as he went to open Parliament, in regal state, more splendid than anything likely to be seen on the stage.

According to the *Dublin Journal*, workmen had been employed
for weeks in enlarging the galleries of the theatre, space had been
taken from the pit to add to the boxes, wax candles instead of
tallow filled the scores of gilded sconces, and there was an aug-
mented orchestra. The fashionable world naturally wished to be
seen on such an occasion in the exalted company of the party
from the Castle, and all the available boxes had been bespoken
days before. Already, says Molloy, at five o'clock

. . . the great, lumbering, showily-painted coaches and sedan
chairs had commenced to invade the narrow thoroughfares,
intent on depositing their burdens of the first rank and distinction at the playhouse doors, where sentries in full uniform were
drawn up on guard.

All was bustle, movement and confusion; the noise of
innumerable voices was deafening. Here were coachmen, red-
faced and powder-wigged, thundering sturdy oaths at their
steeds; footmen shouting and running to and fro; silver and
gold-laced lacqueys, with staffs surmounted by the coronets
of their noble masters, striving to keep at bay the good-
humoured crowd pushing forward to peep through the windows
of the coaches; and plush liveried chairmen cursing their
sturdier fellows who had outstripped them in the race for
place. Horses pranced, the city gamin screamed to each other,
saluted such of the gentlepeople as were known to them, or
who were rendered conspicuous by their dress; a crowd of
orange-women cried their wares; the motley throng gathered
round the pit and gallery doors, shouted witticisms and pleasant badinage, as they crushed each other almost to death; and
the link boys, who had already lighted their flambeaux, darted
here and there, leaving flaming tracks, brief and lurid, in their
fitful wakes.

A short time before the Lord Lieutenant was due to arrive, Peg
Woffington's coach turned into Smock Alley, and Peg descended
with the air of a duchess – 'and yet with as friendly a face as your
neighbour's'. The crowd cheered, the popular actress – who
had been one of themselves not so many years ago – rustled her
silks through the stage entrance, and the crowd turned to see the
rest of the brilliant show. A guard of red-coated soldiers was
already drawn up on each side of the path from the cobbles to the

Spranger Barry
by E. Harding, from
a portrait by Sir
Joshua Reynolds.
(Harvard Theatre
Collection.)

Colley Cibber
by I. B. Vanloo.
(Harvard Theatre
Collection.)

Owen M'Swiney
by I. B. Vanloo.
(Harvard Theatre
Collection.)

Thomas Sheridan
by J. Stewart.
(Harvard Theatre
Collection.)

colonnade of the playhouse. Came a distant cheer, then the cavalry escort, clad in scarlet, clattered to a stop, preceding the ducal coach, painted with the royal cipher. The Duke and his Duchess descended, he glittering with orders, she splendid in satin and feathers, diamonds winking at every step she moved. Sheridan and Theophilus Cibber, clad in Court suits, stood bare-headed, holding silver candlesticks with tall wax candles alight, ready to conduct their Graces into the theatre.

The theatre was crowded to the roof. Two of the principal boxes had been thrown into one, hung with scarlet silk embla-zoned with the royal arms, and furnished with mirrors and gilded chairs.

The Lord Mayor, wearing his red cloak and gold chain of office, sat with his wife, patriotically attired in green satin; around them rustled the Quality in their finery, the men in their gold-frogged satins and curled wigs, the ladies like enamelled figurines, their brocades cascading fine lace at wrist and bosom, their jewels glinting in the wax lights. The pit was filled with the lesser classes; proprietors of the Dublin newspapers, self-appointed critics who would air their views on the morrow in the coffee-houses, students from Trinity ready to ape the men of the world.

As the Castle party entered, the orchestra struck up the national anthem, the Lord Lieutenant bowed graciously, and the rest of the gorgeous company settled down to enjoy Mrs Woffington's Lady Townley.

Peg Woffington was always at her most brilliant on a gala occasion. She never gave of less than her best at any performance: to do so would have gone against the grain for a player who was a dramatic craftswoman as well as an instinctive artist. At a com-mand performance, however, especially before the Duke of Dor-set, who was a patron of the drama and one of her admirers, she reached heights of excellence in a performance which was written into the history of the theatre. Benjamin Victor, the treasurer of Smock Alley and not usually effusive in his praise – he disliked 'incense' – wrote a letter to Peg saying that he had not seen a complete Lady Townley until that night. The newspapers and journals were full of panegyrics on her beauty, her elegance, her deportment, her acting; George Faulkner had to apologize in

G

Faulkner's Journal for not having enough space to print all the verses which had been sent in, praising the matchless Woffington.

Sheridan quickly took advantage of Peg's runaway success to present her in further plays. She appeared as the tragic Andromache, and as Hermione. Night after night she played to crowded houses, and when she appeared in her favourite breeches parts, Silvia in *The Recruiting Officer* and Sir Harry Wildair in *The Constant Couple,* ladies sent their footmen to the theatre hours in advance, to bribe the box-keeper into letting them have seats. Benjamin Victor wrote to the Countess of Orrery in London:

> The brilliant Mrs Woffington is the only theme either in or out of the theatre. Her performances are in general admirable. In *Andromache* her grief was dignified and her deportment elegant; in Hermione she discovered such talents . . . such commanding force, such variety, such graceful attitudes, the very fools stared and felt her powers. In short, poor Bland is inevitably undone, for those fools (her greatest admirers), who had not sense enough to see her defects before, now see them by the comparison. I heartily wish I had force enough to excite a desire in your ladyship to come to Dublin to see this actress.

Mrs Bland had established herself in Dublin as a good all-round actress, and Peg Woffington's meteor-like appearance on the theatrical scene was a disaster for her. 'When seen together, like the comet and the falling star, it was impossible for the audience not instantly to perceive the difference between the brilliancy of a true diamond and that of a Bristol stone. Peg Woffington was now the magnet.' Poor Bland left Smock Alley. Peg Woffington seems not to have taken much notice of the unfortunate actress she had supplanted; this was the cut-throat world of the theatre, and each had to look out for himself.

The packed houses continued – as did the valuable patronage of the Duke and Duchess of Dorset. They attended her benefit, when the demand was so great that the pit had to be 'laid open to the boxes' to accommodate all the expensive 'golden tickets'. Their Graces commanded performances of *Hamlet, The Merchant of Venice* and *As You Like It,* which gave Peg the chance to show what she could do in Shakespeare; she now played the Queen where she had once acted Ophelia as an ambitious girl. The paeans of praise also continued: the Green-room overflowed with worshippers every night. Peg smiled on them but singled no one out. She preferred, for the present, to have a hundred lovers – at a distance. For companionship she had Angelo, who had already made useful friends and was contemplating settling in Dublin for a year or two.

Sheridan had never had such full coffers at his playhouse. Hitchcock noted down the practical rewards which accrued to Smock Alley this season, writing:

> Her [Peg Woffington's] reception was such as surprised the most sanguine expectations of her friends, and astonished even the manager, who was highly pleased with his acquisition. It is almost impossible to describe the raptures the audience were in at beholding so beautiful, elegant, and accomplished a woman, or the happy consequences which resulted to Mr Sheridan.

The happy consequences amounted to four thousand pounds taken in all for forty performances in which Peg Woffington played the principal rôle. Thomas Sheridan had not done badly with an actress whom he had at first hesitated in engaging.

As the season went on, Sheridan put on more plays with Mrs Woffington in the lead: he could be certain of full houses on her nights. Peg worked extremely hard, acting every kind of rôle: from breeches parts to grotesque old women, when she did not hesitate to line and disfigure her beautiful face. She specially enchanted her audience in the range of modish women, whom she interpreted perfectly, with just that slight touch of caricature, the delicate heightening of a foible or a mannerism, that set the wits smiling. Peg did not miss a single performance, through illness or for any other reason; and, as usual, she was punctilious when it came to acting for her fellow-players' benefits, appearing at twenty-four of them during the season.

News came from London that John Rich, who had lost his prestige as the king of pantomime, had now regained the favour of the town by producing a new version of this entertainment. It was called *Harlequin Sorcerer*, and Tate Wilkinson relates:

> There was never anything before like the rage for it. The doors had to be opened three hours before commencing to relieve the streets about Covent Garden of the crowd. It made Garrick and Old Drury tremble – for all they got was the

discontented overflow of children and the grown-up masters
and misses who failed to get in to see the pantomime.

Garrick was not of the trembling persuasion, but Rich's new
entertainment was certainly a threat to his own theatre receipts.
Now that Woodward's Harlequin was failing to draw the crowds
to Drury Lane, he must find something to replace *Queen Mab*.
He looked round for established favourites to provide a strong
counter-attraction to Covent Garden's novelty. There were those
of his cronies who wondered whether Mrs Woffington in Dublin
could be tempted back to London. Peg Woffington was known for
excellent sense where the profession was concerned, and good,
businesslike terms might induce her to make a favourable decision. Was it possible that Davy Garrick himself was having regrets at having lost her? Garrick had married Violette. Had Mrs
Garrick expressed regrets – to say the least – at any mention of
Mrs Woffington's being engaged: was that what was holding
Davy back? There were conjectures, gossip . . . Garrick was
happily enough married, but it was noted that he quickly turned
the subject whenever Peg Woffington's name was mentioned in
company. Were old, deep feelings not yet quite stamped out by
matrimony? Garrick was silent on the subject, but the gossip
went on. It reached Dublin, and there were some who looked
curiously at Peg, wondering whether she would return to London
at the end of the season, on the chance of being taken on at Drury
Lane. Peg Woffington showed no sign of wishing to leave Dublin,
and Sheridan did not wait before re-engaging her for the following
season.

Owen M'Swiney wrote to Peg in 1753, telling her he had made a
Will leaving her a sum of money in Consols sufficient to produce
two hundred pounds a year. There was, however, a stipulation.
M'Swiney was a Protestant, and he laid down that Margaret
Woffington must become a Protestant to benefit by the legacy.

Peg was very much surprised, for during their long intimacy
M'Swiney had not appeared to be in the least religious, nor had he
ever discussed religion with her. She herself had never been other
than a nominal Catholic, and her mother's renewed devotion to
the Faith, after years of lip-service, had seemed to Peg to be a

nod towards the conventions of her neighbours. Why not? It gave the old lady something to do, and kept her from being lonely. Peg Woffington had few scruples in agreeing to renounce her tenuous adherence to Catholic doctrine, and she accepted M'Swiney's conditions.

She was by this time on very friendly terms with Sheridan and his wife, sometimes dining with them before the play. Mrs Sheridan was a woman of considerable character; her son, Richard Brinsley, then a child, inherited a good deal of talent from his mother as well as from his father. Peg discussed M'Swiney's will with the Sheridans, who said that if she had decided to conform to the terms of the will, she should make the change now and do it quietly, so as not to offend the main body of their audiences, who were predominantly Catholic. Sheridan suggested that she should travel to his country house at Quilcagh, fifty miles from Dublin, and be formally received into the Established Church by the Protestant vicar of that parish. Peg's chief concern was to spare the feelings of her mother, and she agreed to the suggestion. A few days later she left Dublin for Quilcagh with Sheridan, in his carriage. They were, of course, seen by many.

Scandal quickly flared up. It was noted that Mrs Sheridan had not accompanied her husband to Quilcagh, and there was an immediate rustle of excitement throughout the theatregoing public. What a tidbit! The manager of Smock Alley eloping with his leading actress! Poor Mrs Sheridan! It was an unexpected turn of events, as everyone had thought the manager and his wife to be uncommonly happy, matrimonially speaking. Still, with Peg Woffington's changeless beauty *and* reputation, it was not, after all, surprising.

'Poor Mrs Sheridan' went about her daily business, not unduly perturbed, having quietly made all the domestic arrangements for Peg's stay at Quilcagh. She knew as well as her husband that a rumour of this kind would do far less harm than the truth, both to Sheridan's pocket and to Peg Woffington's professional career. The human weaknesses of men and women brought a smile to the lips of the scandalmongers, but a recantation of faith would arouse only scorn and the deepest disapproval. Once the couple returned to Dublin, there would be whisperings and shakings of heads for a time, then the 'affair' would be forgotten. Who now attempted to count Peg Woffington's lovers? They were dismissed with a tolerant shrug. But let the lovely Peggy officially leave the Church, and she would never be forgiven.

It turned out as the Sheridans had predicted. Peg went back to Smock Alley, and Sheridan returned to the manager's room. The following season, Sheridan doubled Peg's salary – this time without hesitating or bargaining. Mrs Woffington had filled every house during the season, and the manager had made an unheard-of profit; he intended to keep her in Dublin as long as possible.

Peg gave her mother an increased allowance, and also enlarged her investments. With an income of nearly a thousand pounds a year, she could now afford to live luxuriously, and she did not stint herself. She moved to a large house in Capel Street, furnished it well, bought a carriage and pair, engaged good servants, and began to entertain on a lavish scale. Her evening parties became famous – not less so because they were attended mainly by men. Peg had never disguised the fact that she found most society women boring; she disliked their 'prattle of silks and sattins and the sins of their dearest friends', as well as the restricted range of their interests – due, she freely admitted, to the narrow education they were given compared with their brothers. She had always made up for her own lack of education by a love of reading and a preference for the company of wits, poets, writers, dramatists, statesmen and men of letters. Her intellect was stimulated by their society, and she was not unaware of the fact that she could hold her own in conversation with the best of them. Had not Charles Hanbury Williams praised her quick intelligence? She was now at her zenith: a cultivated, accomplished woman with a remarkable power of drawing the best brains to her house: 'The graceful ease of her manner, the wit of which she was the acknowledged mistress, and the hospitable way in which she entertained, immediately secured for Woffington in Dublin the position she had occupied in London.'

Not quite, however. In London, Mrs Woffington had been received in the houses of many of the Quality, and was on curtsying terms with the Royal Family, being bidden to visit the King in the box at the theatre, and the Prince and Princess of Wales in theirs. It was different in Dublin. The ladies who lived in the houses in Dawson Street and round St Stephen's Green took care that the less respectable side of Mrs Woffington's character was mentioned when her talents were praised, and there was much

silken innuendo. The Woffington might hold her famous receptions, but she was not received at the Castle, nor by the leading
families.

Peg laughed, and continued to entertain the masters and sons
of those families in her crowded withdrawing-room, with its
decorated ceiling, carved chimney-piece, hangings and chairs of
Genoa damask. It was pleasant to have enough money to be
able to live, in reality, like the fashionable dames she acted so
often on the stage; pleasant to respond to the raillery of distinguished men. Some of them had been her lovers. Ah well. It was
also pleasant to reflect that her lovers usually remained her
friends. Peg was at her most scintillating on these occasions,
under the glittering chandeliers which sent out rainbow lights,
while powdered footmen handed round wine on silver trays, and
there was laughter and good talk. Radiantly lovely and exquisitely
dressed, Peg moved from group to group in a company which was,
outside France, the most civilized in Europe.

The women of quality affected to despise the player-woman –
who never attempted to hide her *amours* when they were properly
discreet about their own – but there were ironic incidents. The
best-known concerns the Gunning sisters, Maria and Elizabeth,
legendary society beauties of whom Horace Walpole was to
write:

> There are two Irish girls of no fortune, who are declared the
> handsomest women alive. I think there being two so handsome,
> and both such perfect figures, is their chief excellence, for
> singly I have seen much handsomer figures than either; how-
> ever, they can't walk in the park, or go to Vauxhall, but such
> mobs follow them that they are therefore driven away.

Walpole met the sisters only after they had come to London,
stunning the capital with their remarkable beauty. Peg Woffington
knew them at an earlier period, and had occasion to do them a
service which was subtly ironic, in the circumstances. They
belonged to a very good Dublin family, but were 'as poor as
poverty'. Their father, John Gunning, 'a thriftless Irish gentleman' who owned a semi-ruined castle but little else, had married

the daughter of the sixth Viscount Mayo. This link with the aristocracy, unbuttressed by a sufficient income to go with it, made life
difficult for the daughter of a viscount. Nevertheless, determined
to give her daughters a proper start in society, Mrs Gunning
left her husband's castle, and rented a house in Capel Street,
Dublin. Her objective was to present her lovely girls at a Drawing-
Room at the Castle. It meant more debts, but the future of Maria
and Elizabeth was at stake. Mrs Gunning felt she must somehow
manage that important introduction to the best society; the rest
she had to leave to fate – and the susceptibilities of the young
sprigs of the nobility.

An invitation duly came from the Castle, and the two Miss
Gunnings would have been delighted, 'but there was an obstacle
which at first sight seemed unsurmountable. Nature had given
them wonderful beauty, but fortune had denied them decent
dresses.' What to do? They had no money, or friends from whom
they could borrow suitable attire. Someone mentioned that Mrs
Woffington, the actress, lived in the same street. She was rich and
known to be generous. Would she . . ?

Peg Woffington must have smiled when she received a stilted,
polite, semi-condescending yet pathetic letter from the beautiful
Gunnings, asking for the favour. She sent her personal maid,
Kitty, to their house, with a message saying they could come and
choose gowns to their liking. With Sheridan's permission, she
lent them two of her stage costumes; they looked splendid, for
there is evidence in memoirs of the time that the young ladies
made a sensation on their entrance into the ballroom. Mrs
Woffington may not have been *persona grata* in vice-regal circles,
but her dresses went to Court on that occasion.

16
The Beefsteak Club

The 1752–3 Dublin season was perhaps the highlight of Peg Woffington's career. She was now in a position to inform the manager what plays she wanted, and she had chosen a list which gave her scope to display the variety of her talent: Andromache, Hermione in *The Distress'd Mother*, Calista in *The Fair Penitent*, Maria in *The Nonjuror*, and her two famous breeches parts, Silvia in *The Recruiting Officer* and Wildair in *The Constant Couple*. The playhouse was crowded, night after night, and Sheridan did not allow interest to flag. He announced that he would present several of Shakespeare's plays if enough seats were engaged, and his friend and good patron, the Duke of Dorset, gave orders for command performances of *The Merchant of Venice*, *Hamlet* and *As You Like It*.

Peg had studied the comedies of Shakespeare and several of the tragedies, but she had not played in any of them for some time. It took a great deal of concentration to memorize afresh the long parts involved; but she was still a quick study, and she was word perfect long before the final rehearsals. There were rumours in the clubs and drawing-rooms of new amorous attachments, whispers of quarrels at her house with a favoured gentleman of fashion who was furious because his divinity had suddenly become inaccessible 'because of her business'. Her business, forsooth! The fops and beaux could never accept that the celebrated Mrs Woffington was celebrated because of her devotion to her 'business'. They immediately concluded that there was another lover in the case.

The gossips poked their noses round and about in vain. Peg Woffington had never troubled to deny rumours, neither had she ever affirmed them. She kept her private life quite private, when she'd a mind to, and could turn a disconcertingly cool smile on anyone who attempted to ask hinting questions. It amused her to glance at the boxes at the end of a performance, and know that even while they patted their gloved hands together in applause, the ladies were speculating about her latest *amour*. Let them. She would have as many lovers as she pleased, when and where she pleased, as often as she pleased, without asking their leave! The playhouse contained more than the boxes, however. In a full house, the galleries were crowded with the Dublin mob, laughing, shouting and excited, forgetting poverty and misery, their magical evening paid for with a hardly hoarded sixpence. The moment she came on the stage, cheers, clapping and stamping broke in an avalanche of welcome as she stood smiling at them.

'Her elegant deportment is a prologue in her behalf,' wrote George Faulkner in his *Journal*.

The Irish loved elegance. The man in the gallery might not have a sound coat to his back, but he expected to be ravished by gorgeously clad goddesses on the stage. He was never disappointed when Peg Woffington appeared. The ladies in the boxes, in their satins and feathers, noted how the Woffington brought the most perfect taste to her stylishness, and wondered afresh that a woman who had run barefoot through the Dublin streets as a girl should have learnt so much without being bred to a good society.

What may have puzzled these grand dames more was Mrs Woffington's refusal to put on airs, or allow her enormous popularity to make any difference to her natural character. Hitchcock pays tribute to this lack of vanity, so unusual in an actress of the time:

> To her honour be it ever remembered, that whilst thus in the zenith of her glory, courted and caressed by all ranks and degrees, it made no alteration to her behaviour; she remained the same gay, affable, obliging, good-natured Woffington to everyone around her. She had none of those occasional illnesses which I have sometimes seen assumed by capital performers, to the great vexation and loss of the manager and disappointment of the public; she always acted four times a week. Not the lowest performer in the theatre did she refuse playing for.

It was a fortunate circumstance for the Theatre Royal that the

Duke of Dorset was again Lord Lieutenant of Ireland; his frequent commands for performances helped Thomas Sheridan's
prestige. Patronage in high places was very useful, and Sheridan
thought of a plan to make it even more so. He would institute a
Beefsteak Club, such as the theatre managers had in London, and
invite His Grace and other influential men to the dinners.

Such clubs were an institution in the theatre, when the principal
performers dined together one day in the week, generally on a
Saturday, and, according to Victor, 'authors and other geniuses
were admitted members'. The first Beefsteak Club had been established in London early in the eighteenth century by 'merry
Dick Estcourt', a mime and popular comedy actor who gave a
regular weekly dinner to which were invited the chief actors of
the day, together with prominent men and wits like Sir Roger de
Coverley and Sir Robert Steele. The object of the dinner was 'to
spend a few hours in mirth and social friendship'. Estcourt
provided excellent grilled steaks and good wine, and he wore
a small gold gridiron round his neck when he presided at the
board.

There was also the Sublime Society of Steaks, founded in
1735 by John Rich and the Earl of Peterborough. It was held
weekly in a private room at the Theatre Royal, Covent Garden,
and invitations were eagerly sought. Peterborough was an eccen-
tric, a man of varied talents and a delightful companion; he
loved the company of players, and even carried his eccentricity
to the point of marrying one, for the singer Anastasia Robinson
became his wife. Rich never asked more than half a dozen outside guests to meet his leading actors, but they were carefully
chosen – aristocratic supporters of the theatre, who joined in the
discussions on the plays and casts proposed for the ensuing week,
thus giving them the feeling that they had a hand in the running
of the theatre. As John Rich, behind his uncouth manner, was a
shrewd manipulator, his guests generally voted for the programme
which he prompted them to suggest themselves. He also managed
the financial side of this quasi-social meeting in such a skilful
way that each man insisted on paying his share of the dinner.

Sheridan decided to go one better than John Rich and conduct
his Beefsteak Club in style. He fitted up the dining-room in his
spacious house in Dorset Street to take a large company, and
asked thirty to forty of the Quality to dine at his table once a

week. It was considered a great honour to be invited to Mr Sheridan's Beefsteak Club, especially as the Duke of Dorset and his close friends were frequent guests, besides poets, dramatists, painters, wits and political personages.

There were two further innovations: no actors were invited for the purpose of discussing plays or casts, and no guest was expected to pay for his dinner. Sheridan was their host in the strict social sense, and paid all. More, he provided the most intriguing novelty of all. He asked Peg Woffington to adorn the head of the table, the only woman there. News flew round the town that the 'gay, volatile, enchanting Woffington had been elected President of the Beefsteak Club'.

The proceedings were always lighthearted, and poems were brought and declaimed, praising the lovely occupant of the Chair. On one occasion, when the Duke of Dorset was present, the President herself produced a set of verses, which she delivered with graceful bravura:*

To His Grace the Lord Lieutenant of Ireland, etc. etc.
Humble Petition of Margaret Woffington, Spinster.

> May it please your Grace, with all submission
> I humbly offer my petition:
> Let others with as small pretensions
> Teaze you for places and for pensions,
> I scorn a pension or a place,
> My whole design's upon your Grace.
> The form of my petition's this –
> I claim, my lord, an annual kiss –
> A kiss by sacred custom due
> To me and to be paid by you.
> But lest you entertain a doubt,
> I'll make my title clearly out.
> It was, as near as I can fix,
> The fourth of April, 'forty-six –
> (With joy I recollect the day)
> As I was dressing for the play
> In stept your Grace, and at your back
> Appear'd my trusty guardian, Mac†;

* *The European Magazine,* 1752.
† Owen M'Swiney

A sudden tremor shook my frame –
Lord! how my colour went and came.
At length, to cut my story short,
You kiss'd me, sir, heav'n bless you for't,
The magic touch my spirits drew
Up to my lips and out they flew,
Such pain and pleasure mixed, I vow,
I felt all o'er, I don't know how.
The secret, when your Grace withdrew
Like lightning to the green room flew
And plunged the women into spleen,
The men received me for their queen,
And from that moment swore allegiance –
Nay, Rich himself was all obedience.
Since then your Grace has never yet
Refused to pay the annual debt.
To prove these facts, if you will have it
Old Mac will make an affidavit;
If Mac's rejected as a fibber,
I must appeal to Colley Cibber.
By good advice I hither came
To keep up my continual claim.
The duty's not confined to place,
But everywhere affects your Grace,
Which being personal on you
No deputy, my lord, can do.
But hold! say some, his situation
Is changed. Consider his high station.
Can station or can titles add
To Dorset more than Dorset had?
Let others void of native grace
Derive faint honours from a place.
His greatness to himself he owes
Nor borrows lustre, but bestows.

There are a dozen lines more on the same sycophantic level.
It is not known if Peg herself wrote the doggerel lines; the
likelihood is that Sheridan got a hack to compose it.

It will readily be believed [remarks Hitchcock] that such a
select assembly enjoying such entertainment, free of all

expense, and enlightened by the sprightly sallies and jeu d'esprits of so lovely a president, were as happy as any set of mortals on earth could be; each indulged the hilarity of his disposition, and all was wit, repartee, and happy for the theatre, if the public had beheld this assembly in its true light, harmless and void of all design.

Reports of the extravagant luxury of the Beefsteak Club dinners were going the rounds. There were toasts to the English King: the President, an Irishwoman, toasting the hated oppressor! No doubt there was plenty of political talk going on behind the dining-room doors in Mr Sheridan's house. Mocking laughter, too; the servants had passed it on that the laughter in there was something that rose to the sky, so it did. Not for these dark rumours the simple, naïve truth – that the lovely President and Sheridan's guests 'unsuspectingly enjoyed the present moment in all the delights which wit and mirth could inspire'. The actress and her manager, for all their popularity, were beginning to be suspect.

The Lord Lieutenant had already become an object of black dislike. He had introduced a Bill into Parliament for paying a portion of the English national debt out of the Irish revenue. The Bill had been negatived by a small majority of eight, and there was rejoicing in Ireland. Dorset, who had been amiable enough before, was now classed by the Dublin mob as an arch-enemy, and feeling grew against the manager of Smock Alley who went out of his way to entertain the Lord Lieutenant and his gang so lavishly. As for Peg Woffington, the once enthusiastic Dubliners had sour looks for their favourite actress when her carriage rattled along on her way to Dorset Street. She was one of them: she had come from the same back alleys as those in which they still lived. They did not grudge her the success she had earned, but need she go flaunting her more-than-plenty in the faces of those who had little to put in their stomachs? And in the company of the detested English?

17

Disaster

Sheridan opened on 10 October 1753 with *The Beggar's Opera*, several new actresses appearing in the women's parts and West Digges taking Macheath. Digges had come to Dublin with a letter of introduction to Sheridan from Theophilus Cibber. Now about thirty years of age, he came of a family 'connected with the nobility', according to his own account, and had left a life of affluence because 'the stage displayed a thousand charms to his imagination and opened a source of inexhaustible wealth'. An acquaintance with Cibber strengthened this passion, but he knew that if he tried to act in London his family would prevent him, so he crossed to Dublin on Cibber's advice and sought employment with Thomas Sheridan. A good voice, a gentlemanly bearing, and a willingness to accept a low salary secured him a place in the company, and Sheridan was now trying him out.

Peg Woffington did not appear at Smock Alley until later in the season, when she played the Widow Lackit in *Oroonoko*. The hero was taken by Dexter, an Irishman who had been educated at Trinity College, become stage-struck, gone to London, and managed to persuade Garrick in 1751 to give him a trial at Drury Lane. Davies was the prompter there at that period, and he noticed that Dexter, in spite of his eagerness to become a player, was so unconcerned about his début that he was in the pit conversing with his friends until half an hour before the rise of the curtain. This casualness was a measure of his talent, for he seldom rose above mediocrity, 'though he never gave offence', having a tall figure and easy address. He was able to command a wide variety of parts, and was engaged by Sheridan to play in

Dublin for the 1752–3–4 seasons. It was galling for Peg Woffington to have to play with third-rate actors, but she accepted the situation with her usual philosophy, and, also as usual, continued on her own account to give of her best.

One of the plays in rehearsal was a translation of Voltaire's tragedy, *Mahomet ou le Fanatisme*. The play tells of Alcanor, a citizen of Mecca, whose son, Zaphna, and daughter, Palmyra, were stolen in childhood by the false prophet, Mahomet, and steeped in Islamic intolerance. When Zaphna is grown into a youth, Mahomet incites him to kill Alcanor, asserting that he is an infidel. Zaphna stabs Alcanor, and learns as the other dies who he really is. Mahomet poisons Zaphna, and makes love to Palmyra, who rejects him with horror and kills herself. Behind the melodramatic story, Voltaire was able very powerfully to highlight the theme of intolerance, of innocent victims used by evil men for their own ends. There were fiery passages denouncing tyrants and court favourites. Some of Sheridan's friends told him that it would not be wise to produce the play at this particular time, because of the rise of political feeling. The discontent which had been gathering momentum for a considerable time was near reaching boiling point, and the Dublin audiences were notorious for finding political implications when none was intended, with the English king as the villain of the piece. The play had been a success in London, which was the reason Sheridan had included it in the season's programme. He refused to believe that his faithful audiences would be so foolish as to object to what was a 'dramatickally correct piece'. *Mahomet* had been advertised in *The Dublin Journal*, the players had been rehearsing for many days, and he again assured his friends that the audience would not be so foolish as to make a party matter out of a playhouse piece. The rehearsals continued.

Self-assurance and vanity played strange tricks with the usually shrewd manager of the Smock Alley theatre at this critical moment. He was an object of suspicion because of his association with the Castle and the English aristocrats whom he was constantly entertaining. His friends had told him earnestly that he was taking a dangerous risk – the mob would certainly seize upon any excuse to show their resentment and displeasure. Surely he would use ordinary commonsense and refrain from exacerbating them by putting on a play with such an explosive theme?

Again Sheridan refused to listen. *Mahomet* had been planned and
Mahomet should go on.

The first night was 2 February, 1754. Peg Woffington was
playing Palmyra, Sheridan himself took the rôle of her brother,
Zaphna, West Digges was Alcanor, with another leading player
in the company, Sowden, as Mahomet. The play had been well
rehearsed, and in other circumstances everyone concerned would
have been confident of a triumph. Tonight there was a peculiar
atmosphere. The theatre was completely full; the pit and galleries
were packed, and those who could not get standing room remained
outside, unsmiling, waiting. The Duke of Dorset had brought a
party of friends, and the crowd parted silently as the sedan-chairs
were set down, the chairmen opened the doors, and the satin-
clad, bejewelled figures picked their way into the theatre. As
Sheridan was playing, he was not there to bow the Lord Lieutenant to his box. Instead, the theatre servants cleared a way, thrust-
ing aside those who came too close.

The crowds in the pit and galleries were as silent as those
outside; they were under instructions from their leaders, grim-
faced men with averted faces, well practised in the art of creating
disturbances, and fomenting any which were already under way.
In the Green-room the minor players, already changed into their
stage costumes, sat without speaking. Sheridan was in his dressing-
room, putting on Zaphna's robes; he was perfectly calm. Peg
Woffington, dressed as Palmyra, waited at the side of the stage,
out of sight. It seemed strange not to hear the usual sounds from
the other side of the curtain: orange-wenches shouting their wares,
pit and gallery exchanging rough badinage. There was no sound
from the boxes, either; no hum of conversation or trickle of
laughter.

The curtain went up, the performance had begun. Sheridan
made his entrance, looking extraordinarily youthful as Zaphna,
hero of the play. At other times there would have been a roar of
welcome at his first appearance, but now there was only a menac-
ing silence. Sheridan started his first speech, in the energetic,
oratorical style which had always excited his audiences, bringing
wave after wave of applause. Tonight, he ended the speech and

waited, but there was not a single handclap. The manager was genuinely surprised and confused: this had never happened to him before in all his years in the playhouse.

Now Digges came on to the stage, in the character of Alcanor. A ripple moved through the house: Peg felt it. Digges, a competent actor, made the most of his comparatively small part and spoke out. He apostrophized the heavens:

> *If ye powers divine*
> *Ye mark the movements of this nether world*
> *And bring them to account, crush, crush these vipers*
> *Who, singled out by the community*
> *To guard their rights, shall for a grasp of ore*
> *Or paltry office, sell them to the foe!*

There was an immediate uproar in the audience: the mob-leaders had given a signal. Applause broke out with the force of a cataract tumbling over a cliff; there were shouts and whistles, cries of 'Encore!' Digges was astonished – he had never before won even a handclap, let alone a reception like this. At first he could not believe that it was his own insignificant self in an insignificant part which was causing this tumult of approbation, but the pit and gallery left him in no doubt that he was the hero of the evening. They stamped and clapped and again yelled 'Encore!' until he repeated his speech, and then they demanded another encore and yet another. It was a long time before he was allowed to leave the stage and so enable the play to proceed.

Peg Woffington, standing out of sight at the edge of the stage, watched and listened with mounting uneasiness. Unlike Sheridan, she recognized the situation; she knew when an audience was determined to be hostile. By the time her cue came, she had braced herself to go out and face them, and if she felt any trepidation she did not show it. With steady eyes and head held aloof, she acted Palmyra 'with more grace than was ever before shown in it'.

The audience was cold. Hitchcock considered it to be a remarkable circumstance that 'their great favourites, Mr Sheridan and Mrs Woffington, went through their scenes, which are the finest in the play, without the least notice'. Even the Ducal party in the silk-hung stage box kept silent, no doubt thinking it politic to refrain from making a sign of any kind. No sound came

from the audience until Digges reappeared, when there was an
immediate hurricane of clapping and shouts of 'Bravo!' The curtain came down at last, the candles were extinguished, and the
audience dispersed – again in that curious, almost terrifying
silence. There were no meetings in the ante-rooms of the boxes,
where the Quality were wont to remain above half an hour on
other occasions, exchanging views on the play and players. The
Duke of Dorset and his friends visited the Green-room to con-
gratulate Mrs Woffington and Mr Sheridan on their performances
but it was an uneasy scene, and Peg was glad when they took
their leave and she was able to call for a chair and go home to
her house in Capel Street.

Sheridan was angry. He could not – or would not – understand
why the play should have given offence. A few weeks later, he
decided to put it on again, announcing another presentation of
Mahomet for 2 March. His friends were astonished and appalled.
Benjamin Victor, the treasurer at Smock Alley at the time,
found Sheridan's obtuseness 'something mysterious, and what I
could never account for, why he permitted that Play to be acted
a second Time'. A cynic wrote: 'Possibly it was the force of
heredity, since his father [the Reverend Dr Sheridan] had displayed a similar lack of tact by blandly preaching, on the King's
birthday, from the text Sufficient unto the day is the evil thereof.'
Hitchcock says roundly:

> . . . in this fatal instance his usual prudence and good sense
> seemed to have totally deserted him. A manager, as he is the
> steward of the public at large, ought carefully to avoid attach-
> ing himself to any particular interest; but when matters were
> so inflamed that even the most rational persons were preju-
> diced, and could not reason coolly on political subjects, to
> throw such an opportunity in their way seems . . . an unaccount-
> able infatuation.

In fact, Sheridan was in a dilemma. If he permitted encores of
the kind Digges had been surprised into giving, the government
would say he was of the Nationalist party; and as he officially
occupied the position of Deputy Master of the Revels and derived
his theatre patent from the Court, this was out of the question.

On the other hand, if he forbade encores, the Nationalists would at once accuse him of being a government 'creature'.

He would have to come to a decision about the encores, but he was still determined to put on the play in March. Anyone who wanted to see a particular play performed could send their requests to the box-keeper of the theatre, as was the custom in London. Their names would be entered in a memorandum book, and if a sufficient number wanted the play, it would be performed, provided a week's notice was given stating the day of the desired performance. So many people had asked for *Mahomet* to be repeated that Sheridan felt he was obliged to comply with their requests. He consulted a few cronies who usually agreed with all his plans, and they fortified his decision by the opinion that 'they could see no reason why he should lose all the advantage of the time and labour which it cost him to prepare this play'.

As for the matter of encores, Sheridan tried to make the best of both worlds, and left the decision to the actor concerned. On the night before the March performance he called a meeting of the players in the Green-room and read them out a speech which he had written with much care beforehand, and which was later published as a pamphlet, to show the public his reasonable attitude in the affair. He began by saying that the stage was not a proper place for the exhibition of political sentiments, and went on:

> I do not pretend to dictate to you in your private capacities . . . every man has a right to think as he chooses . . . In your theatrical character I have an undoubted right at least to advise you . . . I lay it down as a maxim, that the business of an actor is to divest himself, as much as possible, of his private sentiments and to enter, with all the spirit he is master of, into the character he represents. But if an actor, in order to please the public, should, by any unusual emphasis, gesture or significant look, mark out a passage in his part as a party stroke, he in that instance steps out of his feigned character into his natural one, than which nothing could be more disgusting or insolent to any auditor, who came with no other intent but that of seeing the play; such a performer ought to be looked upon by the public as an incendiary, as one who throws the brand of discord among them . . . the theatre in that case, instead of

being a place of pleasure and entertainment, would become
a scene of riot and disorder. I was in hopes that the example I
had set upon this occasion, would have had so much influence
as to make admonitions unnecessary; for whatever my private
sentiments may have been, I defy any person to charge me
justly, that the least glimpse of them appeared in my conduct,
either as a manager or an actor. It is my business to take all the
precautions and care in my power, that the audience shall enjoy
their entertainment in peace and not by any act of mine, to encourage and foment party feuds.

At this point Digges arose, and said that the manager's remarks
were obviously directed at him. Sheridan admitted that they
were:

'To you, Mr Digges, I must particularly apply, as you were the
first tragedian I ever heard of, who repeated a speech upon the
encore of an audience. I am in hopes that it was the suddenness
of the thing, and want of time to reflect upon the ill consequences
which might attend it.'

Digges then rose again, and asked how he should conduct himself if, on the following evening, the same demand for the encore
of the inflammatory speech should be made.

'Sir, if I should comply with the demand of the audience, and
repeat the speech, am I to incur your censure?'

Sheridan was evasive; he did not want to give a direct answer:

'If it be once established as a rule, that one part of an audience
have a right to encore a speech, upon the same principle, any
other part of that audience may claim the same right. If they have a
right to have it once repeated, why not several times as well as
once? Why not any other speech as well as that one? And why
not as many speeches as they shall think proper?'

Once more Digges asked for a definite compliance or prohibition, but still received no directive from the manager, one way or
the other.

'You have now heard my arguments on that head,' said
Sheridan. 'If you think they are of weight, I suppose you will
act accordingly; if not, remember I do not give you any orders
upon this occasion. You are left entirely free to act as you please.
I leave you to act in that matter as you think proper.'

·   ·   ·

The following evening, crowds gathered in Smock Alley long before the doors of the theatre were opened – as usual when scenes and rioting were expected. Pit and galleries were soon densely packed. The boxes were also full, but the nobility sitting there were quiet and watchful. 'The pit looked capable of dark things, the gallery dangerous; a feeling of excitement and apprehension settled over the whole house; a storm brooded in the atmosphere,' says Molloy. Nor was it long before the storm burst. As before, there was silence when Sheridan made his appearance and declaimed his long speech. Then Digges, as Alcanor, came on to the stage, and there was a tremendous outburst of applause which died down as he spoke the inflammatory lines. As soon as he had finished, shouts of 'Encore! Encore!' broke out from the pit and galleries, together with renewed stamping and clapping.

Digges had been prepared for this, but he seemed to be confounded by the violence of the clamour. He hesitated, stepped forward, and held up his hand for silence. When at last he could be heard, he said 'it would give him the highest pleasure imaginable to comply with the request of the audience, but he had his *private reasons* for begging they would be so good as to excuse him, *as his compliance would be greatly injurious to him,'* as Hitchcock got it from someone who was there.

Did the actor know what he was implying? Contemporary commentators differ about this extraordinary speech. One of them thinks that Digges could not have said anything else: another takes the view that he was so nervous, he hardly knew what he was saying: a third is of the opinion that Digges had a private grudge against Sheridan, and deliberately insinuated that the manager had instructed him to refuse an encore. Whatever his motive, his apologia brought an immediate, ugly reaction. The mob yelled 'Sheridan! Sheridan!' and when he did not come, 'Manager! Manager!' Sheridan had gone behind the scenes, where he remained. He sent the prompter on to the stage to say that the actors were ready to continue with the play, if the audience was willing to listen; those who did not wish to stay could have their money returned and leave the theatre. This curt message enraged the audience still more, and again the cries rang out: 'Sheridan! Manager! Sheridan!'

It has often been remarked, observes Hitchcock, that on the most trying occasions in life, when most we need it, our presence of mind forsakes us.

It might be truly said so of Mr. Sheridan at this critical moment; in all probability, if he had immediately come forward, and obeyed their summons, the uproar would have ceased, and the mischief been avoided. He naturally would have requested to know their pleasure; in answer to which they certainly would have asked, if it was by his orders Mr Digges forbore to gratify their demand. To this, with the greatest truth, he could have replied, no; on the contrary, he knows I left him entirely free *to follow his own inclinations.* Unreasonable as they were . . . yet such a declaration must have silenced them, or turned their vengeance on its proper object, the actor, whose imprudence continued all this disturbance.

Instead of going before the curtain, Sheridan went to his dressing-room. Several of his friends had left their boxes and hurried after him, one of them in particular, Mr Adderley, urging him to return and pacify the audience. Sheridan refused: he was exceedingly angry by now.

'They have no right to call upon me – I'll not obey their call!' he said, and began to take off his stage robes. Adderley offered to go with the manager, to see that he was not insulted; Sheridan replied that he was not in the least afraid of being insulted, but he had no intention of giving in to a rioting mob. Dressing himself in his own clothes, he sent for a sedan-chair, and left the theatre for his house.

The noise in the theatre was now terrifying, presaging violence: the audience had got completely out of hand, yelling for Sheridan every few moments. Peg Woffington, who had been at the side of the stage, waiting for Palmyra's cue, listened to it with fear and anger. The prompter rushed up to her to say that Mr Sheridan had gone. The mob would wreck the theatre! Would Mrs Woffington go before the curtain and speak to them? If they would listen to any of them they would listen to her, their favourite. 'But this was as impolitic a step as could be taken,' says Hitchcock. 'Her known connexions with the Court party precluded all chances of her success . . . here her influence was entirely lost, and beauty, for once, failed in commanding respect and admiration.'

Outwardly calm, and summoning all her powers of charm and friendliness, Peg stepped out on the stage before the curtain, holding out her arms for a hearing. The audience howled at her. Peg Woffington had never before experienced this spitting, biting hostility, and she was appalled. Most of the occupants of the boxes had long since gone; she was facing the real Dublin mob, the shabby, poverty-stricken Irish whose bitter resentments had broken surface. She had always been their darling – and they had turned against her. Their anger was a living thing: a shrill clamour of harsh voices yelling abuse at the President of the Beefsteak Club, the favourite of the Lord Lieutenant – an English duke who lorded it in state in Dublin Castle while the country lived in wretched poverty and near-starvation.

Peg had to retire, humiliated. Digges was now prevailed upon to do something, and it was not until he went before the curtain that the noise died down. He attempted to explain that Mr Sheridan had not *forbidden* him to give an encore of Alcanor's lines; Digges himself had thought it wiser not to hold up the action of the play, and Mr Sheridan was in no way to blame. The audience roughly rejected this belated excuse for the manager. Tumult started again. Sheridan – where was Sheridan? They would have Sheridan. Digges said the manager had gone home. This infuriated the audience still more, and they demanded that he should be fetched. One of the mob-leaders in the pit called out they were willing to wait all night, if need be, but they were determined the manager must appear. Knowing that he lived at a distance, they would give him an hour to come, no more. They were bent on Sheridan's 'submission'.

Digges quitted the stage and sent a messenger to Dorset Square, with an urgent request to return to the theatre. Sheridan refused to stir out again. At Smock Alley, the mob waited the allotted hour, renewed their shouts for Sheridan, and when he did not appear, proceeded methodically to business. Several ladies had remained in the boxes, curious to see what was going to happen; now they were greatly alarmed.

Two of the leaders . . . rose up in the middle of the pit, went over to the boxes, and handed out the ladies with a great deal of politeness; this accomplished, a young gentleman stood up in the middle of the pit, and cried out, 'God bless his Majesty King George, with three huzzas!' At the end of the last huzza they fell to work with such fury, that in less than ten minutes the audience part was entirely demolished.*

Benjamin Victor quickly took the treasury box to a place of safety, and hurried to the Castle to inform the Lord Lieutenant of the danger to the Theatre Royal. The Lord Lieutenant advised him to go to the Lord Mayor. That worthy was ill of the gout, and could not venture forth. Neither the sheriffs nor the city magistrates were at home.

In the theatre, the orgy of destruction went on. The ironic call in the name of King George had been the signal for general action. Cheering wildly, the mob pulled down the curtain and proceeded to smash up the boxes. They pulled down the stage furniture and hacked it into slivers fit only for firewood; they ripped the canvas stage wings apart, pulled out the candle-sconces and waved the lighted candles round their heads with reckless abandon. It was a scene of nightmare terror, and the actors did not wait to see the outcome, they rushed to the back doors of the theatre and left the building as quickly as they could.

Peg Woffington went with them: there was nothing else she could do. She found a sedan-chair, and reached her house in a state of shock and misery. Here indeed was a lesson on the chequered life of a public player; it was the most insecure existence in the world, she thought. Flattered and admired for years – and then the swift change from plaudits to abuse and execration. Peg had no one to whom she could turn for comfort: no husband, no real friend at hand. Lovers? Nobody since David Garrick had ever meant anything to her. Her mother? The good soul never went near a theatre; she spent most of her time in church, or doing good works at the convents. Her sister? Peg was under no illusions about the Honourable Mrs Cholmondeley, who would smile politely and pretend to listen, her thoughts elsewhere. Peg knew that in this black hour she would have to stand alone, as she had always done.

* J. F. Molloy: *Romance of the Irish Stage.*

Smock Alley theatre was almost entirely wrecked, but the damage had been confined to the fittings and furniture, not to the fabric of the building. It was by a miracle that a fire had not been started, not only from the burning candles, but because in a store-room the rioters had dragged a grate of burning coals into the centre of the room and left it to blaze; the flames had been stamped out in time by the box-keeper.

The shell of the Theatre Royal still stood: it could be re-furnished, fitted out again. Sheridan, however, refused to con-tinue in management there; he wanted nothing more to do with Smock Alley and its fickle violent audiences. He would go to London. Benjamin Victor tried to persuade him to change his mind; Victor knew that the Dublin mob, having 'punished' Sheri-dan for the *Mahomet* affair, would consider honour satisfied on both sides, and would be back in hundreds, ready to applaud the next play. Thomas Sheridan was not to be moved; he was deter-mined to give up the Smock Alley theatre, and would 'set foot there no more'. He took leave of the public through the news-papers, in an *Address of Vindication* in which he set out the speech he had made to the actors before the fatal repeat performance of *Mahomet*. He then looked round for a tenant for the theatre.

The obvious person to take it was Benjamin Victor, who went into partnership with Sowden, a leading actor in the company. They were to pay Sheridan five pounds for every acting night, and lend him two thousand pounds as a mortgage on the wardrobe, which was valued at double that sum. Sheridan agreed to repair and refurnish the stage and auditorium, and when the theatre was reopened, in March 1754, the company finished the season with a series of benefits for themselves, to compensate for the nights they had lost. Peg Woffington played in twenty-four out of twenty-six benefits, the first, her own, being a performance of *All for Love*.

On that night, the Duke of Dorset and his Duchess were in the boxes surrounded by their friends, and the rest of the house was full. Hundreds of candles glowed in the new gilded sconces, the scenery was admirably painted, the stage picturesquely dressed. All was as before . . . or was it? The actors were ner-vous. Would the night of *Mahomet* be repeated? Peg Woffington, as tautly strung as the rest, put on a confident air and laughed. The sight of her standing in the Green-room, exquisitely beautiful, her dark eyes twinkling with gaiety, brought back some of their own confidence, and when the sign came from Benjamin Victor in the prompter's box that the curtain was about to rise, they moved bravely towards the stage.

All went well. The pit and galleries applauded as loudly as did the boxes, and Mrs Woffington was called before the curtain again and again. Her earlier anxiety vanished, as she felt her spell over them reassert itself. They could be monsters, but when it came to an attentive, receptive set of people there was nothing like a Dublin audience. The season was almost at an end, but she expected to be back next year. With *Mahomet* forgotten, and Mr Victor in command, there would be fresh triumphs . . .

Peg made arrangements to go to London for the summer, and left Dublin in May 1754, giving up her house in Capel Street and already deciding where she would like to live on her return. She did not know that she would never return to Dublin.

18
London Again

Sowdon, Benjamin Victor's partner, was already in London,
recruiting players for the coming winter season. He was
principally after Spranger Barry, who was experienced and popular enough to take Sheridan's place at Smock Alley. According to
Molloy, 'Mr Barry was fully sensible of his own importance, and
insisted upon eight hundred pounds salary for himself, and five
hundred pounds for Miss Nossiter, a young lady then under his
protection. These were great terms, but necessity obliged the
managers to comply with them.' It was important that there
should be a strong enough company to draw large audiences to
the reconditioned theatre.

Peg Woffington was not asked to return for the winter season.
The Duke of Dorset, on learning of this, wrote expressing surprise
that Mrs Woffington had not been persuaded to continue for
another season at Smock Alley, and Victor gave him the reason:

> When I waited on Mrs Woffington to take my leave at her
> setting out for London, I told her I thought it for her interest
> as well as ours that she should be engaged the next winter
> there. She was greatly disappointed at not receiving proposals
> from me, upon which I told her she would find Sowden in
> London, and if it was her desire to return, whatever terms they
> agreed on should have my hearty concurrence. They met in
> consequence, but as she expected her former salary of £800,
> he very wisely got rid of the subject as quickly as he could. No
> man has a higher sense of her merit than I have, yet that great
> salary cannot be given, even to her, the fourth season, because
> novelty is the very spirit and life of all public entertainment.

Peg Woffington would not cheapen her price: she knew her worth. She took good lodgings in York Buildings, and news quickly spread that Woffington had returned. Peg had come back without a settled engagement in view, but there was now no need to go to the doorkeeper at Rich's house and beg for an interview with the great manager. Soon after her arrival, John Rich waited on Mrs Woffington at York Buildings, and engaged her for the Covent Garden company at the salary she demanded, eight hundred pounds. She was to make her first appearance in the autumn. On inquiring the names of the other players, she found that George Anne Bellamy was still in the company; but Peg Woffington, after three years of success in Dublin, felt well able to compete with that young woman.

The summer passed pleasantly. Peg was not due to appear at Covent Garden until October, so she was free to see her friends and pay visits. Owen M'Swiney was soon in attendance, but he had lost his former robustness, and was often at Bath, where he was trying to recover his failing health. It was Colonel Caesar who was now seen with Peg, and she sometimes went down to Winchester to stay at his country house.

Signor Angelo was once more established in London, with his own academy of fencing. He and Peg occasionally went to the theatre together. One evening they were in a private box at Drury Lane when Peg, struck by the unusual beauty of a girl sitting in a box at the opposite side of the house, pointed her out to Angelo. He took out his quizzing glass – and thereafter could not take his eyes away from the lovely apparition. Laughing, Peg accused him of falling in love at first sight. Angelo spent the rest of the evening gazing at the box opposite, instead of paying attention to the stage. At the end of the performance, Peg encouraged him to be bold and resolute. It was not difficult to find out the identity of the young lady; she was a Miss Masters, the well-dowered daughter of a deceased naval officer. Signor Angelo, obeying due forms, waited on Mrs Masters, and for the next few weeks proceeded to woo the daughter with great ardour. He was, in the end, made happy, and Peg now had two attached friends in place of one.

What she liked best was going down to Teddington; she had reopened her villa, and enjoyed spending the late golden days at the riverside village. She missed Polly. Sometimes she could

THE
FEMALE VOLUNTEER:
OR,
an Attempt to make our Men STAND.

An EPILOGUE *intended to be fpoken by* Mrs. Woffington *in the Habit of a Volunteer,
upon reading the* Gazette *containing an* Account of the late Action at FALKIRK.

Peg Woffington in *The Female Volunteer*.

persuade her sister to come to Teddington for a day or two, but the Honourable Mrs Cholmondeley had many engagements and several children, so it was not easy for her to leave London; she would reel off a list of engagements which she positively could not break. Peg usually took her old friend and dresser Mrs Barrington with her to the villa; their relationship had grown into something solid and enduring, built on tolerance, genuine affection, and an appreciation of each other's essential qualities.

There were a number of parts to study for the forthcoming season, and, as usual, Peg worked conscientiously for many hours a week, no matter what invitations were conveyed to her lodgings. Colonel Caesar was never far away; one source states that he 'resumed his hopeless courtship', and another says categorically that he proposed marriage. It is doubtful if Peg would have tied herself to anyone now. She was thirty-six years old, comparatively rich, and, as she herself recognized, of a roving temperament. David Garrick was the only man she had ever really wanted to marry. She liked Caesar, accepted his escort when she wished to attend a soirée, and unashamedly made use of him when it suited her. Caesar was delighted. He was sufficiently a man of his world to know that he could never possess Woffington for good, whether she took his name or not. All he could do was to serve her and be her friend.

There was a full house on 21 October 1754 for Mrs Margaret Woffington's return to the London stage as Maria in *The Nonjuror*, and the ovation which greeted her on her first appearance lasted many minutes. This was the moment Peg had dreaded, and the loud applause was reassurance that her fame stood as high as ever. Peg knew a great lifting of the spirits, an exultation which was to carry her through the weeks of strenuous work which lay before her. This was her life: her world. She had sometimes felt bitterness at what she secretly considered to be her failure to achieve the happiness which she had seen, again and again, come to the plainest woman: a husband and children. Yet she did not hide the fact from herself – and from understanding friends like Macklin – that her own strong ambitions and temptations had led her along the paths of pleasure and not of happiness. She could not change now. Applause, adulation, freedom to indulge her own desires if she so wished: these had become woven into her way of life, and she would grasp, and enjoy, what success came her way.

Success? It was clear, after a few weeks in the theatre, that she would have to fight hard to keep her place in the capricious world where she had worked for most of her life. Spranger Barry had returned from Ireland to Covent Garden, bringing with him Miss Nossiter, his mistress; they were both friendly in the Green-room, and Miss Nossiter, who did not compete over parts with Mrs Woffington, paid her great respect. George Anne Bellamy showed the older actress neither respect, liking nor civility: she did all in her power to upset Peg Woffington. On 13 November Peg 'ravished the town' in her old part of Silvia, but a few weeks later, on 15 January 1756, it was the Bellamy's turn. Rich put on Lee's tragedy, *Alexander*, with Woffington and Bellamy as the rival queens. George Anne had commissioned her hairdresser's French wife, who was visiting Paris, to bring her back two dresses for tragedy, the finest she could purchase. One of these was a gown of deep yellow, in which 'taste and elegance were never so happily blended', and to this George Anne added a purple cloak. Rich had bought a handsome gown from the Dowager Princess of Wales for Peg Woffington, a straw-coloured satin which looked beautiful by daylight but which became dirty white by candle-light, especially against Bellamy's yellow and purple.

'Thus accoutred in all my magnificence,' complacently relates George Anne in her memoirs, 'I made my entrée into the Green-room as the Persian Princess. But how shall I describe the feelings of my inveterate rival! The sight of my pompous attire created more real envy in the heart of the actress, than it was possible the real Roxana could feel for the loss of the Macedonian hero.'

According to George Anne, Peg Woffington, almost bursting with rage, drew herself up and said with a haughty air:

'I desire, Madam, you will never more, on my account, wear those clothes in the piece we perform tonight.'

To which Bellamy replied:

'I know not, Madam, by what right you take upon you to dictate to me what I shall wear. And I assure you, Madam, you must ask it in a very different manner, before you obtained my compliance.'

Samuel Foote.
(Harvard Theatre Collection.)

Caricature: a Green-room squabble.
(Yale University Library.)

Caricature: *Miss in her teens*. Peg Woffington is the central figure.
(Harvard Theatre Collection.)

Peg repeated her request 'in a softer strain', and the Bellamy agreed to wear a costume that would accord more harmoniously with the ex-royal straw-coloured satin. The next night, she sported the second dress from Paris. This was even more splendid than the first, and Mrs Woffington's rage was re-kindled, and 'Oh! dire to tell! she drove me off the carpet, and gave me the *coup de grâce* almost behind the scenes.'

Though George Anne despised revenge, she did not dislike retaliation. She donned the yellow gown and purple cloak once more, put on her best jewels, and returned to the Green-room. In spite of the fact that one of the *corps diplomatique* was there, waiting to pay homage to Miss Bellamy's beauty, Mrs Woffington's fury could not be kept within bounds. She imperiously demanded how dared Miss Bellamy dress again in the manner she had so strictly prohibited? Miss Bellamy smiled contemptuously, and turned to a newly arrived admirer of her own, a French plenipotentiary.

Peg now really lost her temper. With a look full of meaning, she said that it was as well Miss Bellamy had a *Minister* to supply her extravagance with gowns and jewels and such paraphernalia. George Anne retorted that *even half the town* could not furnish Mrs Woffington with presents equal to those given by the Minister she had so illiberally hinted at – and made as quick an exit as possible, recollecting the well-known distich: 'He who fights and runs away, may live to fight another day.'

The Minister in question stood and laughed, and then His Excellency acted quickly, for the enraged Peg was off in hot pursuit; if he had not interposed his person and covered George Anne's retreat, she would have stood a chance of appearing in the next scene of the play with a pair of black eyes, instead of the blue eyes which nature had given her.

Mr Samuel Foote naturally profited by this little scene, and produced a piece which he called *The Green-room Squabble, or, a Battle Royal between the Queen of Babylon and the Daughter of Darius*, distributing his satire between both actresses.

An unexpected irritation to Peg at this time was Tate Wilkinson, a brash, stage-struck youth with a talent for mimicry. He was the son of a clergyman, his father dying when he was seventeen. Not bred to any profession or business, young Wilkinson determined to go on the stage, and was taken on as an apprentice

H

pupil by John Rich. Wilkinson's chief amusement was mimicking his betters. Giving impersonations of famous players always raised ill-natured laughter: 'The actors and actresses naturally do not approve of the practice, nor admire the talents of such an exhibitor,' Wilkinson naïvely wrote. He was not the first 'exhibitor' of the art. David Garrick had taken off leading actors in his early days, as Wilkinson was quick to point out:

> The peculiarities of Mr Delane, an actor of the first rank, were so severely pointed out by Mr Garrick, in the character of Bayes, that it is said to have actually occasioned Mr Delane's flying to the bottle for relief to his hurt mind; he continued to use it to such excess that he never was himself again . . . Mr Garrick, at the solicitation of his friends and remonstrances of the actors – without whose assistance he could not live, for what avails a general without an army – and from full conviction his own merit required not such aid as mimickry, as it was merely a trifling feather in his cap of fame: he for once in his life did a generous action, and gave up what he no longer wanted.

Tate Wilkinson might disapprove of the great Garrick stooping to the ignoble art of mimicry, but he was an adept at it himself. One day a family friend, Captain Forbes, came to London and invited the young man to dine with him at the Bedford Arms. After a good dinner, when they were both 'jolly with the bottle', Forbes suggested going on to Covent Garden, where Peg Woffington was playing Clarissa in *The Confederacy*. They had the stage-box, which made Tate Wilkinson uneasy; he was used to being a hanger-on behind the scenes at this theatre, and did not wish to be conspicuous. He knew he had made enemies backstage by his tricks, and his fears were soon justified.

A messenger arrived from Mr Rich, asking what he was doing in His Majesty's box? Captain Forbes, warm with wine, sent the messenger back with a truculent reply, stating that Mr Wilkinson was his guest. The rest of the evening was a nightmare to Tate Wilkinson. He had often had the Green-room in a roar with his malicious mimicry of Peg Woffington's manner, and when she came on the stage and glanced up at him, he knew that she had been told of his tricks. Long years afterwards, when he himself

was a theatre manager, he could still feel the embarrassment at
what followed Peg Woffington's entrance:

'She came close to the stage box, finishing her speech with such
a sarcastic sneer at me, as actually made me draw back.'

Then a woman of the town, seated in a balcony above the
box, repeated some of the actress's words in a shrill tone, and the
whole house laughed. Wilkinson relates:

> Like electricity it caught Mrs Woffington's ear, whose voice
> was far from being enchanting. On perceiving the pip-squeak
> on her right hand, and being conscious of the insult she had
> then given apparently to me, it struck her comprehension so
> forcibly, that she immediately concluded I had given the retort
> upon her in that open and audacious manner, to render her
> acting and tone ridiculous to the audience, as returning con-
> tempt for her devilish sneer. She again turned and darted her
> lovely eyes, tho' assisted by the furies, which made me look
> confounded and sheepish.

The following day, when Tate Wilkinson attended John Rich,
he was kept waiting a considerable time in the ante-room. Peg
presently passed through, and without a word, curtsy or bow of
the head proceeded towards her sedan-chair. Then she stopped,
turned and said contemptuously:

> Mr Wilkinson, I have made a visit this morning to Mr Rich,
> to command and to insist on his not giving you any engagement
> whatever – no, not of the most menial kind in the theatre.
> Merit you have none – charity you deserve not – for if you did,
> my purse should give you a dinner. Your impudence to me last
> night, where you had with such assurance placed yourself,
> is one proof of your ignorance. Added to that, I heard you
> echo my voice when I was acting, and I sincerely hope in
> whatever barn you are suffered as an unworthy stroller that
> you will fully experience the same contempt you dared last
> night to offer me.

Mortified and bewildered, Tate Wilkinson watched her go. It
seems not to have occurred to him to go after her and beg her to
listen to the real train of events. Perhaps he was too conscious of
his own indiscretion, rousing laughter at the expense of the 'queen
of the hive'. He was sufficiently punished for it. Rich cast him

off, and though Wilkinson was allowed to go behind the scenes, he was given no walking on parts that season.

The young man now realized the theatre was not the earthly paradise he had formed in his imagination, 'for the mist was removed, and I saw actors, actresses and myself in a different mirror, which convinced me what we all really were'. Even the goddesses of the stage had normal human weaknesses, and were swayed by anger, and occasional petty passions of revenge when their pride was touched. It says much for the young Tate Wilkinson that Peg's treatment of him did not affect the very high esteem in which he held her and his appreciation of her best qualities. He pays her a wholehearted tribute in his *Memoirs*:

> Peg Woffington possessed wit and vivacity, but never permitted her love of pleasure and conviviality to occasion the least defect in her duty to the public as a performer. Six nights in the week had been often her appointed lot for playing without murmuring: she was ever ready at the call of an audience; and though in possession of all the first line of characters, yet she never thought it improper or a degradation of her consequence, to constantly play the Queen in *Hamlet*, Lady Anne in *Richard III*, and Lady Percy in *Henry IV*. Parts which are mentioned as insults in the country [theatres] if offered to a lady [actress] of consequence.

Peg Woffington had enjoyed excellent health for most of her life, but she now began to experience bouts of illness; it is clear that she had an internal malady which the physicians had no power to cure. She was approaching forty, and still had the energy and zest which were so characteristic of her. By 1757, however, there was a perceptible change. She disposed of the Teddington villa and rented a house in Queen's Square, where the devoted Mrs Barrington could look after her when she was unable to appear at the theatre. Also, she had a great longing to be nearer Polly, who came to see her and brought her growing family from time to time. Hannah Woffington still lived in Dublin, contentedly growing older and more devout: she belonged to the shadowy past.

Colonel Caesar was Peg's constant companion. Owen M'Swiney
had died over a year since, and Peg had inherited the legacy he
had promised her. Darnley was no more; Hanbury Williams
had long ago left England. David Garrick had been married
some years, and he, too, was receding in some curious way, a
memory among memories. Peg was thankful for present kindness, and Colonel Caesar was more than kind. As her malady
grew worse, he carried her down to his house at Winchester,
where she usually recovered from lethargy and pain; her gaiety
she never lost.

Charles Dibdin, the song-writer, met Peg Woffington early in
that year. His father, a silversmith at Southampton, knew
Colonel Caesar, and both Dibdins were invited to dine one evening at the Colonel's house. Charles Dibdin remembered the
occasion well: 'Mrs Woffington lived with Colonel Caesar, who
was very fond of her, and it was his great pleasure that she should
invite celebrated men to the house.' The celebrated men on that
occasion were Quin and Handel . . . 'I remember the evening was
a very merry one.' So Peg Woffington and James Quin must have
buried old scores.

The end of her career came a few weeks later, and is described by Tate Wilkinson, who was there. Wilkinson, after a
lean period, had managed to get the part of First Gentleman in
Alexander, put on for a benefit night at Covent Garden. He had
borrowed an old black velvet suit of Garrick's, decorated with
broad gold flowers 'as dingy as the letters on a piece of gilded
gingerbread', to which he had added an old red surtout trimmed
with dirty white fur, a cape of the same hue, and an old flock
muff. The audience hooted and howled at this figure of fun, and
the young man realized he had not been a success.

On Monday, 17 May 1757, Peg acted Rosalind to Mrs Vincent's* Celia at Covent Garden, for a triple benefit. Peg had been
ill that day and should not have undertaken to play, but Rosalind was one of her favourite parts, and she hated having to refuse
a benefit, knowing how much the actors depended on it. Tate
Wilkinson was standing at the side of the stage, just out of the
way, when Peg Woffington passed him to make her first entrance.
She stopped, and ironically congratulated him on his recent
stage success, remarking that such merit would no doubt ensure

* A leading actress at Covent Garden.

him an engagement the following winter. Tate Wilkinson bowed but made no reply; he knew her dislike of him, and was sufficiently humiliated.

He stood watching the performance for four acts, and did not notice that Rosalind was in the least distressed. In the fifth act, as Peg came off the stage, she said aloud that she felt greatly indisposed. Wilkinson offered his arm, and Peg let him support her as far as her dressing-room. She changed from Orlando's costume back to the dress for Rosalind, and as she walked back to the stage she again complained of feeling ill. She finished the act, and began the Epilogue, getting as far as 'If it be true that good wine needs no bush, it is as true that a good play needs no epilogue', but when she came to 'If I were among you I would kiss as many of you as had beards that pleased me', her voice broke, she faltered, endeavoured to continue, but could get no further.

'Then in a voice of tremor she screamed O God! O God! tottered to the stage door speechless, where she was caught.'

She never acted again.

Epilogue

Peg Woffington was 'given over' for several days after her collapse on the stage, but she rallied, and very slowly returned to an existence which was now sadly a shadow of her former life. She kept to her bed for some weeks, but could presently sit out in the parlour from time to time, and was able to attend to the business of making her Will and disposing of various properties she had bought with her savings.

Colonel Caesar looked after her devotedly, leaving his house at Winchester for months at a time in order to be with Peg. The Honourable Mrs Cholmondeley was also a frequent visitor. One cannot guess at the workings of her mind: it is possible that the long-buried family feeling, so strong in the Irish race, struggled to the surface and showed itself in affection and gentleness towards the sister who had given her such a wonderful chance in life. When Peg felt well enough, Polly brought her children, and this must have given the dying woman real happiness.

For Peg was dying, slowly wasting away, helpless as her malady gained on the now frail body. Her courage remained high, and there were occasions when the old spirit flamed. Tate Wilkinson and Samuel Foote had been engaged to appear at a new theatre in Crowe Street, Dublin, which Spranger Barry had built. Tate Wilkinson, still doing impersonations, intended to include one of the famous Peg Woffington. When Peg heard of this, she cried: 'Take me off? A puppy! If he dare attempt it, by the living God, he will be stoned to death!' In fact, Dublin laughed. Tate Wilkinson was a very good mimic, and his impersonation was near enough the mark to earn loud applause. The Dublin public was ready to laugh at wit and a touch of malice did not hurt.

When Wilkinson later came to London and announced he intended to repeat the performance at Drury Lane, where Garrick had engaged him, it is said that Colonel Caesar called upon the manager and informed him that he, Caesar, as Mrs Woffington's protector, would hold Mr Garrick responsible if any such insult were offered the lady. Garrick at once agreed to have the Woffington item in Wilkinson's repertoire suppressed.

Peg had made an arrangement with Colonel Caesar that whoever survived the other 'should have all'. Polly, however, persuaded her sister to make a Will secretly, leaving everything to her and her children, and cutting out Caesar entirely. Various stories flew about of Caesar and Mrs Cholmondeley watching each other's movements as Peg Woffington grew worse, each keeping close to Queen's Square. It was a macabre business, and, in the event, Polly won.

Peg Woffington died on 26 March 1760 and was buried in the parish church at Teddington. On her tombstone she is described as '*Spinster, born October 18th, 1720*', but as no record of her birth exists, this date is probably wrong; she was undoubtedly over forty when she died. An infant son of Polly's was later buried in the same grave.

The actress left over £8,000 and some property; apart from an annuity for her mother, and several legacies to servants and a few others, everything else went to Mrs Cholmondeley, including a quantity of fine jewellery. Polly also claimed Peg's stage jewellery. This was a considerable blow to Mrs Barrington, Peg's close friend for many years; Peg had promised the stage jewels to her. They were set in silver, and were very handsome, but the stones were sham, hardly suited to a lady of fashion. Polly insisted on taking them, nevertheless. It is pleasant to record that Mrs Barrington managed to keep back a quantity of Peg's stage wardrobe, including 'a long blue velvet train' which she had always admired, and which Peg had also promised her.

In the Theatre Museum at Leighton House in London one of the exhibits is a pair of buckles, set with brilliants, which belonged to David Garrick. Peg's? It is known that he wore her gift all through his stage career. One looks at them, and wonders.

Then there are the many portraits in collections and elsewhere: Hogarth, Pond and other artists painted her at various periods. Some are set and stiff, indistinguishable from the usual eighteenth-century portraits of actresses. Others make one look twice. Perhaps Pond has best caught an impression of her vitality, of her sheer joy of living. Peg Woffington was no major historical figure, but she enchanted the playhouse of her time, and some of the gaiety lingers on in the sound of her name.

The only known example
of Peg Woffington's holograph

Author's Note

Sources

When one is dealing with eighteenth-century theatrical history, exact truth is hard to find. Some of the accounts of the playhouse of the period are incomplete, misdated, distorted, embellished, or just plain invented. Even the actual records can be misdated; John Genest, a reliable early nineteenth-century stage historian, comments in *Some Account of the London Stage* on gross inaccuracies in eighteenth-century playbills. Disentangling threads, matching up accounts written by contemporaries, allowing for prejudices, comparing dates, studying playbills: these have filled many a fascinated hour. And at the end of it all, does one get a true picture?

The sources which bring you closest to the living, breathing Peg Woffington are accounts given by people who actually knew her and in many cases worked with her. She talked freely to Charles M'Laughlan, the Irish actor who took the stage name of Macklin, and was at first a friend, and then an enemy of Garrick, as has been related in Chapter 9. Robert Hitchcock, prompter at the Theatre Royal in Dublin, wrote of her from first-hand observation, as did Benjamin Victor, who was at one time treasurer at Drury Lane, and to Thomas Sheridan in Dublin. Tate Wilkinson, actor, mimic, and later manager of provincial theatres, was much younger than Peg but old enough to have come up against her many times; he has left unforgettable impressions of Woffington and her world in his *Memoirs*, and, on the whole, he seems to be fair. (See the bibliography at the end of this volume for books by the above writers.)

Sources can be consulted at the British Museum, the Enthoven Collection at the Victoria and Albert Museum, London, the National Library in Dublin, and in the great theatrical collections in America, including those in the university libraries at Harvard and Yale; and at the Library and Museum of the Performing Arts (The New York Public Library, Lincoln Center, New York).

Eighteenth-Century Theatrical Climate

The conditions of working in the playhouse at this period strike one as appalling. There was no such thing as a free stage; players were deemed, by law, to be rogues and vagabonds, and were treated accordingly, when it suited the Establishment or the powerful gentry to take action against managers or actors who had offended them or interfered with their interests.

Censorship of plays and the monopoly of the royal patent playhouses were a strangulating inheritance from the previous century. It says much for the devotion of the actor to his craft – often an obsessive devotion – that the theatre as such had survived. There had been companies of players and musicians attached to royal and noble houses since medieval times. Serious professional actors 'got money and lived in reputation', and seldom lacked employment in the seventeenth century, a dozen theatres being in existence in London alone. Then came the Commonwealth, with its glum Puritan spirit, and the players disappeared; many of them became soldiers in the Royalist cause and were killed.

With the Restoration, 'unbridled gaiety broke loose again'. Charles the Second encouraged the re-establishment of the theatres, and seven companies were soon giving performances at inns with suitable yards, and at newly-built playhouses in Dorset Gardens and Lincoln's Inn Fields. This burst of theatrical activity was not without its drawbacks, for the King was told by Henry Killigrew, one of his favourites, that

> certain persons in and about our City of London, or the suburbs thereof, doe frequently assemble for the performing and acting of playes and enterludes for rewards, to which divers of our subjects doe for their entertainment resort: which said playes ... doe containe much matter of profanation and scurrility ... and for the most part tende to the debauchinge of the manners of suche as are present at them, and are very scandalous and offensive to all pious and well disposed persons.

In other words, the stage was being used by low players who managed to get a good deal of political satire into their free-spoken pieces. Sir William Davenant, another courtier, was equally indignant, on the King's account, at the licence taken by these mummers and mountebanks, and suggested that it was time there was some control over them. In August 1660 Charles the Second granted two patents, one to Sir William Davenant and the other to Henry Killigrew, 'and their several heirs and assigns for ever', for the forming of two companies of players: the King's Servants, who were to act at the Theatre Royal in Drury Lane under the direction of Davenant, and the Duke's

Company, who were to be at the Duke's Theatre in Dorset Garden under Killigrew.

After the interdiction of the playhouses during the Commonwealth, these two licensed companies were sure of enthusiastic support from the public, for they were under royal and aristocratic patronage. Another advantage was the novelty of having actresses on the stage for the first time. Before the Restoration, no woman had ever been seen upon the English stage; female characters had been performed by boys or by 'young Men of the most Feminine Aspect'. The appearance of real, beautiful women naturally drew new admirers into the theatre, especially as Colley Cibber says, 'These Actresses were not ill-chosen, when it was well known that more than one of them had Charms sufficient at their leisure Hours to calm and mollify the Cares of Empire.'

There was an unwritten rule that no play acted at one theatre should be attempted at the other; the best plays of Shakespeare, Fletcher and Ben Jonson were divided between them. The two companies prospered for some years, until the variety of plays became exhausted. The public then began to patronize Drury Lane more than Dorset Garden, because the actors were better at the former theatre. Killigrew re-taliated by adding spectacle and music to action by introducing 'a new Species of Plays, since called Dramatick Operas . . . all set off with the most expensive Decorations of Scenes and Habits, with the best Voices and Dancers'. The novelty soon palled, and the arrival of a new puppet show at Salisbury Change in 1684 proved a disastrous counter-attraction to both patent theatres.

Davenant and Killigrew joined forces and asked the King to shut down the puppet show. Charles the Second saw no objection to exercising this piece of favouritism, and ordered the puppet-master to close his booth. He then suggested to the two patentees that they should unite their interests and form one company of players. The patentees agreed at once. The cards were now all in their hands: they held a valuable monopoly. They decided to divide the profits from the productions into twenty shares, ten going to themselves and the rest being divided among the actors 'in such sub-divisions as their different Merit might pretend to'. The two astute men thereafter set out to make more money for themselves by selling their own shares to speculators, who demanded, in return, votes in the management of the company. It was not a happy arrangement.

The patentees made the most of their monopoly for the next five years. Charles the Second died, his brother James reigned for three uneasy years and then fled to France. King William and Queen Mary sat on the throne of England – and the new monarchs were known to be patrons of the drama. Some of the leading players in the combined patent theatres, led by Thomas Betterton, decided to break away. They had no theatre to act in, but they had a friend at Court, no less a personage than the Lord Chamberlain, who obtained for them an audience of King William. Betterton laid their grievances before the King, and the result was a triumph for the seceding players; they were given a licence to act in a separate theatre. The patents granted to Davenant and Killigrew no longer constituted a monopoly. Betterton and his friends jubilantly raised a subscription, and soon had enough money to build a theatre inside the walls of a tennis court in Lincoln's Inn Fields.

Opening with *Love for Love*, a new comedy by one of their strongest supporters, William Congreve, they were successful from the beginning of their venture, and the Theatre Royal in Drury Lane suffered diminished audiences accordingly.

'As it has always been judged their natural interest, where there are two Theatres, to do one another as much Mischief as they can' was a contemporary sentiment followed by action. When *Hamlet*, always certain to fill a theatre, was announced for Lincoln's Inn Fields, the Theatre Royal announced *Hamlet* for the same evening, so as to divide the audience. (In fact, the Drury Lane management thought better of it – how the town would laugh! – and substituted *The Old Batchelor*.) The main rivalry now was to get plays by new authors. The Theatre Royal scooped with Sir John Vanburgh's *The Relapse*, though the Lincoln's Inn Fields playhouse was able to give the first performance of Vanburgh's *The Provok'd Wife,* an earlier play not yet seen on a stage. Betterton and his company would have done very well had not trouble broken out among themselves. The players who excelled in comedy attempted to assert their superiority because they considered they 'came nearer to nature', while the actors who shone in tragedy objected to what they considered to be unnecessary expense lavished on comedy productions. When players were not being exploited by greedy patentees, they became the victims of their own temperaments.

At this time plays had become so licentious that Jeremy Collier, a clergyman, wrote a pamphlet making violent attacks on the stage. King William, who, though fond of the drama, 'entirely coincided with his [Collier's] principles', and was so disapproving that 'indecency ceased to be considered as wit', and, of course, became less fashionable. The Master of the Revels, who licensed all plays for the stage, came forward in support of Collier. He was not at all concerned with morals, but the Court had long been irritated by political satires in plays which poked holes in their own dignity and that of the Establishment. The Master of the Revels took the opportunity of Collier's attacks to begin a cleaning-up operation. He was very thorough, and 'assisted this reformation with a severity, injustice and ignorance equally disgusting, vexatious and ridiculous'. One sentence in a script would sometimes damn a whole scene, and this would have to be excised, to the ruin of the play.

Secession

Disgruntled actors had one weapon which they used when conditions in a company became too intolerable: they seceded to another company, if they got the chance. William Rufus Chetwood strongly disapproved of malcontents, and reproved them in a passage in his *General History of the Stage:*

> O Happy Manager! whose Servants never Disoblige, or Contradict his Will! no clamouring for Parts, or Pay! no Envy reigns among them! no Sycophants to corrupt his Ears with Falsehoods, or cringing Flatterers to tickle his Vices, or swell his Pride and Vanity. But all obey him without Self-Interest, or ever trouble themselves whether they are naked or cloath'd; or ever repine at the Success of each others Performance.

After twenty years as prompter at Drury Lane, Chetwood should have known that his picture of a playhouse run by a benevolent deity and served by saints was an ideal which must have raised many a laugh in his readers, players and public alike. He was – or thought he was – describing the cosy family atmosphere of Punche's Theatre in Capel Street, Dublin, which had, he said, 'been built and occupy'd by these decent and well behaved Performers several Years'. Understandably, the Capel Street house did not last much longer; a successful theatre in the eighteenth century could not be run by altruists and philanthropists. Managers exploited a player's passion for acting by paying him as little as possible: the player was determined to remain in the world of the theatre and try to wring some kind of livelihood from it. Secession to another management was the only threat he could hold over the exploiter.

It needed a great deal of courage to secede, for players might forfeit all arrears of pay due to them. The provident patentees had long found a way of keeping their actors by withholding salaries when houses were thin, and entering the amounts due in a debts book; this made them at least nominally responsible for arrears. Colley Cibber, in the early days of his professional career, was one of many who never received a day's pay in six acting weeks together, and at one period seldom got more than half his agreed salary.

The patentees, however, had an even stronger weapon to point at the head of seceders – the Act which declared players to be vagabonds. In 1733, a number of actors from the patent theatres seceded to the Little House in the Haymarket, and the patentees promptly decided to go to court and invoke this Act. They got more than they bargained for.

One of the chief performers in the breakaway company was Harper, 'a lusty fat man with a countenance expressive of much mirth, and a strong musical voice well adapted to many parts in operas and farces'. He was a rival to James Quin for the part of Falstaff, and altogether a well-known and popular actor. Highmore, one of the patentees of Drury Lane, elected to make an example of this seceding player, and had him arrested on the stage of the Little Theatre in the Haymarket on a Justice of the Peace warrant. Harper accompanied the officer without any fuss, and was committed to prison as a rogue and a vagabond. He said nothing until he came up for trial at the King's Bench. The court was crowded with players as well as with the general public, and the counsel for the patentees made out a righteous case on the desirability of apprehending and incarcerating vagabonds.

The actor had not engaged counsel. With a fine sense of timing, he stated his defence. Without doubt he was a stage player, he said, and so might conceivably come within the Act on that count. But he was also a House-keeper – a householder – and was accordingly entitled to a parliamentary vote. How could he be a vagabond if he was an accredited voter, owning a 'decent house' in which he resided?

The presiding judge had some caustic remarks to make about the patentees of Drury Lane, before acquitting a gentleman of Mr Harper's standing of the ridiculous charge on which he had been apprehended. Mr Highmore had obviously chosen the wrong actor to 'make an example of', and his Lordship advised him and any other theatrical patentee to be more careful in future, before wasting the time of the court. Harper left the building amid the loud congratulations of the crowd, and on the following day the prints were full of the discomfiture of Highmore and his fellow-patentees.

Riots

Riots in the playhouse were always a hazard, and could flare up at any time. The audience went to the theatre determined to get their money's worth, and if they felt they were not getting full value, they had no hesitation in causing a tumult, or, in extreme cases, of smashing up the furniture and fittings – Sheridan's experience, related in Chapter 17, shows how far they were prepared to go. They sometimes came to the theatre on purpose to cause a riot. Davies, Garrick's biographer, says:

A Riot in a playhouse is very different from a tumult in the street; the latter is a sudden fray arising from ignorance or mistake, generally soon mended, and often without any mischief done to anybody;

whereas the former is almost always the result of a conspiracy, proceeding from private resentment, and in its consequences pernicious to the object against whom it is levelled.

Even such a popular actor as Garrick was not immune from violence in the playhouse. He had made an enemy of a critic called Fitzpatrick, who had been friendly to him at first, but who took offence at something the actor had said or done. Under the pseudonym X.Y.Z., Fitzpatrick proceeded to abuse Garrick in a print called *The Craftsman*, and published further spiteful outpourings in a shilling pamphlet entitled: *An Inquiry into the real merit of a certain popular Performer, in a series of Letters, with an Introduction, to David Garrick, Esq.* The actor replied with *The Fribbleriad*, a poem which held up a Mr Fizzgigg to ridicule. Fitzpatrick, furious, retaliated in the one way he knew would cause the most mischief: he planned a riot at Drury Lane.

He circulated a printed advertisement throughout the taverns and coffee-houses in the neighbourhood of Drury Lane, whipping up indignation against the managers of the two patent theatres for presuming to charge full prices for the performance of a revived play; the custom was to allow admission for half-price after the interval, except in the case of new plays, which required fresh scenery and therefore put the management to extra expense. Fitzpatrick and some of his friends took boxes at the theatre, and waited until Garrick had come on to the stage; he then got up and began to harangue the audience from his box on the 'imposition' of unwarranted full prices. When Garrick, also addressing the audience, tried to explain that the expenses of the theatre had gone up nearly threefold, Fitzpatrick and his confederates shouted the actor down, and soon there was the familiar uproar and vandalism – the breaking of lustres, the tearing up of seats and benches. If one of the actors, Moody, had not prevented one of the rioters from setting fire to the broken seats, the theatre itself would have gone up in smoke. The play had to be stopped, and the audience given their money back.

The next night, a new tragedy, *Elvira*, was put on, and the rioters, headed by Fitzpatrick, again turned up in force. They cried out: 'Will you, or will you not, give admittance for half-price, after the third act of the play, except during the first winter a pantomime is performed?' Garrick had lost a considerable sum the previous evening, and he thought it wise to agree. Fitzpatrick was still not satisfied. He demanded that the actor Moody should go down on his knees and ask their pardon for daring to stop one of their numbers from 'showing his righteous indignation the previous evening'. Moody said: 'I will not, by God!' and strode off the stage.

Garrick, to appease Fitzpatrick, had to promise that Moody should not appear again while he was under the displeasure of the audience. This was serious for the courageous actor, and he determined to go and see Fitzpatrick, who had chambers in the Temple. A contemporary account is given of the interview:

Moody: I suppose, Sir, you know me.

Fitzpatrick: Very well, Sir, and how came I by the honour of this visit?

Moody: How dare you ask me that question, when you know what passed at Drury Lane last night, where I was called upon by you to dishonour myself, by asking pardon of the audience on my knees?

Fitzpatrick: No, Sir, I was not the person who spoke to you.

Moody: Sir, you did: I saw you and heard you. And what crime had I committed, to be obliged to stoop to such an ignominious submission? I had prevented a wretch from setting fire to the playhouse, and had espoused the cause of a gentleman in whose service I had enlisted.

Fitzpatrick: I do not understand being treated in this manner in my own house.

Moody: I will attend you wherever you please; for be assured, I will not leave you till you have satisfied me one way or the other.

Moody then demanded that Fitzpatrick should sign a declaration stating that he, Fitzpatrick, had behaved in a most unjust and improper manner, and to request his friends to withdraw the prohibition against Moody appearing at Drury Lane. Fitzpatrick refused to sign any such document, but agreed to meet Moody at the Jamaica coffee-house the following day. An intermediary was able to make peace between the two, and Moody was allowed to return to the Drury Lane stage.

Fitzpatrick, having tasted the honey of power, was by no means a reformed character. He proceeded to keep himself in the public eye as 'a reformer of theatre prices' by taking his gang to Covent Garden and demanding that the manager should submit to the same regulations as Garrick at Drury Lane. The manager refused, pointing out that 'the nightly expenses were prodigiously increased since the days of former managers, and the public ought not to grudge the full charge, when no expense in actors, cloaths, scenes, music, and every decoration of the stage, had been spared, for their entertainment.'

The audience would not listen; they gave the manager one more chance to agree to their demands, and when he again refused, proceeded to wreck the house; it took the theatre carpenters four days to repair the damage. The manager, who had known what would happen, was also prepared to fight. He caused Fitzpatrick, and several other of the rioters whom he knew by name, to be brought before Lord Mansfield on a Chief Justice's warrant. His Lordship solemnly warned Fitzpatrick that if a life was lost in any riot instigated by him, his own would be answerable for it. Fitzpatrick changed his tactics. After the playhouse was repaired and reopened, he and his friends attended every night, laughing and singing and interrupting the play incessantly, so that in the end the manager had to comply with their demands, and the half-price practice was restored.

Life Behind the Scenes

Players had no inhibitions about bringing their private spites and grievances on to the stage, and lashing out in public if they got the chance. Audiences enjoyed scenes outside the play, and immediately took sides. A temperamental actress, Mrs Montague, a contemporary of Peg Woffington's, found this out one evening when she had decided to be more difficult than usual – it being one of her tenets that audiences took more notice of wilful actresses than of the 'everydays'. She had been given the part of the Queen in *Henry the Second* for the benefit performance of a fellow-player, Mrs Hudson. Mrs Montague liked neither Mrs Hudson nor the part allotted to herself. She sulked, and refused to learn her lines. Just before the play began, it was announced that Mrs Montague was indisposed and therefore prevented from studying the part of Queen Eleanor, and she begged to be allowed to read it.

There was a Hudson faction in the house which was immediately inflamed; they set up a howl, and the entire audience was soon shouting for Mrs Montague. Muttering 'Who's afraid?' Queen Eleanor went on to the stage, carrying her script, and informed the audience that she *would* read the part. The audience then told her, loudly and clearly, that if she did not act the part properly, as was her duty, they would send to the nearest tavern and ask the cook-wench there to come to the theatre and read the part instead. Mrs Montague saw the point, and made an effort – but it was the prompter's evening, and she was 'hissed heartily'.

One reason for Peg Woffington's success in the playhouse was her contempt for this kind of unprofessional behaviour; she would have considered it cheating to fail to memorize and study a part thoroughly. Fully aware of her beauty, grace and charm, Peg never used them as substitutes for the art of acting. When the audience crammed the house to see Woffington play, their senses were enchanted by the perfection of her person – and their minds by the intelligence of an actress who was mistress of her craft.

Note on the Illustrations

Peg Woffington was painted by prominent artists of her time, though not many of the original paintings seem to have survived. There is a fine Mercier at the Garrick Club in London, and – most splendid of all – the magnificent portrait by Pond owned by Lord Lansdowne, reproduced opposite page 22.

A great many mezzotints exist, made after original portraits by Eccard, Van Bleeck, Marcand and others. These are to be found in the Harvard Theatre Collection, Yale University Library, the New York Public Library, the Enthoven Collection and the Print Room in the Victoria and Albert Museum, and other collections.

The portraits chosen for illustrations were painted by artists who knew Peg well, and who, one feels, came nearest to a true likeness of this beautiful woman. Hogarth and Pond, especially, seem to have caught the personality of the living Peg Woffington: the charm, the glint of mischief, the independent spirit, the good nature, are all there.

The pictures of Drury Lane Theatre and Covent Garden Theatre facing pages 119 and 151 are not strictly contemporary, as can be seen from the shape of the carriage in the former print and the dresses in the latter illustration. Both theatres, however, looked like this in Peg Woffington's time, and they have been chosen from scores of others because of their clarity and sense of period.

List of Parts Played by Peg Woffington

Rôle	*Play*	*Author*
Marcia	Cato	Addison, Joseph
Lady Rhadamont	A Fine Lady's Airs	Baker, Thomas
Ann Bullen	Virtue Betrayed	Banks, John
Queen Mary	The Albion Queens	Banks, John
The Lady	The Scornful Lady	Beaumont, Sir Francis
Bellamente	The Emperor of the Moon	Benn, Mrs Aphra
Helena	The Rover	Benn, Mrs Aphra
Queen Elizabeth	The Earl of Essex	Brooke, Henry
Angelica	The Gamester	Centlivre, Mrs
Charlotte	The Refusal	Cibber, Colley
Narcissa	Love's Last Shift	Cibber, Colley
Amanda	Love's Last Shift	Cibber, Colley
Elvira	Love Makes a Man	Cibber, Colley
Angelina	Love Makes a Man	Cibber, Colley
Florimel	The Comical Lovers	Cibber, Colley
Mrs. Conquest	The Lady's Last Stake	Cibber, Colley
Hypolita	She Would and She Wouldn't	Cibber, Colley
Flora	She Would and She Wouldn't	Cibber, Colley
Clarinda	The Double Gallant	Cibber, Colley
Lady Dainty	The Double Gallant	Cibber, Colley
Lady Sadlife	The Double Gallant	Cibber, Colley
Lady Townley	The Provok'd Husband	Cibber, Colley (adaptation and completion of Vanburgh's *Journey to London*)

Rôle	Play	Author
Phillida	Damon and Phillida	Cibber, Colley
Maria	The Non-Juror	Cibber, Colley (adaptation of Molière's *Tartuffe*)
Lady Betty Modish	The Careless Husband	Cibber, Colley
Nell	The Devil to Pay	Coffey, Charles
Angelica	Love For Love	Congreve, William
Lady Frail	Love For Love	Congreve, William
Millamant	The Way of the World	Congreve, William
Lady Pliant	The Double Dealer	Congreve, William
Lady Touchwood	The Double Dealer	Congreve, William
Laetitia	The Old Batchelor	Congreve, William
Almira	The Mourning Bride	Congreve, William
Zara	The Mourning Bride	Congreve, William
Leonora	Sir Courtly Nice	Crowne, John
Elvira	The Spanish Friar	Dryden, John
Cleopatra	All For Love	Dryden, John
Jocasta	Oedipus	Dryden, John (with Nathaniel Lee
Mrs Loveit	The Man of Mode	Etherege, Sir George
Belinda	The Man of Mode	Etherege, Sir George
Aurelia	The Twin Rivals	Farquhar, George
Mother Midnight	The Twin Rivals	Farquhar, George
Oriana	The Inconstant	Farquhar, George
Sir Harry Wildair	The Constant Couple	Farquhar, George
Lady Lurewell	The Constant Couple	Farquhar, George
Silvia	The Recruiting Officer	Farquhar, George
Mrs Sullen	The Beaux' Stratagem	Farquhar, George
Cherry	The Beaux' Stratagem	Farquhar, George
Charlotte	The Wedding Day	Fielding, Henry
Miss Lucy	The Virgin Unmasked	Fielding, Henry
Mariana	The Miser	Fielding, Henry
Celia	The Humorous Lieutenant	Fletcher, John
Estifania	Rule a Wife and Have a Wife	Fletcher, John
Aminta	The Sea Voyage	(probably Fletcher)
Polly	The Beggar's Opera	Gay, John
Mrs Peachum	The Beggar's Opera	Gay, John
Macheath	The Beggar's Opera	Gay, John
Clarinda	The Suspicious Husband	Hoadly, Benjamin
Jacinthia	The Suspicious Husband	Hoadly, Benjamin
Lady Randolph	Douglas	Home, John
Mrs Day	The Committee	Howard, Sir Robert

Rôle	Play	Author
Ruth	The Committee	Howard, Sir Robert
Aura	Country Lasses	Johnson, Charles
Roxana	Alexander, or The Rival Queens	Lee, Nathaniel
The Lady	Comus	Milton, John (adapted by Dr John Dalton)
Rosetta	The Foundling	Moore, Edward
Florella	Greenwich Park	Mountfort, William
Monimia	The Orphan	Otway, Thomas
Belvidera	Venice Preserv'd	Otway, Thomas
Andromache	The Distress'd Mother	Philips, Ambrose
Laetitia	The Astrologer	Ralph, James
Lady No	The London Cuckolds	Ravenscroft, Edward
Arabella	The London Cuckolds	Ravenscroft, Edward
Lothario	The Fair Penitent	Rowe, Nicholas
Calista	The Fair Penitent	Rowe, Nicholas
Jane Shore	The Tragedy of Jane Shore	Rowe, Nicholas
Alicia	The Tragedy of Jane Shore	Rowe, Nicholas
Lady Jane Grey	Lady Jane Grey	Rowe, Nicholas
Aspasia	Tamerlane	Rowe, Nicholas
Penelope	Ulysses	Rowe, Nicholas
Oriana	The Fair Quaker of Deal	Shadwell, Thomas
Widow Lackit	The Fair Quaker of Deal	Shadwell, Thomas
Belvidera	The Humours of the Army	Shadwell, Thomas
Ophelia	Hamlet	Shakespeare, William
Gertrude	Hamlet	Shakespeare, William
Cordelia	King Lear	Shakespeare, William
Constance	King John	Shakespeare, William
Lady Percy	Henry the Fourth	Shakespeare, William
Desdemona	Othello	Shakespeare, William
Queen Margaret	Richard the Third	Shakespeare, William
Lady Anne	Richard the Third	Shakespeare, William
Queen Catharine	Henry the Eighth	Shakespeare, William
Portia	Julius Caesar	Shakespeare, William
Isabella	Measure for Measure	Shakespeare, William
Kate	Henry the Fifth	Shakespeare, William
Helena	All's Well That Ends Well	Shakespeare, William
Lady Macbeth	Macbeth	Shakespeare, William
Portia	The Merchant of Venice	Shakespeare, William
Nerissa	The Merchant of Venice	Shakespeare, William

Rôle	Play	Author
Beatrice	Much Ado about Nothing	Shakespeare, William
Rosalind	As You Like It	Shakespeare, William
Viola	Twelfth Night	Shakespeare, William
Mistress Ford	The Merry Wives of Windsor	Shakespeare, William
Adriana	The Comedy of Errors	Shakespeare, William
Veturia	Coriolanus	Shakespeare, William (adapted by James Thomson)
Phaedre	Phaedre and Hippolytus	Smith, Edward
Isabella	The Fatal Marriage	Southerne, Thomas
Victoria	The Fatal Marriage	Southerne, Thomas
Phillis	The Conscious Lovers	Steele, Sir Richard
Penelope	The Lying Lover	Steele, Sir Richard
Belinda	The Artful Husband	Tavener, William
Violante	The Double Falsehood	Theobald, Lewis
Sigismunda	Tancred and Sigismunda	Thomson, James
Sulpita	Albumazar	Tomkis, —
Lady Brute	The Provok'd Wife	Vanburgh, Sir John
Lady Fanciful	The Provok'd Wife	Vanburgh, Sir John
Belinda	The Provok'd Wife	Vanburgh, Sir John
Clarissa	The Confederacy	Vanburgh, Sir John
Berinthia	The Relapse	Vanburgh, Sir John
Palmyra	Mahomet	Voltaire (translated by James Miller)
Silvia	Marry or Do Worse	Walker, William

This is not a complete list of the parts which Peg Woffington played during her thirty years' career in the theatre; there were many more, like Melantha in *The Frenchified Lady* and Flora in *Ye Village Opera* which probably did not reach half a dozen performances, were never revived, and whose authors are unknown.

Besides her rôles in plays, Peg spoke numberless Prologues and Epilogues. It was considered an honour to speak a Prologue or an Epilogue. Colley Cibber was once offered the first choice of parts by Vanburgh in a new play, and preferred to take two very minor parts *and* the Prologue and Epilogue.

The harsh note which sometimes came into Peg Woffington's voice apparently did not tell against her when managers were deciding who should be given the important responsibility of opening or closing a play. In the flow of a longish speech, without supporting players to help break it up by dialogue, was Peg able by sheer effort of will to control this flaw? It is interesting to speculate.

Among the many Epilogues which she delivered were one written by Garrick on the opening of Drury Lane under his management, one spoken as a Female Volunteer during the Rebellion, one on Shakespeare's women characters spoken after *The Merchant of Venice* during a Command Performance in 1744, one written to follow *Hamlet* when Spranger Barry acted the part for the first time in London, and one addressed to 'the Young Gentlemen who call themselves The Town', spoken by Peg Woffington attired in men's clothes, after the play *The Artful Husband*.

Bibliography

Bibliographical sources include:

Bellamy, George Anne, *Apology for the Life of George Anne Bellamy.* London, 1785.

Chetwood, William Rufus, *A General History of the Stage.* Dublin, 1749.

Cibber, Colley, *Apology for the Life of Colley Cibber.* London, 1740.

Clairon, C. J. Hippolyte, *Mémoires De Mlle Clairon, Actrice Du Théâtre Français.* Ponthion, Paris, 1798.

Cooke, William, *Memoirs of Charles Macklin, Comedian.* London, 1806.

Crawford, Jack, *Lovely Peggy: A Play.* Yale Press, 1911.

Cumberland, Richard, *Memoirs.* London, 1807.

Daly, Augustin, *Woffington, A Tribute to the Actress and the Woman.* Limited edition privately printed for the author, 1888. [Probably New York.]

Davies, Thomas, *Memories of the Life of David Garrick.* London, 1780.

Davies, Thomas, *Dramatic Miscellanies.* London, 1783–4.

Delaney, Mrs. [Mary Granville] *Autobiography and Correspondence,* London, 1861.

Dibdin, Charles. *A Complete History of the English Stage.* London, 1800.

Doran John, *Annals of the English Stage,* London, 1865.

Fitzgerald, Percy, *A New History of the English Stage.* London, 1882.

Galt, John, *The Lives of the Players.* London, 1831.

Genest, John, *Some Account of the London Stage,* 1660–1830. Bath, 1832.

Gentleman, Francis, *The Dramatic Censor.* London, 1770.

Hitchcock, Robert, *A Historical View of the Irish Stage.* London, 1788.

Hoole, J., *A Monody: To the Memory of Mrs. Margaret Woffington.* Printed for the author, 1760.

Hoole, Samuel, *Anecdotes by John Hoole*. London, 1803.
Ilchester, Earl of (and Mrs Langford-Brooke), *Life of Sir Charles Hanbury Williams*. London: Butterworth, 1928.
Kirkman, J. T., *Life of Macklin*. London, 1799.
Lewes, Charles Lee, *Memoirs*. London, 1805.
Matthew, Brander (and Laurence Hutton), *Actors and Actresses of Great Britain and the United States*, (volume entitled *Garrick and his Contemporaries*) New York, 1886.
Molloy, J. Fitzgerald, *The Life and Adventures of Peg Woffington*. London, 1884.
Molloy, J. Fitzgerald, *The Romance of the Irish Stage*. London, 1897.
Murphy, Arthur, *Life of David Garrick*. London, 1801.
Nicoll, Allardyce, *A History of Early Eighteenth Century Drama, 1700–1750*. London: Cambridge University Press, 1929.
1750–1800. London: Cambridge University Press, 1937.
Nicoll, Allardyce, *The World of Harlequin*. London, Cambridge University Press, 1963.
Reade, Charles, *Peg Woffington, A Novel*. London, 1852.
Reade, Charles (and Tom Taylor), *Masks and Faces, 1852*.
Stockwell, La Tourette, *Dublin Theatres and Customs*. Tonne: Kingsport Press, 1938. [A magnificent source-book, now out of print, but obtainable through the public library system.]
Van Tieghem, Philippe, *Les Grands Comédiens 1400–1900*. Paris: Pyf, 1960.
Victor, Benjamin. *The History of the Theatres of London and Dublin*. London, 1733.
Walpole, Horace, *Letters*. London, 1877.
Wilkinson, Tate, *Memoirs of His Own Life*. York, 1790.
Williams, Sir Charles Hanbury, *Works*. [Copy in the British Museum]
Wyndham, H. S., *Annals of Covent Garden Theatre*. London, Chatto and Windus, 1906.
A Bibliographical Account of Irish Theatrical Literature. Bibliog. Soc. Ir. Vol. I. No. 6. Dublin, 1920. [In the National Library of Ireland, Dublin.]
Biographica Dramatica, 1747–66. London, 1812.
Lawrence W. J., Articles in:
Atheneum, July 1903
Notes and Queries, Vol. X, 1904
New York Dramatic Mirror, June 1906 and August 1906
Gentleman's Magazine, August 1906
Weekly Irish Times, December 1907
Connoisseur, April 1908
New Ireland Review, August 1908
Fortnightly Review, February 1919.

Mackliniana, The European Magazine, January, 1795, May, 1800, June, 1800.

Mémoires of the Celebrated Mrs Woffington, Anon. Published S. Bladon, probably 1761.

Thespian Dictionary, or, Dramatic Biography of the Eighteenth Century. London, 1902.

The London Stage: Parts 2 & 3, South Illinois University Press MCMLX [Sets also in the Enthoven Collection, Victoria and Albert Museum, South Kensington, London, and in the Reading Room of the British Museum]

JOURNALS, NEWSPAPERS, ETC.

Various other journals of the period, especially:

Dublin Daily Advertiser Various copies 1732–1760

Dublin Evening Post Various copies 1732–1760

Dublin Gazette Various copies 1732–1760

Dublin Weekly Journal Various copies 1732–1760

Faulkner's Dublin Journal Various copies 1732–1760

Dublin Post and Advertiser Various copies 1732–1760

British Magazine, 1747

European Magazine, various dates, 1750–1760

Index